CULTURE FOR THE

LEFT-BRAINED LEADER

CULTURE

for the

LEFT-BRAINED
LEADER

Strategy, Tactics, and Implementation
for Transformative Results

ANDREW YJ KIM,
DDS, MS, MBA

HOUNDSTOOTH
PRESS

CULTURE FOR THE LEFT-BRAINED LEADER
Strategy, Tactics, and Implementation for Transformative Results

ISBN 978-1-5445-1975-3   *Hardcover*
      978-1-5445-1974-6   *Paperback*
      978-1-5445-1973-9   *Ebook*

To my wife, Sarah.
Without her support, this book would not be possible.

TABLE OF CONTENTS

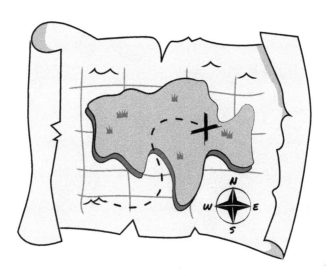

"WHAT GOT YOU HERE WON'T GET YOU THERE!"

A Book for Left-Brained Leaders Who Have Hit a Plateau and Can't Figure Out Why

If you picked up this book, I bet that you have a unique situation. Not everyone picks up a book called *Culture for the Left-Brained Leader* looking for some answers. You've probably had a unique journey to even have heard about this topic or look for solutions in this realm.

- You have a startup, worked really hard to become successful at it, and it's time to grow and scale but nothing is working;
- You have a business, but it seems to be running you more than you're running it;
- You're having trouble getting your company to look at the long-term horizon together, and it's frustrating; or
- You're in charge of leading a culture change, but you don't know where to start. Everything out there on this topic seems to make no sense.

I bet you're very good at your job. You're likely a high performer and very logic-oriented. You're probably very good with processes and strategy.

But you have probably hit a plateau. Your current approach worked up until a certain point, but it doesn't work beyond that. Something is off, but you're having trouble pinpointing it. The same repeating issues are arising. You realize that the same approach will not work anymore, and something needs to change.

You're right, something does need to change. The best description of this phenomenon can be summarized in the saying, *what got you here won't get you there*.

You're exploring the possibility that the answers to your challenges may have something to do with "culture." You're making the connection that it can create a lot of value. But nothing out there makes sense, and you want to understand why.

First of all, congratulations in even recognizing that culture can be a game changer and that you're looking for answers. Many struggle to see this connection between culture and business in the first place. It takes a unique set of experiences and insights to even recognize the value of culture and its potential impact.

However, you're probably frustrated with the confusing material out there. Most material on culture fails to adequately describe the logical connection between culture and business productivity. It tends to represent fragmented viewpoints, have many logical gaps, or function as inspirational books.

That's why you were drawn to the second aspect of the title: *Left-Brained Leader*. As implied by the title, we're going to make sense of this topic. You're probably someone who is mobilized by understanding how things work, rather than reading an inspirational book that has many logical gaps that leave you just as confused as before reading the book.

Why Should You Do This? How Will You Benefit?

Imagine having a company or a team that has your back. Not only do they have your back, but they also look out for problems before they occur, conceptualize their own solutions, and coordinate to get them implemented. They even look at the long-term horizon with you.

Sound impossible? Well, without culture strategy, it is. You may be used to having to micromanage them. In fact, you may have settled with the idea that it's just the way it is.

But with culture strategy, it does become possible. This may be challenging to conceptualize if you've never experienced this type of dynamic and lived those benefits before. But say it is possible (and we'll describe this phenomenon throughout the book). Imagine what you can do with it. You could:

- Grow and scale your business,
- Free up your time and achieve a balanced life, and
- Make a larger impact and leave a legacy.

These are massive benefits that can make a tremendous impact on your life. Too often, leaders get stuck before achieving these things.

But let's not get carried away yet. Once you imagine what is possible, ask yourself which components make this up. Take a moment to ponder this. You'll probably stumble here.

Yes, that's where it gets complicated. Building this type of organization is difficult to rationalize, and there is definitely a lack of material out there that adequately describes the actual strategies, tactics, and implementation that build up to this type of business. That's why this book was written, to better explain it, so that you can better understand it, and help you achieve it.

What This Book Will Teach You

In today's business world, the idea of *culture* is talked about all the time and overused by the media and flashy individuals almost to the point that it devalues the word. They tend to make the topic sound like a bunch of *fluff* because they are focusing on building excitement and hype rather than the fundamentals. So, it gives the perception, especially to analytical and goal-oriented folks, that culture is a bunch of touchy-feely topics that bear little relevance to completing tasks or getting the job done. However, that's really not true.

The truth is that this is a very complex and nuanced topic. This isn't what business media makes it out to be. They tend to hype up how it's all about having the coolest slides or in-office catering, like certain successful progressive or technology companies have done. If that were the case, then we would all have transformative cultures by doing those things, but that simply isn't the case. Companies that truly succeed at this are the minority! In reality, culture is so much more than that. It's evident that it creates value—people don't deny that. But, few can rationalize it. If people do not understand it, they have trouble buying into it.

Unlike other material out there, this book focuses on culture strategy at an enterprise level with a focus on its strategies, tactics, and implementation. Many people have a misconception that culture strategy can be done with isolated efforts. Unfortunately, such incremental efforts are largely unsuccessful, as the sustainability of culture strategy depends on continuous reinforcement through healthy interfaces throughout all the teams of the organization. Otherwise, the momentum for such a movement is stalled or even killed.

This means that if we want to be successful, we need to get everyone on board. This includes the highest level of senior leadership, middle management in charge of the teams, the majority of our team members, and various departments. Even our organizational policies need to be designed to support culture strategy if we want to leverage the enormous value that it can create.

Through this book, you'll have the opportunity to learn a holistic standard of implementing culture strategy at an enterprise level to drive real change and create organic, sustainable, innovative, and exponential value.

You'll also discover that to adequately break down the components of culture strategy, we need to broach the topic in five parts. This is an extremely vast topic, and I'm not going to dumb it down for you. Exclusion of any of these components will be an incomplete perspective of the topic, and it wouldn't do it justice.

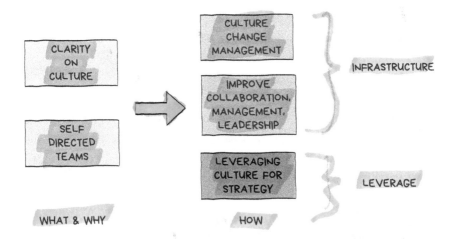

We need to start out with the fundamentals of culture strategy. This involves *what* it is and *why* it's important. Having clarity on these foundational topics will guide our thinking in connecting the dots with relevant issues on an everyday basis and implementing this strategy.

This is further broken down as follows:

- **Clarity on Culture**
  Part I: Why You Need to Start with Culture
- **Self-Directed Teams**
  Part II: Why the Self-Directed Team Is Critical to Culture

Once we've discussed these topics, we should have greater visibility on what we are trying to modify. Lack of clarity on these topics will run the risk of failing to address the real issues when we actually implement the changes.

Then, we can shift our discussion to describing *how* we are going to implement culture strategy. This is further broken down into subgroups: infrastructure and leverage.

Within the topic of infrastructure, we are building a newer and stronger foundation through culture that is capable of greater productivity. To describe this, we need to discuss:

- **Culture Change Management**
  Part III: Facilitating This Transition
- **Improving Collaboration, Management, Leadership**
  Part IV: The Difference Is in Everyday Moments

Once we establish this, we're not done yet. Sure, we get a lot of value just by reaching this point; however, there's more value that can be extrapolated. Now, we can shift our discussion to explain how we can *leverage* this new infrastructure to maximize productivity.

- **Leveraging Culture for Strategy**
  Part V: Connecting Culture with Strategy

These may seem like two separate topics at first glance, but I assure you that they're not. The main point of this book is to demonstrate how to maximize productivity through culture strategy, and this means that we need to demonstrate how the two topics of culture and strategy interlink. This is a sophisticated mechanism that requires a harmonious balance between the two.

By the end of this discussion, we will have converted an organization that was plagued with disengagement into one that is capable of organic, sustainable, innovative, and exponential growth. This may sound nebulous to many. If you have doubts on whether this is possible, read on and assess the logic yourself.

What This Book Will Not Teach You

If you want a book to inspire you and give you the motivation to make a difference, then this book is not for you. If that is your objective, there are countless books out there on culture that do a better job with that. It mobilizes some types of people, and I respect the intent and purpose of those other books.

These are the other things that this book is not:

- A shortcut or a get rich quick scheme
- A quick, easy read
- A short, fragmented view of the topic
- An inspirational book focused on hype and excitement
- A people book (rather, it's a productivity-through-people book)
- A human resources book (but rather, a cross-functional strategy book)
- A stock solution book

This book is for you if want to *understand* how culture works. There's a lack of books out there that truly explain it. This book focuses on real fundamentals that build the essential foundations of culture strategy. It won't be an easy path, but it will be a fruitful one. As the saying goes, *nothing worth having comes easy*.

How I Arrived at Culture Strategy

This wasn't an easy path for me, either. I got into business as an entrepreneur with a start-up. For those who have started their own business from scratch, you'll remember that every single detail matters, including the placement of each object, every detailed process, verbiage to customers, and so on. I conceptualized everything that my team would do, how I would monitor this, and how I would correct discrepancies. This leads to decision-overload, a stressful situation where you're bombarded and overwhelmed with the sheer number of decisions that need to be made. This is in contrast to an acquisition, where certain processes or work dynamics may already be in place. Because I had no pre-existing relationships or systems, I had to literally build everything from the ground up, which meant every detail mattered, and decision-overload felt unavoidable.

In addition, I had some preconceived notions when I started my business. I believe myself to be a well-traveled individual with many different outlooks on life and business. I've been fortunate to have received extensive corporate training and an MBA in finance and strategy. I've been a part of many organizations from big to small and seen their internal functions. I've also studied industry-specific systems relevant to the business I was starting. I developed the notion that business was mainly about the effectiveness and efficiencies of systems.

But I came to realize very quickly that this was simply not how businesses actually ran. I found myself in a very unhappy situation where I was overloaded and overwhelmed. Yes, I had good systems that were supposed to work. Yes, I had detailed procedures. I had everything mapped out. But the business was not working the way I thought it would.

It was because I overlooked the people aspect of the business. I wasn't engaging their inner drive, emotions, desires, and goals in life. Trying to get people to follow procedures felt like I was herding cats all day long and playing middleman for every little disagreement that occurred between different team members. I was in a situation where my business was running me more than I was running my business.

And so, I began to look for a different way. I began looking for help from experts and consultants, and they encouraged me to look at my challenges differently. Before, I was looking at the challenges and thought, *Why can't people just get along? Why can't they just follow the procedures?* Rather than putting the blame on them, I was challenged to look into myself and explore alternative topics, some of which I would have never explored on my own, such as culture, engagement, and emotional intelligence. Interestingly, I was one of the biggest naysayers about those topics. I thought to myself, *I have a real business to run, with real procedures, and real goals to meet. You can't simply care and the challenges will be overcome. You can't just* feel *your way out of everything.* But you know what? I took a leap of faith. I thought, *Maybe these people know something I don't. Let's give it a go and see what happens.*

Even when I was receiving training, I found myself resisting the concepts. Along the journey, I came to realize that many of the concepts didn't make logical sense at first. It sounded like fluffy nonsense because the topics didn't follow a clear, logical pattern. But I persisted and continued to follow the advice. Eventually, after painstakingly absorbing these ideas, implementing them, and being coached on them, I began seeing logical patterns to these topics.

Now, let's fast forward a bit. A lot has happened since then. I stabilized my business and built additional ones. My businesses no longer controlled my life. I used this approach to build the businesses and life that I've always wanted. I've had many different experiences, crashed and burned, licked my wounds, and got back up again. I had countless realizations, and eventually saw that I went the right direction.

Upon these realizations, I grew a desire to share the many learning points that I've experienced because they have the potential to create tremendous value. That meant I would have to help others reproduce it. In essence, I had *transformed the culture of my organization*. However, the problem with sharing these learning points was that available literature, material, and frameworks did not adequately explain the logic behind what I had gone through. I would have to create it myself!

In an attempt to break it down in a reproducible manner, I developed *culture strategy* to handle the topic of culture transformation in a strategic, tactical, and implementation-focused manner. Due to my background and analytical mindset, I approach these topics from an extremely logical perspective that resonates with senior leaders. I realized I wasn't the only one who had been blocked by the fact that nothing out there made sense!

I've gone on to help other organizations achieve the same transformation. They struggled, thinking, *I want to do this, but nothing makes sense! What do I do?* They needed an approach that was focused on strategy, tactics, and implementation. Furthermore, I refined the approach so that it could be done at scale and at an enterprise level.

I've compiled my thoughts in this book, which is meant to be the first of its kind, putting logic behind this abstract and subjective topic from a practitioner's standpoint. This is not another *fluffy* culture book of the type that is already so prevalent. Culture has many moving pieces, and implementing it requires a logical perspective and breakdown of the topic.

When we have a stronger understanding of culture, we are more successful in implementing it, whether that's in your own life, with your team, or in your organization. This is a great chance to get everyone behind it, including the naysayers and the people who don't believe in it. Culture has the potential to truly transform your business and make a large impact in people's lives. We just have to get past mainstream media and flashy people using it as a buzzword for hype, fluff, or touchy-feely effects. It's time to get behind it with rationale and logic, so we can get more people to buy into the ideas and implement culture strategy within our organizations.

The Value Is in the Depth: A Deeper Dive into Topics You May Already Know

Within the confines of this book, I can show you the frame and structure to set this up, but it's up to you to fill it with furniture, decorations, and life. Throughout the book, you'll be challenged in many ways. Even as you implement its lessons, it will force you to reevaluate your methods. This may feel uncomfortable.

On top of that, you may have already been exposed to many of the concepts. However, I'm going to ask you to dig deeper into the topics because that's where the real value is. I used to think that I already knew this stuff when I embarked on this journey. But in retrospect, I didn't know it then. It took a very humble mentality to adopt a flexible and solution mentality.

Flexible Mindset + Solution Mentality = Success

This book will ask you to dive for a deeper understanding of what you already know. It'll require connecting the dots with your everyday life by contrasting the concepts with your everyday actions. It'll encourage you to see things differently. It may have you question the assumptions that you held dear. It may even have you question the very questions that you ask. It'll challenge you to be accountable for all of the difficulties you've had as it lays the clear path that you may have not been walking. It'll be uncomfortable, as you may see the flaws in the current ways you've been doing things.

Even as you implement it, it may be challenging. As you make realizations and implement the strategy, bear in mind that the rest of your organization and world didn't make those realizations simultaneously with you. Therefore, there may be pushback. As uncomfortable as it may be, I encourage you to push on, as this creates real value. There's light at the end of the tunnel, as this method is not like a hamster wheel. It creates real purpose, exponential value, and freedom. I can only show you the path, and it'll be up to you to decide to walk it.

PART I

WHY YOU NEED TO START WITH CULTURE

CULTURE: THE MOST MISUNDERSTOOD VALUE MAXIMIZER

1.1. How Culture Affects Productivity and Behavior

When the word "culture" is brought up, what comes to your mind?

Is it a ceremonial celebration of a hallmark event?
Is it the art and architecture that give personality to a
given region?
Is it the warmth from having a sense of belonging from
commonalities of people?

Everyone has a different definition of culture. In fact, this word has such an open-ended connotation that it triggers all sorts of thoughts from varying people. The truth is that maximizing productivity through culture is likely the last thing that comes to one's mind. It's no wonder people have a difficult time connecting this word with productivity.

Most people tend to have a different perception on the definition of culture. Not to be cliché, but let's reference the *Webster's Dictionary* definition. Webster's defines it as how a particular society has its own beliefs, ways of life, art, and so on. If we take a moment to soak in that definition, we might naturally wonder how that ties to productivity.

What the heck does that mean?
How does that impact productivity?
That sounds like a fluffy concept that doesn't get real results.

In fact, some folks may take it as far as thinking:

That's just for social rituals to fulfill people's emotional need to feel comfortable.
That's unpredictable for reaching goals because it requires micromanagement of people's emotional volatility.

Though that may sound extremely robotic to some people, I must admit that I, too, was guilty of that train of thought. So, let's start our discussion of culture strategy by getting on the same page for the definition of "culture." I find that the best definition is:

> *Culture is what a group of people believes to be acceptable and unacceptable behavior.*

If you take a moment to contemplate that definition, it is extremely profound. That's because suddenly there's a possible tie-in to the concept of productivity. People can usually make the connection that beliefs of acceptable and unacceptable behavior can impact tasks. In fact, this has the potential to be more profound than anything else. This can even impact large-scale societal order, and it's more powerful than any law, system, or policy that can be designed. That's because people can resist and maneuver around policies, and they're actually very skilled at it! The truth is people don't maneuver around what they believe to be acceptable and unacceptable behavior. They don't do this around culture because it engages the inner core of what they believe in.

The natural inclination for managers is to focus on tasks, procedures, or systems. It appears to be the quickest and easiest way of getting things done in a quality manner. They tend to think that by simply assigning tasks to their team members and quality assuring those tasks, they can create a predictable manner of completing an overall objective.

However, such a manager quickly encounters challenges that prove it's not that simple! People have their own beliefs, thoughts, feelings, motivations, and lives. They can resist you despite your best efforts. It's not as simple as handing over a set of procedures, monitoring them through direct observation or data, and picking out where they could use improvement.

We all wish it was as simple as that, but it simply isn't the case! Even if you run a tight ship, the moment the team knows you're not looking, they're going to do something else. Even if you try to create an elaborate data collection process, there are countless ways to hide underneath the radar and have poor work go unseen, ending with substantial lost value. Besides that, productivity is the culmination of much more than the tasks themselves. It requires a great deal of coordination among people. It is difficult to micromanage such interaction points because it would quickly end up in a "he says, she says" game.

However, if we approach management from the perspective of influencing what people believe to be acceptable and unacceptable behavior, we get access to a much broader and deeper range of production-related behaviors. This includes the tasks themselves, but penetrates into a much greater scope than that. It includes unmonitored behavior, coordination between people, reinforcement of the culture, noticing issues, problem-solving, and much more! The greatest beauty in all of this is that it gets reinforced whether or not the manager directly observes or has data regarding this.

Though we will go over processes on how to accomplish this in much greater granularity throughout the book, take one moment to ask yourself:

> What would it take to influence what people believe to be
> acceptable and unacceptable behavior?
> Would an announcement of expectations suffice?
> *Or* would it take using your everyday moments to reinforce it?

By getting on the same page on the definition of "culture," you eliminate a great deal of resistance regarding the topic. Also, these insights are useful tools to encourage managers to have paradigm shifts that allow them to approach their teams differently in their everyday moments.

This Concept Is Not New

After you've had some time to let that definition settle in, it's important to note that the concept of management through what people believe is not new. In fact, it has been documented for thousands of years. Let's review the accomplishments of Confucius, a Chinese politician and philosopher who served in the governance of China in approximately 500 BC. Through management of the vast territories that were

China, he realized there simply weren't enough enforcers to govern such a large empire with enforcement alone. By introducing cultural values, he influenced what people believed to be acceptable and unacceptable behavior. Ultimately, he increased stability and prosperity while reducing the need for heavy enforcement.

In fact, this has been such an established concept throughout military history that it was a common military strategy to target the intellectual leaders after a territory was conquered. They engaged them (or removed them) to create commonalities in acceptable and unacceptable beliefs. This tactic has also been seen in historical strategic alliances between empires and religion for the governance of a territory, as religion had a hand in establishing norms in acceptable and unacceptable behaviors in ways that the empires could not. That's also why the establishment of democracy tends to be successful in some environments and not in others—because the cultural factors can overpower policies.

The concept of governance or management through the beliefs of acceptable and unacceptable behavior is not a new concept. However, what is new is a stronger understanding of the right combination of behaviors that optimize productivity. We see that very clearly in many progressive and innovative companies that have the potential to disrupt their industry.

It is such an impactful topic that some major and successful companies have based their core strategy around culture to achieve market competitiveness and sustainable profitability. Well-known examples include Southwest Airlines, Zappos, and The Walt Disney Company. Many technology companies use it as a tool to stay competitive. In fact, these companies know that if they get this one thing right, then everything else comes together and they dominate the market. They take it so seriously that they've found creative ways to invest in influencing culture, such as having cool slides, buffets, and ping-pong tables. Though such tools may help promote certain atmospheres, they're very far from the fundamentals that culture strategy represents.

In today's business environment, culture can greatly impact organizational productivity. If you look at it from the perspective of acceptable and unacceptable behavior, you can see how it can impact the way people make their day-to-day decisions and, ultimately, their productivity. This impacts not just how they produce as an individual, but also how they collaborate. When we are working with an organization or team, we are not working by ourselves. We actually have to discuss our findings, generate ideas, plan, and coordinate to have our goals come to fruition. All of those steps require collaboration, which introduces the possibility of communication breakdowns. This includes all of the informal hallway chats, heart-to-heart talks, meetings, and happy-hour discussions. There's no way to design systems around all of that.

Only a powerful culture can penetrate all of those layers. When we achieve this through the right combination of beliefs of acceptable and unacceptable behaviors, the resulting collaboration represents intangible assets through the value of synergy. We begin to see an optimized version of productivity through organic and scalable value creation. When we establish these behaviors as the new norm, we know that we were truly successful in implementing culture strategy.

1.2. Perception of Culture by Companies and Leaders

It's quite clear that the concept of culture can elude even our most capable business leaders. That's why it's not surprising to observe a very wide range of perspectives when it comes to their understanding of culture and how it relates to the business. I find four categories of perceptions from business leaders.

1. **Unaware!** – Many business leaders are unaware of this concept or outright deny it! They're either oblivious or living in denial. Largely, this stems from a lack of awareness and knowledge of the subject matter, or a fixed mentality in favor of a methodology of producing results that they are accustomed to. In this situation, we need to focus on the awareness of the importance of culture strategy.

2. **Aware, but don't know what to do about it** – In this category, business leaders are aware that culture strategy can produce tremendous value. They have observed this topic as a growing trend or were convinced by statements from other leaders they respect who claimed that culture strategy was their main success component. In this situation, we need to establish the desire to implement change and equip them with the proper knowledge.

3. **Aware, but misdiagnosing or mistreating the underlying causes** – This category of business leaders is aware of the value of culture

strategy and they're even trying to implement it! However, due to the elusive nature of this strategy, they misdiagnosed the situation and are either bandaging the existing symptoms of the business or delivering the wrong treatment. In this situation, we need to increase their knowledge of culture strategy to gain greater clarity.

4. **Aware, already doing it, and trying to refine their culture further for greater value** – In this category, business leaders are already aware of, implementing, and succeeding at culture strategy! Often, such leaders trust their gut instincts for their decisions without being able to rationalize it. They are looking for more ways to refine their culture for greater value. In this case, a deeper knowledge of the subject matter can help them achieve it.

No matter what your situation is, it's important to understand that culture management is a process and a journey. Even as we make breakthroughs in our own understanding of the matter, we are faced with the need to help others achieve similar breakthroughs. It's important to recognize our own struggles in making such realizations so we can help others create the same value, because culture strategy requires that we come together as an organization.

1.3. The Risks of *Not* Repairing Culture

It is undeniable that culture is an elusive concept, and the companies that are succeeding at it represent the minority in the current market. However, times are changing. There is a growing trend within the business landscape toward a greater number of companies that focus on culture strategy. Already, it has taken over the market in many industries through disruptive models. For example, we can clearly see this in the retail industry. Many brick-and-mortar shops and brands are shutting down due to struggles maintaining relevance with market demands.

However, companies that focus on culture strategy are taking over market share and have a greater appeal for good talent.

If you're already facing the challenges associated with losing market relevance or access to talent due to competition focusing on culture, it should be a no-brainer that it is urgent to act now and hope that it is not too late, as the industry environment will only get tougher.

If this has not affected you or your company, then you can choose to be proactive and implement culture strategy now. Or, you may choose to wait until the market begins to force you to make such a change (either through loss of market share or challenges in attracting good talent), but that would be highly reactive. It can be costly to wait until the market pressures demand action! This is because culture change doesn't happen overnight.

As we dive deeper into the moving pieces in implementing culture change, it will become increasingly evident that this may take a long time! This is especially the case if you are a large company, as you will have more complexities due to your scale, and this change can take years. If you begin implementing this in the downturn, it may be too late!

A more proactive stance would lead you to implement culture change before the pressures are tangible. Companies that have a strong focus on culture strategy tend to dominate the market and even weather downturns extremely well. A proactive stance could lead the company to a state of abundance. Wouldn't that be the best position to be in?

So, whichever type of leader you currently are, I invite you to actively pursue culture strategy for your company. Now, you understand that culture can be defined as what a group of people believes to be acceptable and unacceptable behavior. Behavior directly impacts productivity, and that is why culture is an essential foundation for strong businesses. This concept is not new. It goes back thousands of years, but it's still as relevant and impactful today as it was when Confucius used it to unite an enormous empire. Age-old wisdom can help you stay competitive, take over market share, and have a greater appeal for good talent. So, let's get into how you can live and breathe culture strategy to succeed in your business.

CHAPTER 2

TO LIVE CULTURE, YOU NEED TO SEE THINGS DIFFERENTLY

2.1. Which Is Real Infrastructure: People or Systems?

I remember when I first started my business. I was eager to build a business that delivered a great service and product. I planned on delivering this through being extremely organized through the best systems and procedures, streamlining data acquisition to accurately measure quality assurance, and telling my team which areas they could improve on whenever discrepancies formed. I was sure this was the way to go.

I looked into the best systems that the industry had to offer. Not only did I do that, I cross-referenced them with best practices from *other* industries. Then, I adapted them to my customized situation. Afterwards, I filled positions by plugging people in and ensuring they were compliant. I believed this would breathe life into the organization with strong processes and dedicated people.

This worked very well for a while and we met our short-term goals. We actually grew very rapidly, built a good reputation, provided great services, and exceeded our business goals. Then we got to the point where we needed to grow further. Suddenly, we encountered challenges we'd never encountered before. I learned that the systems I had introduced were dependent on me personally maintaining them. The demands of growth began to spread me out too thin, and I was unable to maintain those systems. We hit a plateau, and we couldn't grow any further.

This actually led to a very challenging time in my life. I found myself in a situation where I was stuck. As a business owner, I was accountable for everything in the business. Financial and operational pressures began hitting home and affected my personal life. To grow, everything needed to function and sustain itself without me, because I couldn't be everywhere at once. I discovered that systems wouldn't hold when I wasn't there in person to reinforce them.

It took a paradigm shift to solve this problem. I was investing in systems infrastructure first, then trying to develop the people infrastructure after that. I realized I had to do it in the reverse order, because what I had built had a weak foundation. I had to invest in people infrastructure first, then  systems infrastructure second. This was a very difficult paradigm shift to make. It was hard for me to let go of the systems. With them, I could identify inefficiencies and room for improvement from a mile away. I was concerned that letting go would cause other issues.

I was able to reconcile this when I realized that shifting my focus to people infrastructure didn't involve completely letting go. It was just a different way of approaching the challenges. I could focus my efforts on building the most elaborate people infrastructure, which turned out to create much more long-term value and broke the vicious cycle of being stuck.

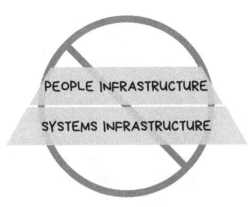

Not a good approach: systems infrastructure first, people infrastructure second

Recommended approach: people infrastructure first, systems infrastructure second

- **Systems infrastructure** involves setting up organizational systems, policies, procedures, data, and documentation.

- **People infrastructure**, on the other hand, involves people development, optimal communication, coordination, and synergy through relationships and culture development.

2.2. Different Lens, Different Trajectory

Approaching situations through a people infrastructure is a skill that requires looking at things through a different lens. It is very impactful because it puts everything in a different perspective and reprioritizes how a manager diagnoses situations, problem solves, and implements solutions. In an isolated manner, it may appear unimpactful, but on a scaled or enterprise level—that is, on an everyday basis—everything can change.

It requires a deeper analysis of the situation. Naturally, if a process breaks down and causes an issue, a manager will likely focus on the immediately preceding task that went wrong and try to address it. This usually provides a quick fix to the situation. However, this overlooks deeper-lying issues and ends up simply putting a bandage over them, brushing them under the rug, or treating the wrong condition. This is an unsustainable way of problem solving that cumulatively ends up with culture dysfunction.

On the other hand, when approaching problems with an eye for people infrastructure, the manager would be inclined to identify the deeper root cause of the issue. He would identify where the breakdown in people development and collaboration occurred.

- **Visible root cause lens** = Task focus
  There's an overemphasis on the immediately preceding event as a single point of failure.

- **Deeper root cause lens** = People development and collaboration focus
  There's a deeper analysis into the underlying issues.

To illustrate this concept, let's discuss a common situation that people can relate to. Imagine that you are a manager of a team. You have a team member who has been with you for half a year and is underperforming on his tasks. This is a typical frustration that managers encounter, and you may be hasty in judging the team member with the following thought:

The job isn't that hard. What is wrong with him?

This type of thinking will likely lead you to give a stern statement demanding performance improvement without uncovering the real issues. A deeper analysis of the root cause may get us to uncover significant findings, such as:

- There is a lack of training available,
- You haven't engaged the team member's motivation,
- The employee needs coaching on self-management, thinking, or communication skills,
- The team dynamic is dysfunctional,
- There's a distrusting environment,
- There are unsustainable organizational processes, or
- There are other, deeper-lying issues.

Viewing the issue through this lens will lead you to have a different kind of conversation, diagnosis, plan, and outcome. It is likely that you can identify a deeper root cause that would not have otherwise been visible. The result is that you can proceed in a direction that leads to mutual alignment and continuous engagement.

You may think that's not how the real world works, and that you can't do that for every situation. I'm not saying you can rescue every situation through this approach. However, there are many situations that good managers can actually salvage, and they can go on to create excellent results with a broad range of people and situations. Managers who are fixed in the visible root cause lens with a task focus often find themselves unable to stabilize a situation that a skilled manager with a deeper root cause lens can.

Unfortunately, there are times when the situation with the employee is still unworkable despite making your best attempts at resolving the issues. This usually requires action from Human Resources. Delineating the difference will require situational assessments and adaptation skills, but this should occur only in a minority of cases.

This deeper root cause lens can be applied to countless more situations. Hopefully, this one example gives you a basic idea of how the deeper root cause lens creates a different trajectory. In fact, this gave me new eyes to diagnose everything in my same scenario differently. At first, it took a lot of intentional effort to see things in this manner. Once I got the hang of it, however, it was just like learning any other skill and it became second nature, just like riding a bike.

Furthermore, I began to recognize that almost all situations are a result of developmental or collaboration issues. That meant that almost everything involved developing people and their collaboration skills. Accomplishing goals through people development and coordination felt very odd and vulnerable at first. It appears like a slower and inefficient way of getting things done.

In the beginning, you might be telling yourself, "What would take me a week may take a month using collaboration and coaching techniques. I don't have the time for this!" However, if you follow that mentality, you will create a perpetual dependence on your presence to get things done. Then, you would be spread out too thin, plateau your potential, and have no bandwidth to work on anything else. You may feel like you are over-worked and alone, thinking no one else cares about the team as much as you do. You may feel stuck or even bring your stress home, which could ultimately affect your personal life.

It's tough to let go and use situations as opportunities to develop and coach people. In fact, the value doesn't become tangible until later. Even when it becomes tangible, it's not obvious as there's no clear moment that shows it's working. However, there'll be a moment when you realize the issues that you used to have no longer occur. That's why it's import-ant to continue to *stay the course*. It ultimately gives people a chance to develop, have ownership over their skills, and learn from their expe-riences. It creates a path for the development of people infrastructure within the organization.

Does this seem like the same old cliché leadership talk? Does it sound rather unimpactful? In a single, isolated situation, this may appear to be the case. However, imagine the cumulative impact throughout the entire organization on an everyday basis. It can definitely result in an enormous impact when scaled. Not only that, but it can lead to organic, sustainable, innovative, and exponential growth patterns that many leaders always dream or talk about.

2.3. Culture Is the Infrastructure That Holds Every Other Capability Together

As your organization shifts its focus toward people development and collaboration, the culture strategy will begin to mature and take shape. This creates an opportunity to leverage relationships rather than direct them. The following are significant benefits in leveraging relationships rather than directing:

- You can transfer ownership of various systems and capabilities to the team(s), which means they can initiate their own system updates or integrations as necessary.

- You can bring in capabilities from outside your field of expertise and keep them unified under a common goal through collaborative focus.

This means the leader does not need to be a subject matter expert in every technical capability within the organization. It allows for the possibility of assimilating and aligning multiple capabilities under a common, overall vision through healthy collaboration, as opposed to micromanaging every technical function. You don't need to master every technical body of knowledge under the sun to run a successful organization because that is not humanly possible.

This is why culture strategy is the king of all strategies! It becomes the uniting centerpiece among various departments and divisions. It's also why you often need the backing of the CEO to champion this initiative forward.

You may be thinking, *How is it even possible to consolidate the technical and operational capabilities of other departments using culture? If you don't know what they do, they will recognize that and get away with doing a poor job! Or they will serve their own interests and compete with each other.*

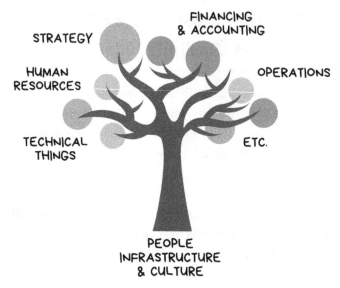

Analogy: a tree that represents culture infrastructure branching to everything else, visualizing how it can assimilate and align all other capabilities

Such thinking is evidence that you are still stuck in the systems infrastructure mentality. Indeed, this would be challenging if you have that mindset, as there will be clashes between differing perspectives.

That mindset would foster an environment where people do not adequately develop ownership over their skills and ideas. They would also lack the ability to reconcile their differences through trusting collaboration. In fact, this would breed distrust. Under those circumstances, it may become extremely difficult to strike a balance under a common, united goal. However, if we use people infrastructure as the centerpiece, it is possible to reconcile and unite the differences of differing technical capabilities through collaboration.

Have you ever seen a CEO of a large, multinational corporation (MNC) who is a subject matter expert in every component of the company? The answer should be no. And, in reality, that scenario is not even possible as there are too many components. Then, how do they effectively lead such large companies? It's not through being a master of everything. It's because they unite the different components together.

Culture strategy takes it one step further than that. The enormous value of culture strategy comes from the fact that it unites different business components through mutually trusting collaboration that leverages the capabilities of people and consolidates multiple areas of technical expertise. Through this, it minimizes the organizational bureaucracy commonly seen in many other organizations. Thus, it creates a sustainable ecosystem for innovative and collaborative efforts to organically balance its priorities and resources for exponential growth. That's why:

> *Culture is the strategic infrastructure for organic,*
> *sustainable, innovative, and exponential growth.*

2.4. Different Types of Culture. Which One Is Your Organization?

Some may say, "Hey! We have a real business to run. We don't have time to focus so much on the people."

Without a doubt, organizations need to demonstrate competitiveness to reach goals and penetrate the market. However, some people take that notion and carry a misconception that being a people-focused organization means they are not a goals-focused organization. Such people think that the two cannot coexist.

That cannot be further from the truth. The relationship between being people-focused and goal-focused is not antagonistic! Rather, the relationship is better described as two different dimensions that can overlap with each other. In fact, there are *four* types of cultures that exist.

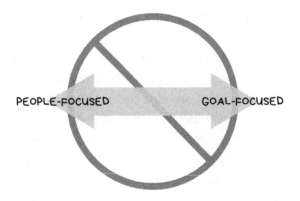

PEOPLE-FOCUSED   GOAL-FOCUSED

- **Synergistic Collaborative:** This is the culture that this book recommends. In this culture, a goal-focused mentality is maintained and accomplished by creating synergy through collaboration and people development. It has the potential to yield greater market competitiveness through the value of synergy.

- **Traditional Competitive:** Historically, most profit-based companies exhibit this form of culture. It has a strong focus on goals and achieves this through a strong sense of hierarchy and competitiveness. We do see a higher tendency toward this culture in traditional organizations, which tend to manage through authority and goal-orientation.

- **Social Club:** This type of organization has a strong people-focus but lacks a goal-oriented spirit. Many people misconstrue people-focused organizations as this type of organization exclusively. It is commonly seen in extremely social organizations that don't need a strong goal focus to sustain them, such as some nonprofit organizations and social clubs.

- **Isolated Silos:** This type of organization lacks both people-focus and goal-focus characteristics. There is neither a push toward an objective nor collaboration. This is sometimes seen in organizations that lack motivating leadership and well-developed objectives to sustain them, such as certain public sectors (some Department of Motor Vehicles offices come to mind).

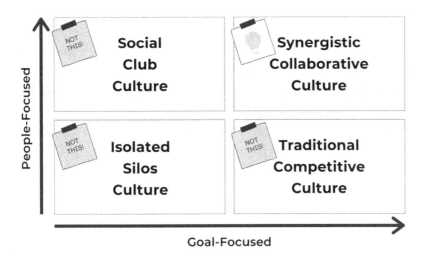

2x2 box diagram: people-focused versus goal-focused

This is a modification of a framework presented by Robert Goffee and Gareth Jones, as discussed in the November-December 1996 issue of *Harvard Business Review*, among other places. If you're interested in diving deeper into the different characteristics of culture types, their research is an excellent resource that takes the topic in greater granularity.

Why People Who Are Accustomed to One Form of Culture Don't Naturally Acclimate Well in Another

It is important to understand that each type of culture has its own beliefs of what are acceptable and unacceptable behavior. This creates a great deal of tension when you try to mix them. For example, if you transplant someone who is accustomed to a Traditional Competitive culture into a Synergistic Collaborative culture, a great deal of clashing ensues. Even in the opposite direction, when someone from a Synergistic Collaborative culture is transplanted into a Traditional Competitive culture, they often do not sustain themselves when left to their own devices.

Therefore, mixing cultures without plans for reconciliation is usually not successful. Neither is trying to achieve culture change with uncoordinated, incremental efforts, as it tends to create artifacts of mixed culture categories that clash with each other. Rather, true culture change usually involves restructuring the foundation of a company to recreate the common definition of acceptable and unacceptable behaviors.

In this book, I am describing what it takes to create the Synergistic Collaborative culture, which is highly people-focused *and* goal-focused. When a company succeeds in creating this culture, there is a need for ongoing culture alignment. People naturally have varying mindsets of acceptable and unacceptable behavior. Many people may not be accustomed to this type of culture and will spontaneously revert to what they are used to without alignment maintenance. This can be achieved through reinforcing the concepts on an everyday basis, making it a part of onboarding, developing leaders and managers to champion it by living by example, refereeing it, and implementing the culture strategy at an enterprise level.

Based on the four types of cultures, ask yourself the following:

Which is your culture?

Which culture do you want your organization to be?

Can you mix your current culture and your desired culture? Will incremental efforts in reconciling them be impactful?

Occasionally, I encounter people who represent a Traditional Competitive culture, and have been trying to implement a Synergistic Collaborative culture without success. If that is your case, ask yourself:

Have you truly transitioned to a people-focused mentality?

Has that permeated at an enterprise level?

Do you see how incremental efforts can lead to an unsustainable situation?

If you answer *no* to any of these questions, we may be able to identify where your challenges are arising from. We may be overlooking the true nature of culture strategy or forgetting to reassess the foundation of the company as it relates to this strategy. In essence, you may be underestimating the scope of work for this change.

You Can Create Strategic Infrastructure

Changing your team's culture does take a lot of work. There's no denying that. It requires a shift from placing systems infrastructure first to prioritizing people infrastructure. That means the foundation of your business becomes people development, optimal communication, coordination, and synergy through relationships and culture development. Systems, data, processes, and documentation then sit on top of that foundation. A culture change requires you to look at situations through a deeper root cause lens, instead of a visible root cause lens, so you can identify underlying issues and change your trajectory.

Culture strategy creates an opportunity to leverage relationships rather than direct them, so you don't need to be a subject matter expert in every capability within your organization. Nor do you need to focus only on goals or on people; the two approaches are not antagonistic. When built together from the ground up, you can create a Synergistic Collaborative culture that works with both approaches to yield greater market competitiveness. You create a strategic infrastructure for organic, sustainable, innovative, and exponential growth.

Now, imagine trying to push this kind of culture in an enterprise level, which goes beyond your personal reach, interactions, and observations. All of a sudden, it becomes an enormously complex and deep topic that engages many subtopics. You may be wondering to yourself, *How would you even accomplish that?* That's what the rest of this book is about.

CHAPTER 3

WHAT YOU NEED TO KNOW WHEN DECIDING TO IMPLEMENT CULTURE STRATEGY

3.1. What You Can Gain from Culture Strategy

Through culture strategy, you can gain access to the most impactful mechanism to create value in business. As renowned management consultant and author Peter Drucker said, "Culture eats strategy for breakfast."

This quote highlights how culture is a formidable internal strategy that overpowers other strategies. This is because culture strategy propagates and amplifies all our other efforts. Even if we set out on a well-planned strategic direction, if we cannot handle it internally, there is a high likelihood of failing to meet business goals or even imploding as a team or organization. How many times have you set out on a strategic direction but became bogged down by internal matters?

This phenomenon can be an elusive concept to many, so to illustrate, we will compare it to a lever mechanism. Culture strategy is so powerful because it truly creates a leverage mechanism within the business. This is a concept from physics, which amplifies the manual force that is applied by several times over.

"Give me a lever long enough and a fulcrum in which to place it, and I shall move the world."

—Archimedes

No matter how much manual force we apply, we cannot overpower the force of a lever. For example, can you open an oyster shell with your bare hands? Don't you need to get an object in-between and lever it open? Trying to do business without culture strategy is like trying to open the oyster shell without a tool. Sure, you can do it if you're strong enough. But isn't it easier to use leverage to open it?

When you are trying to prop up a business through manual force, you may find yourself in a situation where you are trapped, overworked, or even regretful. You might have team members who are not motivated and do not have your back. Perhaps you're dealing with the same issue over and over again. Sound familiar to your situation?

By implementing culture strategy, you can break out of this cycle by creating leverage mechanisms within the business. Imagine the potential impact if you had these mechanisms throughout your organization. Not only could you make a stronger impact, but it would require less force of will from you. To make this possible, you need to start by building a newer and stronger infrastructure.

Infrastructure

A stronger infrastructure is built upon a collaborative culture and self-directed teams. As an overview, this involves the institutionalization of good management, accountability, engagement, and collaboration to create a landscape of *self-directed teams* throughout the organization. These self-directed teams are critical building blocks that enable the leverage mechanism. They are comprised of a *manager* and *contributors* (team members) who can organically problem solve and sustain the business. Without them, there is nothing to leverage.

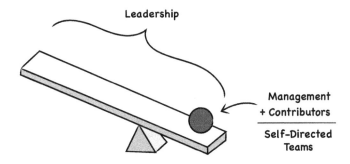

Leverage

Now, we have the foundation for *leaders* to leverage results from managers and teams. Leaders are the agents that leverage value from these self-directed teams. They accomplish this by guiding team-level problem solving as opposed to traditional directives. This is a very refined skill compared to the traditional approach. They specialize in maintaining this culture, building on to the people infrastructure, and influencing results through buy-in. When properly positioned, they can generate maximum impact through this lever mechanism.

Furthermore, leaders can amplify the results from leverage through a new paradigm of *strategy* that is only possible with a well-developed culture. Rather than approaching strategy in a top-down, linear manner, leaders focus on leveraging the results through an ecosystem of strategy throughout the organization. This captures greater value through improved adaptability, innovation, ownership, and alignment, and a well-defined enterprise-level strategy.

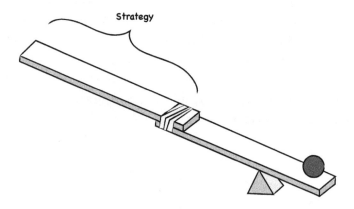

Imagine creating this leverage mechanism at an enterprise level and conceptualize the impact that it could make. Such value can be difficult to quantify with projections. But it's clear that the impact of organic, sustainable, innovative, and exponential growth at an enterprise level can lead to continued market dominance. In fact, many leaders who have grown massive companies through culture strategy have claimed that if you get culture right, everything else comes into place.

Prove It! Where's the Evidence?

Since culture strategy focuses on the infrastructure and DNA of the organization, it's extremely difficult to design a comprehensive research study that measures its results. It's not like changing a sales process to improve conversion rates, adjusting a marketing feature to see leads generated, or improving a manufacturing process to evaluate the percentage of products within specification. Rather, it targets many subjective components that are very difficult to measure. And since it aims to improve the infrastructure of the organization, it can improve all manners of the business—sales, marketing, product design, customer satisfaction, retention, and more. In fact, one of the greatest value adds for culture strategy is the increased relevance to customers and talent, thereby increasing market share and access to talent.

There's an increasing amount of anecdotal information and case studies that demonstrate the exponential potential of culture strategy. There's also a growing trend of businesses jumping on the culture bandwagon to remain market competitive. There are other businesses that are losing market relevance filing for bankruptcy, because their internal infrastructure couldn't keep up with the rapidly changing landscape of today's marketplace.

The best well-conducted study that tried to explain this phenomenon came from the Gallup Institute, which compared world-class companies to other companies. They rationalized the value of culture strategy from the perspective of engagement.

The study looked at the breakdown of employees based on three categories of engagement. *Actively Engaged* employees are key employees who continue to think for the company, identify issues, problem solve, and do their utmost for the company. *Passively Engaged* employees are doing the minimum to get by, may notice issues, but don't collaborate, don't problem solve, and maneuver around policies. *Actively Disengaged* employees actively create problems within the organization by starting conflicts, creating divisions, or intentionally performing subpar work.

Based on those definitions, what percentage of employees do you think the study found were Actively Engaged, Passively Engaged, and Actively Disengaged?

Average Company
Actively Engaged: 33 percent
Passively Engaged: 49 percent
Actively Disengaged: 18 percent

These numbers show the spread of employees within those categories for the average company. This information may come as a surprise to some. Now, what do you think the spread is for world-class companies?

World-Class Company
Actively Engaged: 67 percent
Passively Engaged: 26 percent
Actively Disengaged: 7 percent

These world-class companies have tendencies to dominate the market. By having a greater proportion of Actively Engaged employees who are looking out for the company and fewer Passively Engaged and Actively Disengaged employees, such a difference in performance of the market can be made.

How do they accomplish this? Well, that's what culture strategy is about. In essence, it institutionalizes good leadership, good management, accountability, self-direction, engagement, and more. These attributes may be difficult to quantify, but looking from the angle of the Gallup study, the massive impact of culture is undeniable.

3.2. What You Do with This Infrastructure and Leverage Mechanism Is Up to You!

Imagine you have these leverage mechanisms set up throughout your organization. Though leveraging is a more refined skill and more difficult to learn than traditional management techniques, once you overcome these hurdles, it takes significantly less time and energy to produce the same results. At this point, you'll recover your time and energy. What will you do with this? You'll realize that it is up to you!

You can use this newly formed infrastructure to grow and expand further. Maybe you'll choose to further your ambitions to make your mark on the world. You can choose to regain balance in your life. Perhaps you sacrificed so much of your personal life that it's time to revisit the things that matter to you the most. Or, you can refocus on your personal or business mission. You can get back to the very reason you started the business or got into leadership in the first place. Now, with a team that has your back, you can refocus on your purpose as an organization. When you do this with the right team, you can make a greater impact.

Maximizing Your Impact or Getting Your Time Back

One of the major advantages of culture strategy is the ability to recover your leadership margin.

> **Margin** – Extra amount of time, energy, or bandwidth allowed for use as needed.

This is possible because it creates an ecosystem of self-direction, which frees leaders from granular tasks. This is significant as it allows leaders to do the following:

Accomplish More Impact with Less Time Involvement

This maximizes the impact or gain per utilization of your time, energy, or bandwidth as a leader. Culture strategy creates a framework for maximizing this because it gives you a way to focus on higher-ticket items such as strategy and mobilizing teams with leadership techniques. It creates a sustainable way to push multiple fronts simultaneously, and it's a predictable way to "clone" yourself and be in multiple places at once. This is your ticket to scaling.

Recapture Balance in Life

A common misconception regarding high performers is that you have to sacrifice your personal life to get far in your career. That may be the case with the traditional model of doing things, as it heavily relies upon sheer will in perpetuity. However, culture strategy creates a different frame that creates margin, which can be utilized to recapture balance in life or to accomplish more. It's your choice!

I've had interesting conversations with successful entrepreneurs who sacrificed their relationships with their family for their business. Now, many of them say they would give up everything to reconnect with their loved ones. I think that's a powerful realization that came after the fact. If only they had seen this earlier and chosen a path of doing business that involved culture strategy, they could have had both. The benefits of culture strategy stretch far beyond the organization itself.

Purpose-Driven Benefit: Make the World a Better Place

When I embarked upon making a difference with culture strategy in my business, I did so with productivity in mind. It was during and after implementation when I realized the humanitarian benefits that are possible with culture strategy.

We Serve Our Customers Better

I realized that the quality of our service improved. That's because we had a team that was attuned to the needs of the communities, and we problem-solved around them. That meant we took a larger market share, but also that we were making a better impact on the community.

We Create a Home for Our Employees

I also realized that employees make culture strategy-focused companies their home. Companies that focus on culture strategy are still the minority in the marketplace, and many employees have become disheartened by the dysfunction that exists out there in other types of organizations. When employees see the benefits of culture strategy, they treat it like an oasis. We say the following:

> "We see each other in our jobs more than our own families. So, be happy wherever you are. If you're not, life is too short to be unhappy in a job, so you're welcome to look elsewhere. But if you choose to be here, be sure it's because it makes you happy, and give it your all!"

That tends to be a far better retention perk for good talent than anything else out there. It was nice to realize that this strategy has this collateral benefit. In fact, I've heard from many employees that the quality of their personal lives improved from the purpose and lessons they gained from our company.

It was nice to learn that this strategy can have a large, positive societal impact by the ripple effect from the broad reach of companies.

3.3. What Are the Risks with Culture Strategy?

The more you understand how powerful this strategy can be, the more you see the importance of implementing culture strategy. The deeper you understand how culture creates value, the greater the impact you will be able to visualize. However, the converse is true: the deeper you understand it, the more challenges you'll be able to visualize. Nothing in this world has no risks or downsides.

I'm a firm believer of knowing the risks of any major decisions, so I can set realistic expectations and better prepare for the challenges. Therefore, it's important to understand the downsides of culture strategy, as we will then be in a better position to mitigate the associated challenges. Let's evaluate the risks together.

Drawback #1: It's Difficult to Quantify and Measure

Oftentimes, organizations use data to diagnose issues, get on the same page, and measure success. It's a way to keep matters objective and evaluate the truth in situations. Unfortunately, this is very difficult to do with culture strategy. What are we going to measure?

Not surprisingly, the true value of culture strategy is difficult to measure and quantify. The gains associated with successful culture implementation tend to have lagging results—it can take a long time to see the impact—along with being affected by multifactorial variables. This is applicable to both the causes (independent variables) and results (dependent variables).

In addition, since culture is an infrastructure-related strategy, it impacts everything. At the same time, it mixes in with everything else going on within the organization, which can yield misleading information.

Since it doesn't have clear-cut measurables, it is advisable to either adopt a holistic view of the strategy or choose related measurables that are priority issues for the organization at the moment and focus on them. That is because, based on specific situations, there may be certain measurables that are important to you. It's not a one-size-fits-all. It's not as clear-cut as many other initiatives with clear target objectives.

Drawback #2: It Doesn't Work with Incremental or Isolated Efforts

If we want to make a comparison, culture change can be likened to reworking the foundation of an old home with a poor infrastructure. It's not a simple, cosmetic fix, and truly requires work at the deeper, inner foundations to be done properly. Depending on the situation, sometimes it can even be more difficult than starting from scratch!

This isn't a strategy that can occur in isolated, uncoordinated increments if we truly desire enterprise-level impact. Because of this, culture strategy truly requires buy-in throughout the entire organization, and the highest level of authority backing it. This includes buy-in at senior management, different departments, middle management, and the majority of employees. Otherwise, we simply achieve cosmetic fixes or bandaging.

Culture strategy influences how tasks are accomplished at all levels of the organization. Without buy-in, there will surely be pushback and resistance. On top of that, culture strategy draws upon deeper-level concepts, which adds to the challenges of educating people to visualize the potential benefits and getting them on board.

Drawback #3: It Is Hard

Culture strategy has a high difficulty level associated with it. Though it has the potential to bear enormous fruit, there are also nontrivial risks associated with it. It requires a great deal of skill to successfully manage the high degree of complexities. Therefore, you must recognize the technique- and operator-sensitive nature of this strategy, and prepare to build those skills or have competent talent push them forward.

Enterprise-level culture strategy is extremely technique and operator sensitive as it is difficult to implement. It requires a strong understanding of the topic. It needs to be implemented by people with great ability to see strategic connections between leadership, change management, organizational policies, operations, strategies, and so on. It also requires excellent leadership with the ability to influence, achieve buy-in, manage momentum, and maneuver around organizational political factors.

Underestimating the high complexities and skill requirements associated with culture strategy will likely result in a poor success rate. You need to build these skills, have your best people to pull this off, or have the right advisors. This isn't simply a strategy where you send others to a simple training and expect it to come together. Though it has enormous returns, it also has a high failure rate due to mismanagement.

Drawback #4: People May Resist, and You May Lose Some People

Managing culture change carries the risk of resistance and turnover. It requires changes at a deeper level, and human psychology tends to resist such changes even when there are clear advantages.

From one angle, if an organization is wrought with poor engagement and incompetency, profound changes may be a good thing. However, it doesn't change the fact that it may be a challenging transitional experience.

Other times, it may be important to be delicate with the transition, as such resistance and turnover could cripple the organization. It is important to recognize when such risks exist, and to have a plan to mitigate them.

Drawback #5: Financial Benefits Are Materialized in the Long Term

The impact of culture strategy's financial implications on business performance is a critical decision-making factor. It is evident that culture strategy has the potential to create an exponential growth trajectory. However, it is likely to have a delayed realization of exponential growth. Thus, if a company is already in a rapid downward spiral, it may be too late to implement such a strategy. It can take significant time to implement culture strategy. That's why it's important to be proactive, diagnosing the need for improved culture early and initiating such a strategy before the symptoms of poor culture become debilitating.

In addition, care must be taken to minimize the possibility of negatively affecting short-term productivity. Culture strategy may have risks associated with possible turnover, resistance, time for people to become accustomed to the new management culture, and decreased productivity due to absences for training of employees. Managing such risks can help mitigate their likelihood and impact. Therefore, it is important to recognize them and have prudent mitigation plans.

Drawback #6: There May Be a Need to Reserve Financial Resources

It's also important to understand the financial implications on the expense side. This strategy may incur an initial expenditure to gain access to necessary, specialized knowledge (for example, training or consultants), assessments, and quality talent to push the initiative forward, and to set up necessary training and education programs to develop your people.

However, a greater financial impact will likely be experienced on sustained expenses after the initial implementation. A large component of this strategy leverages value from margin. Initiatives include training, coaching, facilitating, aligning, and planning. If the organization runs at constant full capacity, there is no room for developing and leveraging these capabilities. Therefore, relevant teams need to be staffed slightly above capacity to accommodate functional gaps during such moments.

Sometimes, compensation needs to be equalized with the market. If a company already has competitive compensation packages, this is irrelevant. However, if a company has an absolute priority to keep expenses efficient, it may inadvertently result in below-market-rate compensation, which can impact retention. Since this strategy relies upon the development of people, the company needs reasonable retention to accomplish its goals.

Naturally, such financial decisions can make a financial officer anxious, as there may be a delicate balance to achieve profitability and reach stakeholder expectations. Therefore, it is prudent for this to be a partnered effort among relevant parties, to achieve mutual trust for the attainment of the long-term exponential goal.

We don't always have to increase our budget. There are ways to create margin without doing so. The expense of implementing culture strategy can be mitigated if inefficient processes and misalignment can be identified and removed. These inefficiencies create a great amount of waste, and correcting them naturally opens up additional bandwidth and margin. This may help some organizations create additional margin without increasing budget.

Cumulative Business Impact

It's important to understand the overall business implications of culture strategy. Clearly, there are enormous gains for your company from a financial standpoint. Growth can become organic in nature. When executed properly, an exponential growth pattern can be exhibited after an initial expense and possible production slowdown period. This is how some progressive companies have grown at such unprecedented rates to become gigantic corporations that outcompete the traditional conglomerates that used to be viewed as untouchable.

Below is a summary of pros and cons that have been discussed so far.

Table: Summary of Pros and Cons of Culture Strategy

Pros	Cons
Framework to create value via synergy and proper allocation of talent based on skills.	Initial costs for education, necessary talent, and skills development.
Framework for adaptability and innovation.	Delayed initial return on investment.
Increased market competitiveness for customers.	Higher upkeep costs with a higher average cost of labor, expertise, training, and alignment efforts.
Increased market competitiveness for talent.	Possible slowdown of existing short-term production.
Framework for self-directed teams.	Challenges in measuring success and keeping track of value created.
Framework for scalable growth.	Extremely operator and technique sensitive, requiring exceptional strategic and change management capabilities.
Framework for organic value creation.	
Framework for exponential growth.	
Framework to inject strategic capabilities within teams.	Buy-in required at all levels of employment.
Ripple effect of value creation throughout the organization.	

3.4. Factors That Can Add to the Complexities of Culture Change

It's also important to recognize and understand other factors that add to the complexities of culture strategy. This proactive mindset allows us to do a better feasibility and scope analysis. It also helps us be better prepared to address potential issues and anticipate a realistic expectation for this strategy.

Large Corporations with Rigid Processes and Mindsets

If you are in an existing large organization, you may be thinking to yourself, *This will require stepping backwards to deconstruct and then reconstruct the culture. This will be hard to pull off.* You may be right. This is why, ideally, people infrastructure should have come before systems infrastructure in this strategy. It is similar to trying to fix the foundation of a home with a poor foundation. One of the greatest challenges with a large company is in its difficulties in adapting. Thus, it does have added challenges in adapting to a new culture.

Larger companies have more complicated buy-in and approval processes. If there is large-scale resistance, this may be a challenging mountain to climb. Buy-in needs to occur in all layers of the organization, from contributors to middle management to senior management. Thus, there may be stakeholders who vehemently object to this type of change. In such situations, it is prudent to craft a change management program to manage possible risks. That's why we sometimes need to create a separate governance board, implementation team, and communication plan with targets.

If there already is a desire for this type of change, but the organization lacks the tools or understanding, it may be easier. In fact, the company may already be trying to implement a similar strategy. However, due to a poor understanding of the methodology and moving parts, they may be having challenges with implementation. In such situations, introducing the methodology may be better received.

Another reason that larger companies have added complexities is that there are usually deeply entrenched processes holding up its functions and capabilities. They may be so deeply entrenched that it may be difficult to modify them suddenly. In such cases, we may need to superimpose culture strategy on top of the existing processes, rather than having it be the main foundation. This may involve incremental process and policy updates as mutual trust is built between different layers of the organization. Bear in mind that this may reduce the risks associated with culture change, but it will also reduce the potential impact.

If this is more challenging, why would larger companies do this? Many are interested in culture strategy because they have already realized that market conditions are changing, and their competitiveness for talent and consumers is dwindling. Newer innovative and disruptive organizations are outcompeting them, and the company's long-term prospects look questionable. Therefore, it's time to adapt to recapture the relevance to the market on those various fronts.

Extremely Deep-Held Beliefs

Initially, I used to think that being a part of a Synergistic Collaborative culture would be a no-brainer. I thought everyone would want to be part of it because there are so many advantages to such a culture. I came to learn the hard way that this is simply not the case. This culture requires everyone to adopt a collaborative mentality and develop a stronger baseline in communications, self-management, and thinking skills. Even managers and leaders need to develop competent skills in getting buy-in, maintaining an environment of developing people, coaching, facilitating, reinforcing this culture, and so on. They may not be accustomed to this. Developing these skills is similar to developing other new skills in life in that there are challenging moments. They will encounter uncomfortable, vulnerable, and embarrassing situations in the learning process. They will have to put in effort to overcome these hurdles and become competent. Remember what it was like learning how to drive a car, and all of the challenges associated with it? It is like that all over again.

People tend to be creatures of habit, and this may be more challenging if we've been doing things a certain way for a long time. People may have preconceived notions of how teams and managers should operate, and they cannot adapt to anything else. For example, managers and leaders from Traditional Competitive cultures may be accustomed to using authority to accomplish everything rather than focusing on buy-in. They may resist as it can be a painful process to develop these new skills. Sometimes, an unhealthy ego prevents them from continuous development, or they may not be willing to expose their vulnerabilities in the learning process. They could have trust issues in life or distrust in people due to previous bad experiences. Any or all of these can inhibit them from developing mutually beneficial mindsets for continuous growth via culture strategy.

Hybrid Cultures

An example of hybrid culture is seen when large corporations try to develop a strong culture in an isolated setting through a subsidiary joint venture, acquisition, innovation team, or similar structure. The largest challenge for those scenarios is at the interface between the two groups. Oftentimes, the umbrella organization may apply top-down management on a culture that thrives through bottom-up management. This may interfere with the way the subsidiary does things and can erode the trust and strategic purpose of the culture. When we're faced with this sort of situation, it's important to:

- Protect the interface between the innovative team and the corporation.
- Manage expectations from other parts of the organization (they may perceive that the subsidiary is receiving special treatment and deem it unfair).
- Effectively facilitate any transition of capabilities that may be built through this innovation team.

Cutthroat Industry with No Room for "Disruption" or Market Segmentation

There are applications for Synergistic Collaborative culture in almost all industries. Even in extremely challenging industries, we can often find innovative "disruptions." A culture like this has greater adaptability to higher levels of customer service and innovation, so it is possible to attain higher forms of efficiency to bring expenses down via automation (with technology) or targeting higher market segments (through improved customer relations). So, if your industry can leverage that, it is definitely possible, even in many commoditized industries. For example, the US airline industry is a widely known commoditized industry, and Southwest Airlines made headway via its people strategy.

I do admit that some industries may be so commoditized that they have little room for differentiation through customer service or innovation. This is especially true when businesses within the industry have such cutthroat environments that they have extremely thin profit margins and little room for innovation, due to insufficient return on investments. Then, it may be challenging to find an application for culture strategy. However, disruption still occurs in many commoditized industries via culture strategy all the time, often in the most unexpected areas.

Extremely Traditional and Hierarchal Beliefs in Surrounding Communities

The overall culture of a country, state, city, or community can have a huge impact on people's perception of acceptable and unacceptable behavior. For example, in locations that are prevalent with Traditional Competitive culture mindsets, there may be increased complexities and challenges with culture strategy. This can impact the scope of culture alignment and people development efforts that is required to successfully implement this initiative.

Sometimes, we can adapt variations of culture strategy to the local mindset. Many organizations have still found ways to create variations of Synergistic Collaborative cultures, despite their local mindset obstacles.

Alibaba.com in China is one such company that had to overcome massive resistance to establish itself as the e-commerce giant it is today. To accomplish this, they had to overcome many great alignment challenges.

Complex Resistance Situations

There are definitely unique situations that add to the complexity of implementing culture strategy. Along this journey, there may be a need to make a hard stance to push for buy-in to the strategy and get people to play their part. However, there are situations that can make it more difficult to make this hard stance. Such situations can include:

- Labor unions,
- Organizations where replacing "bad apples" is not an option,
- Culture change with external partners,
- Physically dangerous or high-tension situations,
- And more.

In such situations, stakeholder management and refined communication become increasingly important to maximize alignment in a seemingly perpetual conflicting situation. It is critical to deliver messages that address the core of their concerns while highlighting mutual goals. Whatever your situation is, be sure to properly size up the scope of the challenges, so that you can better prepare to overcome them.

In summary, culture strategy is an infrastructure and lever mechanism that leverages the value of self-directed teams. What you do with this is up to you. There are drawbacks and, at times, additional complexities, which you are now aware of, but these risks can return great rewards. As anecdotal information and studies show us, Actively Engaged employees create world-class companies. We've seen that these team members are key to exponential growth, but what exactly makes them so critical to success? That's what we'll look at next.

PART II

WHY THE SELF-DIRECTED TEAM IS CRITICAL TO CULTURE

CHAPTER 4

ANATOMY OF A SELF-DIRECTED TEAM

The following realization was pivotal in how I came to view the "art" of predictably establishing *self-directed teams*. It took me a long time to recognize, as it was another deeper-level realization.

> *Balanced perspectives of problem solving are needed*
> *for the formation of self-directed teams.*

Now, people can take this to mean many things. It is important to properly understand the weight of that statement as it impacts the ability to predictably form a fundamental component to the self-directed team. This chapter will be focused on clarifying this point.

I used to hire people who made me comfortable. Like other managers, I looked at a candidate's resume, skills, years of experience, recommendations, and references. I would interview them to see if we could get along and work together. I'd ask questions to gauge their knowledge and how they thought. When we built a team in that manner, we did well initially. We built a growing business that delivered great service and built a good reputation.

However, the challenges came when it was time to grow. I needed to step out because I couldn't be in multiple places at once, but the team we built didn't hold without me. In fact, issues occurred without my presence that I'd never seen before, and the team could not problem solve on their own. That baffled me. I attempted to rationalize this phenomenon and tried many things to fix it. I was stuck for a very long time. Then one day, it finally dawned on me. I had unknowingly created a homogenous team because it felt comfortable.

Now, it's important to recognize that *a homogenous team actually shares the same blind spot.* In reality, no one consciously knows that they're building a homogenous team. It's an unconscious set of decisions that leads one to such a situation.

> *Managers unknowingly build homogenous*
> *teams because it feels comfortable.*

My team was similar to me. My employees shared my strengths but also my weaknesses. As a business owner, I was willing to go through countless painstaking trials and tribulations to gain the skills to cover my natural weaknesses, but other people weren't willing to go to such great lengths to acquire these skills. It was too painful for them.

Eventually, I realized there were other people who naturally filled those voids because those perspectives were within their comfort zone.

- There were other people who could effortlessly accomplish things that I found extremely difficult.
- On the flip side, such people will likely find things that I deem extremely easy to be very challenging for them.

However, filling these voids wasn't as easy as simply bringing other people in. They were different from me. They talked differently, processed information differently, and saw the world differently. Because of that, they made me uncomfortable. It created tension, and that tension needed to be reconciled. I had to address these differences and get everyone to work together.

Different people actually make
managers feel uncomfortable.

Eventually, I learned how to reconcile those differences and create a team that covered a broader spectrum of problem solving. Even though that was uncomfortable, reconciling differences in perspectives with people development and collaboration was a lot easier than pushing homogenous people through extreme trials to develop skills in their natural weaknesses. When I made these realizations and put them into practice, I made the transition from having traditional teams to self-directed teams.

Now, I'm not suggesting you should take everyone under the sun into your company just because they think differently. I'm not saying this simply for the sake of being diverse or inclusive. This needs to fill a void from a functional business perspective. That means you need to be skilled at recognizing the voids.

At the same time, there does need to be foresight in evaluating your ability to reconcile these differences and whether such reconciliation is possible with a potential hire. If you only find yourself comfortable reconciling an extremely narrow range of people, it may be prudent to consider developing your management skills further.

Good managers can reconcile a broader range of
people variations to develop self-directed teams.

It Requires Introspection to See This

This is a deeper realization that can be very difficult to see. A manager who is stuck in the weeds of all the action is often blind to this because they never step out and see if the team can hold without them. In fact, some managers actually hold multiple teams together with their sheer willpower, trying to do everything at once, without such realizations. This is an unsustainable situation. It is likely that after more challenges are thrust upon them, they will implode or hit a brick wall. Then it will be so painful that they will have no other choice but to see it this way. I recommend trying to see it before that happens. The sooner you recognize the voids in your team and your management skills, the sooner you'll be prepared to make a larger impact by building self-directed teams.

4.1. Difference between the Anatomy of Traditional and Self-Directed Teams

Anatomy of a Traditional Team: Hierarchy and Technical Skill Focus

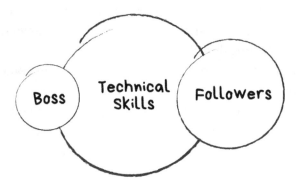

Hierarchy Focus

Let's look at the anatomy of a *traditional team* together. This is actually how most teams are comprised. It is a very linear way of creating teams. You'll notice how there is a focus on hierarchy and technical skills within this formation.

- **Boss** – The boss is the *manager* of a traditional team. The boss uses authority to get people to do the necessary tasks so the job gets done. They expect their followers to do what they need, and they typically prefer to have a team that doesn't disagree with them.

- **Followers** – Followers take instructions from the boss. They are often more focused on not stepping on the boss's toes than on what really needs to be done and collaborating with others.

Technical Skill Focus

The boss and the followers focus on the skills and experience required for tasks. There may be a large focus on evaluating situations based on the visible root cause lens (which is task focused), and getting things done through processes and procedures. Data is likely a large focus for quality control. This can be a predictable way to get simple, routine tasks done.

It's not atypical to see an overemphasis on the technical skills of a job in this form of team. The entire team is not accustomed to solving issues with good collaboration. Thus, they try to overcompensate for every issue with further emphasis on technical skills. Interestingly, this further adds to the homogeneity of the team without their realization. It also adds a tremendous amount of burden on becoming a technical master at everything, which can sometimes lead to unrealistic expectations.

Weakness

The drawback for such a team becomes extremely apparent when unforeseen circumstances are thrown at the team. This type of team formation creates an unintended homogenous environment. It lacks balanced perspectives in problem solving, and subsequently the team will struggle with situational adaptations.

Sometimes, those symptoms are not clearly visible if the boss is micromanaging multiple perspectives through sheer will. However, that's an unsustainable situation as it creates an overdependence on the boss, and there is no room for growth for the rest of the people. In addition, if the team is large, it is impossible for the boss to identify, problem solve, and direct every issue.

Commentary

This type of team formation is an artifact of the Industrial Age and functioned adequately throughout the greater part of history. However, in today's market environment, we are reaching a turning point from market pressures that demand solutions to highly specified and dynamic pain points. This requires teams that can create adaptable solutions. Therefore, more and more organizations are focusing on creating self-directed teams that can collaborate around such problem solving, and they are outcompeting other companies that have not followed suit. If current traditional teams do not adapt to this changing landscape, they may find themselves in a situation where they become obsolete.

Anatomy of a Self-Directed Team: Balanced Perspectives and Collaboration Focus

Balanced Perspectives

In the *self-directed team*, it is important to have a balanced set of perspectives for a holistic representation of problem solving. Different perspectives contribute to this in their own way. More detailed descriptions regarding the spectrum of problem solving will be discussed in the next subsection.

Then, the most common question is, "Who's the boss? Is it the most dominant person?" There should indeed be a person who is accountable for the team and is granted formal authority and a management title. However, it doesn't necessarily have to be the most dominant person, and they should not carry the same "boss" feel as in traditional teams.

Rather, everyone should contribute to the spectrum of problem solving in their own way. Their differences of opinions and perspectives will introduce a new set of challenges that will need to be reconciled; therefore, the functional management duties should be given to the individual who is most accountable and can best reconcile differences between these perspectives to bring the best out of everyone and achieve a self-directed team status.

A Team That Lives and Breathes the Idea of People Infrastructure and Deeper Root Cause

In Chapter 2, we discussed the concept of people infrastructure and utilizing the deeper root cause lens (which involves people development and a collaboration mentality) to approach issues. The self-directed team is a unit that lives and breathes these concepts. It should be the manager's primary goal to achieve this unity.

This is opposed to the traditional team, which is focused on approaching issues with the visible root cause lens (which is task focused).

Technical Skills Are Still Important, but *Not* as Heavy of a Focus

You'll realize that in the diagram of the self-directed team, there is still a focus on technical skills. However, it is no longer the primary focus of the team. Rather, we add balance to the team with an added focus on collaboration.

When teams truly collaborate, it eliminates the need for everyone to be a master at everything. Interdependency, trust, and teamwork are born from this. It creates a motivating environment where people are eager to share their knowledge, and organic skill transfer occurs.

Weakness

The biggest weakness for this approach is that it requires better management skills and a supporting organizational culture to predictably create such teams. They are more challenging to create, and so it takes deliberate effort to create this type of team.

Commentary

This team has the ability to self-direct. That means that they can identify their own issues, problem solve, and implement solutions on their own.

Such teams are outcompeting others in the current market. They sustain through hardships, grow on their own, develop creative solutions to deliver better value, and collaborate in a healthy manner toward a common, strategic goal. That's why investing in culture strategy to institutionalize the predictable formation of such teams can lead to organic, sustainable, innovative, and exponential growth.

Traditional managers may have blind spots regarding their team. Interestingly, many managers who have a traditional team incorrectly believe they have a self-directed team. They've made incremental efforts to improve the team dynamic, and gotten different personalities to cooperate with one another. However, they haven't truly reached a self-directed team status. This blind spot is usually the result of the following:

- They may have minimized conflicts, but the synergy between the team members has not been properly harnessed through people development and collaboration.

- They still cling onto their need to always be "right," and are actually more hierarchal than they realize.

The real test is in having the manager step away for an extended period of time and evaluating whether the team sustains themselves or is doing better by the time the manager returns. If you can't do this with a great deal of confidence, there is room for improvement in properly developing your team.

4.2. The Value of Balanced Perspectives

To truly understand how a balanced set of perspectives impacts self-direction, it's important to visualize the full spectrum of problem solving.

- **Notice issues** – The team needs to be able to identify issues on their own. They can't wait for the manager to identify every issue.
- **Problem solve** – Without an overdependence on the manager, the team needs to be able to conceptualize solutions. They can't wait for the manager to think of every possible solution.
- **Get people on the same page** – Without an overdependence on the manager, the team needs to get on the same page. They can't expect the manager to be a perpetual cat herder.
- **Create accountability for doing the work** – There are a lot of tasks that need to be completed to meet objectives. The team needs to demonstrate accountability for the plethora of tasks and push them forward in a reliable manner. They can't play hot potato with the responsibilities or make excuses whenever things don't work out.

Once we recognize that the self-directed team needs to be able to do this on their own, we can visualize how certain people naturally fill various aspects of the spectrum. Let's explore different perspectives using an applied version of a well-known framework, DiSC. It provides a framework of four primary characteristics of team members and recommendations on how to manage them.

The Goal Pusher

Who they are: These people are typically very ambitious and big-picture oriented. They are usually very confident and have no issues telling people what to do. They are extremely goal oriented and are extremely skilled at reaching their objectives.

Why they're important: A team cannot stay afloat if it is not reaching business objectives. Goal Pushers bring in a competitive spirit and a desire to reach goals. They are also skilled at identifying big-picture issues and recognizing the highest priorities in any given moment.

Their blind spot: Goal Pushers tend to achieve their goals at any and all costs. They may have a tendency to "leave a trail of dead bodies behind." They also may be insensitive to details, fine-tuned customer service, and team morale.

Let's imagine that you have a group of goal-oriented people within the team. Typically, they will start butting heads, competing against each other and arguing to get their way. Obviously, a situation like that can create a toxic environment.

When you have too many Goal Pushers, you'll reach objectives, but you may introduce an environment of unreasonable and dysfunctional amounts of conflict. Everyone will want to have their way and meet their agenda because everyone will want to be right.

The Analyzer

Who they are: These people are extremely logical and rational. They are excellent at analyzing situations, evaluating whether things make sense, organizing, and analyzing data to ensure objectivity.

Why they're important: A team can be led astray through false claims, lack of information, and debilitating inefficiencies. Analyzers ensure the team stays objective by analyzing situations, organizing data, and evaluating efficiencies. They are also skilled at identifying detailed issues that can compound to become larger ones.

Their blind spot: They tend to slow things down because they get so deep in a topic that they lose track of the overall picture. That's where the term *analysis paralysis* comes from. This can lead to going down a rabbit hole and becoming over-fixated on a situation. Analyzers tend to think the world is going to fall apart over a detail, and they engage in endless debates when left unchecked. They can also be insensitive to other people's emotions, and may have challenges collaborating with team members and providing customer service.

The Enthusiast

Who they are: They're the life of the party and always the center of attention. They're great at bringing people together and getting people on the same page. When it comes to work, they're always thinking about who needs to do what.

Why they're important: Enthusiasts can make anything fun. Naturally, they like to bring people together to work on anything and everything. They're great at getting people on the same page, encouraging buy-in, creating alignment, and improving morale.

Their blind spot: These people can get carried away in the moment. They might spend too much time talking. If you have too many of them, it will be like "happy hour" all day long, and no one will get anything done. Because they can get carried away in the moment, they also have a tendency to overcommit without thinking things through.

Enthusiasts may also have challenges with follow-through. As they can get carried away with an upswing of morale, they can be affected by a downswing and get bored. They may give up easily or appear fickle to others.

The Stabilizer

Who they are: These people are extremely considerate and prefer stable environments. They have a strong affinity toward routine situations. They often derive comfort from knowing that if they do a specific set of tasks, they will get predictable rewards (such as stable pay, staying out of trouble, and recognition).

Why they're important: Stabilizers create stable and peaceful environments due to their considerate nature and preference for routine situations. Bosses of traditional teams often view them as the most employable as they are not confrontational and they perform their routine duties. Their considerate nature also makes them great at detecting customer-service or staff member issues. In fact, they are usually the first detectors of these issues as their instincts are honed toward empathy.

Their blind spot: Stabilizers' affinity toward peaceful and routine situations gives them added challenges in pushing for goals. They often prioritize a peaceful environment over any goals. If you have too many Stabilizers, they'll get along great, but goals will likely not be met and the business can suffer. Sometimes, they view pushing for goals as a moral conflict, as it often requires going through people and "rocking the boat."

Because of their nature to avoid conflict, there often needs to be a significant effort to create safe zones for Stabilizers to feel comfortable speaking up. If they don't feel that safety, they will likely opt to remain quiet and stay out of trouble. So, even if they notice issues, they may not speak up.

They tend to get anxious whenever there is change because they prefer predictable sets of work and rewards. They get extremely concerned when there is any form of change, and they often need a great deal of reassurance.

Stabilizers also tend to struggle with myopia and have challenges seeing the big picture. That's because big-picture prioritization and thinking often requires deviation from the routine. Also, their empathetic nature can create a tendency to over-focus on people's emotions.

Balanced Perspectives and Collaboration Are Required for True Self-Direction

A good balance of these perspectives allows for a fuller representation of the problem-solving spectrum. When this is achieved, we have a higher likelihood of establishing a self-directed team that is capable of situationally adapting to issues thrown at them. You may ask if there are times where people exhibit a mixture of the characteristics. Absolutely! But even when people exhibit a mix of characteristics, they tend to have a primary characteristic. Therefore, this frame is still helpful as a guideline to visualize the balanced perspectives better.

The Platinum Proportion – For the typical team, the following ratio of people is recommended:

- 16.7 percent (1/6) Goal Pushers
- 16.7 percent (1/6) Analyzers
- 16.7 percent (1/6) Enthusiasts
- 50 percent (1/2) Stabilizers

This ratio of people tends to create a good balance for most teams. It accounts for the varying perspectives needed, while simultaneously recognizing the larger volume of routine tasks that need to be completed. If this ratio is compromised, you may notice a higher likelihood of the team failing to meet goals or self-imploding.

Though it may be difficult for some teams to maintain this ratio due to the nature of certain jobs having stronger affinities for specific profiles (for example, engineering tends to have more analytical people), we should try to maintain a balance when possible for a higher likelihood of self-direction.

Other times, certain teams don't have enough people to maintain this ratio yet. Evaluate whether this is relevant to your team and organization. Apply the Platinum Proportion as it makes sense to your situation.

The Value of Self-Direction

Let's say you had two teams, one with the anatomy of a traditional team, and the other a self-directed team. Let's say they currently both meet the same business objectives.

> Are the two teams equal in value?
> If not, which is worth more?

At first, you might think that both teams are equal in value because they both produce the same results. However, that is not true. Even if they produce the same, the self-directed team is worth more.

The self-directed team has the ability to situationally adapt to issues that occur, as team members have the ability to problem solve by themselves. Their team has the infrastructure for collaborative synergy throughout the organization by creating a mechanism for leverage.

This value may be difficult to visualize if you look from the vantage point of short-term goals. However, if you monitor this over a longer period of time and experience multiple market-shifting situations, it becomes obvious that this team is more valuable as you witness them adapting to the market better.

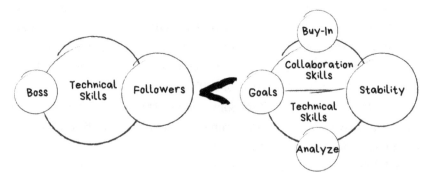

4.3 Management: The Need to Reconcile Differences with Greater Collaboration and Coaching Skills

In the previous section, we illustrated the importance of different perspectives, how they differ from each other, and how they represent varying aspects of the problem-solving spectrum. Now that you have a representation of the full range of problem solving, everything's done, right?

Wrong! Because the team is less homogenous, they tend to think differently. This means there is an increased amount of *tension points* that will exist throughout the team.

Tension Point Management

What is a tension point? You know when you say something to someone, but they hear a completely different message to what you actually said, and they get frustrated, then you get frustrated? That's a tension point.

For example, imagine an Analyzer wants to focus and work, but an Enthusiast keeps chatting him up. The Analyzer is frustrated that he can't focus and that the Enthusiast is not getting any work done. The Enthusiast is also puzzled at how cold the Analyzer is and tells him to "relax and stop being so serious." The Analyzer is fed up and escalates this to you. Does this situation sound familiar?

> *Many managers often end up with a traditional team*
> *to avoid dealing with these tension points.*

Whether they are conscious of it or not, managers often end up with a traditional team. Why? They chose people similar to them to avoid the challenges of managing multiple perspectives. In the short term, this may feel more comfortable and easier, but it leads to unsustainable situations.

However, refusing to manage these differing perspectives creates its own problems. When different types of people are left to their own accord, they do not naturally collaborate and achieve the high performance of self-directed teams. This is why you need good management skills to reconcile these differences.

This needs to be done through people development and collaboration.

This doesn't resolve organically. Managers need to reconcile tension points, coach, develop people, and guide the team toward a self-directed team status.

Creating Self-Directing Teams by Guiding the Team through the Different Stages of Maturation

To truly harness the value from self-directed teams, we need to become experts at taking teams through various phases of maturation toward the highest state. This is similar to reaching the Performing Stage in psychologist Bruce Tuckman's Four Stages of Team Development, which provides a frame for guiding teams through these different phases. Unfortunately, most traditional teams never make it that far. Let's explore a summary of the various phases of Tuckman's Four Stages of Team Development:

- **Forming** – This is the honeymoon phase. During this phase, people are excited and are extremely cordial with each other as they are getting to know each other.

  The manager's main role is to set clear expectations for the team.

- **Storming** – In the Storming phase, people begin to test each other's boundaries and bump shoulders with others. Depending on the degree of conflict, this can be the most stressful phase, as disagreements have a tendency to escalate.

  The manager's role here is to make sure conflicts don't get out of hand. As long as they are reasonable, let them happen, and allow team members to establish dynamics with one another. If they are getting out of hand, the manager must step in and stabilize the situation. In high-conflict situations, this may involve a great amount of effort.

- **Norming** – During this phase, boundaries have been established and people are tired of conflicting with each other. The team becomes peaceful as they are avoiding conflict. However, don't let this peace deceive you. This is actually the most dangerous phase because most teams—especially traditional ones—get stuck here. This is where disengagement and demotivating environments arise and become the norm.

  The manager's role in this phase is to encourage people to continue to bring things up. Conflict is good as long as it is done in a healthy manner. That's how the best ideas are born. The manager can identify areas for people to develop through coaching, so that they can begin taking ownership of their work and behavior, and reach higher than they thought possible.

- **Performing** – You actually have to get here to achieve the self-directed team status! This is the phase where people have a great deal of ownership, engagement, and motivation. There is a free flow of collaborative problem solving that the team performs on their own, and the manager may no longer be needed.

  In such a case, the manager's role is to plan succession and slowly step out, so they can work on the next big thing.

It's important to emphasize the importance of reaching the Performing Stage. In essence, that's what a self-directed team is. However, it is also important to recognize that most teams never make it this far. They get stuck in the Norming Phase. This is a common situation for traditional teams.

It's important to reflect upon this and ask:

What phase is your current team in?

What can you do to take your team to the Performing Phase?

Now you understand the anatomy of a self-directed team, and how balanced perspectives of problem solving are essential to their formation. With this awareness, you can avoid the trap of unknowingly building homogenous teams because it feels comfortable. You can fill the voids in your own skillset with people who are different than you, and you won't be surprised when these people bring new challenges to the team dynamic.

Instead, you will focus on reconciling this broad range of people. You will combine the four types of personalities—the Goal Pusher, the Analyzer, the Enthusiast, and the Stabilizer—to create a good balance of perspectives. You will manage tension points through people development and collaboration. With this, you will then be able to guide your team through the four stages of Forming, Storming, Norming, and Performing without getting stuck along the way. It takes great management skills to facilitate this type of team development. We will discuss the nuances of those skills further in Part IV, so you understand how to make the Performing Stage a reality for your team.

CHAPTER 5

LEVERAGING THE SELF-DIRECTED TEAM

I remember waking up one day. I just had a good night's sleep. I felt rested and rejuvenated, not as stressed as before. This might seem corny, but I began to notice how beautiful the day was—it was sunny outside.

I wasn't used to this. Not too long ago, I spent every waking moment worrying and stressing out about the business. It's amazing how numb you can get to the little nice things in life when you're preoccupied with other things.

The peacefulness felt awkward at first. I was used to the hustle and bustle, and I found myself worrying. *What's going to go wrong with the business?* But nothing did. I almost felt guilty about *not* being stressed, almost apologetic. I wasn't used to this. In the past, the business was running me, rather than me running the business. Now, I began feeling a sense of freedom.

The business wasn't running me anymore.

I found myself getting bored. I was used to being a go-getter, but I had freed myself from the business's daily issues. This is the natural progression of culture strategy. I was happy about that, but it felt odd. I couldn't help thinking to myself:

What's next?

Then, I realized that the self-directed team became an infrastructure that was capable of much more than just operating in isolation. It produced a mechanism capable of leverage. That's when I realized my work was far from done. I was no longer in the daily grind, but now I had to play a different game, a bigger game, this time through the art of leveraging self-directed teams.

It gave me the opportunity to successfully lead multiple teams simultaneously. I found that the vehicle for leading multiple teams was very different from managing them. We all know that micromanaging a single team is unpleasant. What's worse than micromanaging a single team? Micromanaging multiple teams—that's even more stressful. Some do this by demonstrating an extremely strong resilience, force of will, grit, or whatever you want to call it. However, with that approach, it can and will eventually catch up to them. That's how people end up sacrificing their personal lives, family, and health for the sake of career and business.

I didn't want to do it that way. If I was going to manage multiple teams, I wanted to do it right. This involved *leveraging* multiple self-directed teams, which was very different from *directing* multiple teams, and that appealed to me. That's what this chapter is about.

5.1. Leadership, a Bigger Game: Leveraging Self-Directed Teams

Just from creating a self-directed team, you'll experience tremendous value. There will be greater adaptability in problem solving and fewer escalated issues. Oftentimes, that's enough of a reason to apply culture strategy.

However, we haven't even begun talking about the enormous potential that culture strategy can capture. We're really just at the tip of the iceberg. Self-directed teams set the groundwork for so much more. They become the vehicle for leverage.

Self-Directed Teams Lay the Foundation for a Bigger Game

To explain this, we need to differentiate between leadership and management. You'll find people define leadership and management as inconsistently as they do culture. Therefore, let's take a moment to differentiate their scope of responsibilities as discussed in this book.

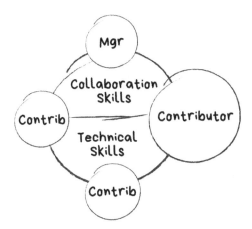

- **Manager** – A manager oversees one self-directed team of multiple contributors. They hold the self-directed team together by managing their collaboration, development, and team dynamic.

- **Contributor** – Contributors are team members with a collaboration-focused mentality in a self-directed team.

- **Leader** – Positioned outside the self-directed team and day-to-day activities, leaders have the capacity to oversee and leverage value from multiple self-directed teams, each with a manager responsible for a team of contributors. This is possible because they use a different set of skills and approach to management.

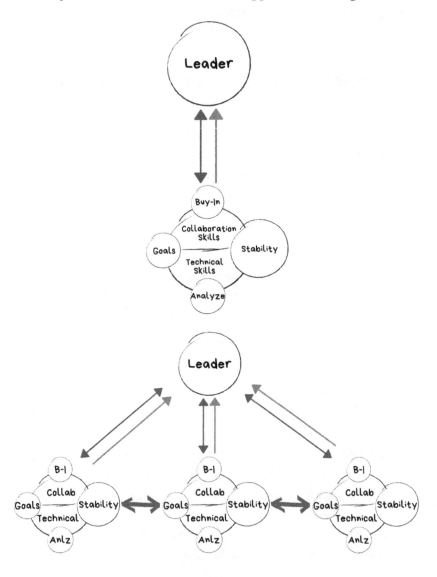

Unfortunately, this is not how most of the world defines it. It's important to recognize how the world sees these definitions, so we can be understanding and get on the same page with them. Otherwise, these concepts can lead to confusion. Let's explore how such terms are used differently by other organizations.

- There are people with management titles who are not responsible for any team.
- There are people with a lead or supervisor title who manage a team but are not called managers.
- Sometimes, functional authority is not given to the leads or supervisors and is instead maintained by a manager who oversees multiple teams.
- There are people with management titles who are responsible for multiple teams.
- There are people with management titles who utilize the skills of leadership within their team.
- There are not many formal titles with the word leader in it.
- There are leaders who oversee their teams with skills more relevant to management than leadership.

As you can see, terminology is very unstandardized. There are all sorts of reasons why companies do it the way they do. All in all, we are explaining this to get on the same page, so we can differentiate the relevant skills and concepts within this book. Now, I admit that the definitions I've used above are oversimplifying a concept that is actually very nuanced. We will discuss these details throughout the book. However, just to move forward with this chapter, let's use those definitions of manager, contributor, and leader.

Even with a Single Team, Transitioning from Management to Leadership Has Tremendous Benefits

When you step out of management and get into leadership, you'll see many benefits. Suddenly, you'll have a sense of freedom through recovered time and bandwidth. For the most part, your team can run without you. In fact, they will take ownership and propose solutions to you. There will be very few escalated issues. Business revenue will be increased and customer satisfaction will remain high.

Let's compare that with being the big boss with a traditional team that has a "manager" deployed there. You'll likely be dealing with a lot of disengagement and a large number of escalations. Likely, you're still putting out countless fires, and you're frustrated with your team. There's a pile of problems whenever you have a site visitation. In such an environment, how could you ever possibly think about growing the business further or recapturing balance in life?

If your goal was to stabilize a single team and recapture balance in life, you may achieve your objectives simply through this transition from management to leadership. This is often the case for small business owners with a single team who wish to recapture time for their families and personal life, while still being moderately involved with the business.

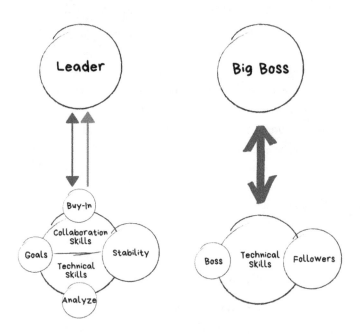

With Multiple Teams, This Transition Can Give You the Infrastructure for a Much More Sustainable Situation

In a situation that involves a greater number of teams, the value of leverage and self-directed teams is more pronounced. To help make this point, let's evaluate what the situation looks like when managing multiple traditional teams. In this model, the "big boss" has to deal with many operational escalations coming from multiple teams. In addition, different teams may have tension between each other, and those issues often get escalated to the boss. No wonder big bosses get stressed! In the long run, this is unsustainable and will implode at a certain point.

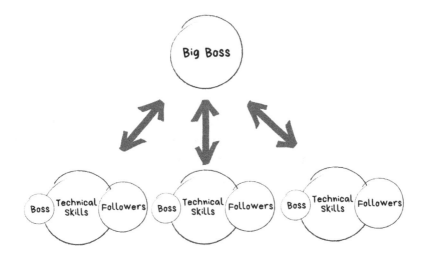

In the self-directed model, the teams handle most of the operational kinks, and they even collaborate with other teams. Thus, day-to-day escalations significantly decrease. Self-directed teams propose solutions and pitch for necessary resources when needed. This creates a much more reasonable workload for a leader to handle when dealing with multiple teams.

It is true that the initial conversion to self-directed teams will be a challenge. However, once the conversion is successful, it becomes an extremely efficient way of overseeing teams. This opens up the leader's energy to refocus their efforts in other higher ticket items.

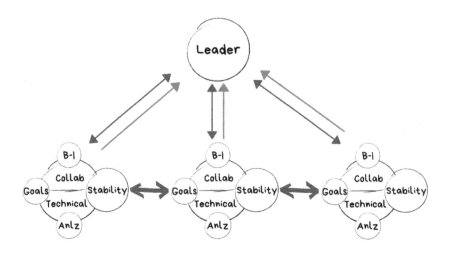

5.2. Identifying Levered Value

By creating a self-directed team, you're already receiving benefits from having fewer escalations and greater coordination among teams. However, we can be even more intentional in capturing benefits from levered value, which is where the amazing potential of culture strategy lies. This is especially the case if your aspirations are to grow and expand the business further.

What Is a Levered Value?

The concept of leverage can be game changing. We can produce an exceptional amount of value that is not dependent on time and sweat. Remember the analogy of opening an oyster shell? Sure, you can pry it open with your bare hands, but why not use a tool to wedge in-between the shell and lever it open? That difference is levered value.

> **Levered Value** is business value that is captured from leveraged activities rather than from the sweat of the work.

To better demonstrate what levered value is, let's imagine that we have two separate, self-directed teams. On their own, they produce one unit of value. So, collectively, they should equal two units, right? Well, if you treat them as stand-alone, isolated silos and are not capturing levered value, then yes. However, if you focus on capturing this levered value, they can equal much more. Long story short, you're making $1 + 1 = 3, 5, 10$, or more. You get the picture.

Levered value is the additional value that is captured, which can be a pronounced amount of value. Leadership is all about harnessing and capturing this value. When leaders focus on levered value, we can generate more total value from the individual components of a business, which are worth far more than they would be if added up individually.

Identifying Different Forms of Levered Value

The first step in harnessing levered value involves identifying it. There are different spectrums of people in relation to this topic.

For some, this can be extremely elusive and difficult to conceptualize. If that's your case, block out some time, ponder on it, write down the possible levered value you have conceptualized, connect the dots with your situation, and figure out what it's worth. We will describe some examples of levered benefits momentarily to get your brain jogging.

On the other side of the spectrum, some leaders see potential levered value very easily, but they have challenges getting buy-in from others and capturing this value. They can use the following list to generate ideas, but it may be more worthwhile to focus on skills in capturing the value in the following section.

Levered Benefit #1: Synergy between Interdependent Teams

In many instances, teams do not function as isolated silos. They impact other teams. In such cases, there are opportunities to create value by ensuring the different teams are going in the same direction and working together. This creates synergistic value between them. We accomplish this by applying the principles of culture strategy on a multiteam level. This introduces collaboration in another dimension, which involves multiple teams. It may involve participation from multiple parties, including team members, managers, departments, and more. Here's what you want to achieve with such efforts:

- **Superior collaboration and coordination between teams** – Naturally, within organizations, the "left hand" doesn't talk to the "right hand." When that happens, it almost looks like common sense goes out of the window. This can greatly increase problems and chances of failure. Getting interdependent teams on the same page through alignment efforts achieves superior collaboration and coordination. That results in greatly increased success rates in reaching objectives and producing value. Sometimes, self-directed teams need a little guidance from leaders to channel their collaborative efforts, which can smoothen cross-functional coordination.

- **Consolidation of the best processes** – Different teams can have similar types of processes. At the same time, certain teams may possess a know-how for handling certain processes that yields superior results. Thus, synergistic value can be produced through the consolidation of such processes to spread this value across multiple teams. That way, multiple teams can benefit from the superior process capabilities. This can be done by grouping the associated tasks with this specialized team or sharing their know-how.

- **Cross-pollination of ideas** – Knowledge capital is one of the most valuable assets within an organization. It is the "brain trust" of the company and should be shared with others to learn through various experiences. However, too often such knowledge sharing doesn't occur due to lack of communication, lack of mutual trust, protectionist behavior, or knowledge hoarding. These are unhealthy tendencies that significantly stunt the potential growth of the organization, which results in more failures and slows people development. Through healthy cross-pollination of ideas, synergy can be created by leveraging the knowledge capital within the organization.

They say experience is learning from your own mistakes, whereas wisdom is learning from the mistakes of others. Though we can all learn everything from our own mistakes, it will be time-consuming and costly. It is much faster to learn from the mistakes of others, which requires people to be open to sharing such experiences. There are countless experiences occurring throughout the organization. We can build synergy through cross-pollination of ideas, which allows people within the organization to choose a wiser path and greatly increases the rate at which we absorb knowledge through lessons learned. This gives us the opportunity for others to capitalize on the lessons of a single team and apply them throughout the organization. That inherently creates value by maximizing future success and minimizing future failures.

Levered Benefit #2: Transferring Ownership in Processes

Processes are meant to generate predictable results that can be scaled for repetitive tasks. However, if we approach processes with a traditional, top-down directive, then it can create rigidity in problem solving. In addition, processes need to be maintained and monitored for compliance, which can take up a significant amount of bandwidth for our key leaders. Therefore, a form of levered results can be harnessed within self-directed teams by transferring ownership of processes to them. This works for a multitude of reasons:

- **Teams buy into the processes** – By owning the processes, self-directed teams will be engaged and be bought into them. This increases accountability and reduces the burden of getting their engagement.

- **Teams maintain the processes** – When self-directed teams take ownership of processes, they also perform maintenance and monitor the tasks associated with them. This creates a more sustainable distribution of work burden for process maintenance.

- **Teams apply the processes better** – Self-directed teams that own their processes are better apt to apply them in their everyday moments. When they own them, they understand their ins and outs, so are better prepared to adapt to various situations. This captures additional value by improving the team's problem solving.

- **Teams update the processes** – Self-directed teams are in a position to identify glitches in processes. When they own the processes, they are also able to update them and make them more relevant. This enables continuous adaptation of the processes, which results in better quality capabilities that have greater depth and relevance to the team members' everyday jobs.

- **Teams transfer the process know-how** – As the organization grows and adapts, there will be a need to transfer the knowledge of the processes to other teams and members. This spreads out the burden of process integration, which can otherwise be an overwhelming task.

Levered Benefit #3: Bottom-up Innovation

The next best idea can be just around the corner. When I look back at my team, I see that many of our best ideas didn't come from me. Sure, I had a hand in guiding them to fit within the organization. Sure, there were some tidbits that originated from me. However, most came from my team. When I first started out as a business owner, I took pride in knowing every detail of my business. Now, I take pride in the fact that

I don't know everything because my team created solutions and integrated them into the organization.

One of the most powerful characteristics of culture strategy is the ability to draw out and refine innovative thinking at all levels of the organization. In essence, this is leveraging the ideas of self-directed teams. This can be beneficial in multiple ways:

- **Discovering solutions that would not have otherwise come about** – How many times have you racked your brain trying to figure out problems that you don't see solutions to? Also, how many times have you implemented your idea, but it didn't work? If you harness this levered benefit, you can harness good solutions from angles that would not have otherwise been considered.

- **Increasing ownership and engagement** – When teams implement their own solutions, they own them! Thus, there are the same benefits of transferring ownership of processes to teams. Teams show greater engagement, adaptability, and application.

Levered Benefit #4: Ownership and Sustainability in Expansion

Expansion and growth can be challenging for business leaders. They generate opportunity, but they also create additional challenges as they increase the scope of work. This is due to the work associated with the growth efforts, but also the work required to continuously oversee a greater number of teams. This can involve an overwhelming number of tasks, which can cause an implosion without sufficient infrastructure.

Capabilities from self-directed teams can be leveraged in these expansion efforts. The ownership of the capabilities is within the teams, and this makes expansion a shared responsibility. Expansion occurs with a continued emphasis on culture strategy, which maintains the people infrastructure of the business and serves as a sustainable growth model. Let's look at the benefits:

- **Higher success rates** – Since you have engaged people who are actually doing the tasks to help transfer knowledge capabilities, the capabilities being transferred are of better quality and are more adaptable, allowing for better integration.

- **Distributed weight of expansion efforts throughout the team** – This creates a much more reasonable and sustainable way of growing and expanding. Too often, businesses grow to feel the pain of a lack of infrastructure. After expanding, they self-implode. This type of reckless growth can create an unsustainable management culture, which can result in an unfavorable situation that resembles a "revolving door" of new talent entering and leaving due to unreasonable distributions and expectations of work.

- **Replicating self-directed teams in the new teams** – When we replicate the formation of a self-directed team in the new team, we can better integrate them with the organization and reduce day-to-day escalations to the leader. Teams demonstrate greater performance and improved collaboration with other teams.

- **Sustainable growth strategy** – Through a combination of sustainable job duties, better processes, and improved collaboration in knowledge transfer, we experience a more predictable way of achieving our growth objectives. It also creates opportunities to develop our talent internally with a continuous stream of stretch projects, organized succession planning, and development of future management/leadership talent. This smoothens out the necessary knowledge, process, and relationship transfers that need to occur as the organization grows. These topics will be further discussed throughout the book.

- **Continuity of culture strategy** – Scaling businesses have a greater challenge in maintaining their culture strategy due to their increasing size. Growth means we are often bringing in more people, which can make culture alignment more challenging. By leveraging self-directed teams for expansive efforts and simultaneously utilizing succession programs, we can promote internally developed talent to represent the culture strategy as we continuously grow the organization and positions open up. When this is implemented properly, it will greatly reduce the rigidity and political bureaucracy that often manifest in larger organizations.

Levered Benefit #5: Strategic Direction

Stand-alone, self-directed teams generate a tremendous amount of value. When they are guided with a strategic direction, they can generate significantly more value. It helps to have a clear enterprise-level strategy to accomplish this. This casts a vision and keeps everyone moving in the same direction to capture strategic value. This clarity creates a common understanding of the priorities of the organization, reduces confusion, and fosters healthy interactions between teams. Furthermore, it reduces internal politics and bureaucracy. With strategic direction, we can:

- **Capitalize on market trends and opportunities** – Strategy can leverage self-directed teams by guiding them to capture market trends and opportunities. This is important because not all value is based on hard work, but rather on smart positioning. When we've adequately built the culture and people infrastructure, we can mobilize self-directed teams to capture this value faster and in a more relevant manner.

- **Maximize engagement** – A well-positioned strategy is purpose driven and can capture engagement throughout the organization. This motivates team members to achieve our strategic vision and serve customers better. When we have greater engagement, we are one step closer to building a world-class organization that can adapt to any issue.

5.3. Capturing Levered Value

Once we identify the desired levered value, we have to work toward capturing it. For some people, identifying the levered value is easy to conceptualize, but capturing this levered value is harder.

The nature of mobilizing and capturing levered value from self-directed teams is very different from managing traditional teams, due to their self-directed nature and the fact that they organically solve problems. Therefore, the name of the game becomes mobilizing and aligning with them without interfering with their self-direction. In other words, don't mess with their groove. Instead, focus on empowering them.

This requires a completely different way of overseeing teams. If you're used to telling people what to do all of the time, you might mess up the interface with the manager of a self-directed team. As you read this section, you'll realize the main emphasis is on communication and influence. We will touch on some concepts now, but we'll go through this in greater detail throughout the book.

Capturing Levered Benefits Tip #1:
Enable Upward Rather Than Downward Management

One of the biggest differences in managing traditional teams versus leveraging self-directed teams is that the flow of delegation can go upward. It requires a mindset shift to enable upward management rather than utilizing a downward-management approach. This involves developing and encouraging teams to take extreme ownership of their own roles to identify issues, problem solve, coordinate, and propose resources/support they need to produce results.

At first, this may appear impossible to those who are not accustomed to it, as it is a special characteristic of successfully created cultures. Some find it very difficult to believe that something like this could be possible without actually seeing it with their own eyes. I, too, was a naysayer before I saw organic problem solving through this method.

However, if we've truly developed our managers and self-directed teams, they can propose solutions and make cases for necessary resources to facilitate their solutions and issues. To truly accomplish this in a healthy manner requires a mutual, trusting relationship, and confidence in their abilities. If we've built sufficient people infrastructure but haven't empowered those people to adopt this partnership mentality, then it is time to make a leap of faith. Here are some ways you can promote this:

- **Empower teams to design their goals, objectives, and tasks** –
  Self-directed teams have the ownership and competence to
  solve problems. Based on their competency level, they can even
  propose the tactical approach, objectives, or goals. This can be
  done in a manner while staying in line with the overarching goals
  of the organization. You must evaluate teams on a case-by-case
  basis to understand their current development level, and make a
  judgment call on involving them in this.

- **Have resources that can be deployed quickly** – The leader has a
  unique responsibility to balance limited resources for allocation
  between competing priorities from various teams and initiatives.
  Resources need to be deployed based upon the strategic priorities
  of the organization. Such resources can include access to training,
  supportive culture alignment initiatives, funds, access to team
  members, access to knowledge capabilities, and so on. Such
  deployment of resources should be a partnered effort between
  the self-directed teams and the leader, rather than letting a lack of
  critical resources become a constraint. This equips the self-directed
  team to be more adaptable to the obstacles they are faced with.

Capturing Levered Benefits Tip #2: Continuous Development of Your Managers and Teams

I'm sure you're a high-performing leader who is used to being better than others in many skills. That got you very far in life up to this point.

However, if you want to go further, you need to develop others and even have them surpass you in their respective skillsets. That's the only way to unlock the true potential and leverage of self-directed teams. That means we need to invest in others. That is how we continuously build onto the existing infrastructure, so that we can leverage it more. We do this by:

- **Developing other managers and leaders** – As a leader, the managers of your self-directed teams are critical in sustaining and growing your organization. Therefore, it's essential to invest in developing their skills, along with deepening your relationship with them. When this is done properly, it further increases the leverage potential of the managers and their self-directed teams.

- **Developing the self-directed team further with specialized projects** – The manager should take the greatest accountability in developing their team members, as they have regular access to them. However, the leader can also help influence their team members' development through involving them in stretch projects, training, and strategic efforts.

Capturing Levered Benefits Tip #3: Reevaluating How We Communicate and Conduct Our Meetings

Mobilizing self-directed teams occurs very differently from mobilizing traditional teams. In the latter, we could use unilateral directives to meet our objectives. This would succeed in mobilizing traditional teams, though we would have a lack of situational adaptability and increased incidents of fires due to a lack of self-direction. If we used a similar approach on self-directed teams, it would actually disrupt them. With these teams, we must mobilize them to leverage results through a different approach. This approach includes:

- **Creating clarity, insights, and transparency** – This is a shift from unilateral planning and directives. In the traditional method, teams don't need to know why decisions are made or what the considerations are. They don't even need to understand such decisions. They must simply do what they are told. However, this doesn't work with self-directed teams. Their self-direction gets more powerful the better they understand a situation. That's why clarity, insights, and transparency are critical components to encourage their understanding and mobilize them. They use that information to strengthen their efforts.

- **Co-planning solutions** – Rather than just creating a plan in isolation and delegating tasks, it's more important to focus on co-creating plans and getting everyone on the same page. Co-creation increases ownership and the ability to situationally adapt because people usually know their own ideas inside and out. On the surface level, this may look like it takes more time, but it saves a tremendous amount of effort during execution, as there are fewer problems that require do-overs. There's a saying, "Why do people never have time to do it right, but always have time to do it over?"

- **Using everyday moments for coaching and developing** – Are we using these situational moments to coach and develop people? When we are confronted with various situations, rather than giving a directive and settling the issue, these moments are great opportunities for coaching and development. Are we doing this? We can only go as far as the capability level of our people. Therefore, it's worthwhile developing them. If our people can't keep up during meetings, it will be difficult to establish the upward-management flow.

- **Getting buy-in and addressing our people's concerns** – Rather than announcing or directing, it's about connecting, educating, inspiring, and empowering. This requires understanding your audience and knowing their world, their way of thinking, and their terminology (so you can speak their language). It's also about packaging the concept in a way that is important to them. In short, to connect with them at a deeper level, it must answer the question, "What's in it for me (WIIFM)?"

Capturing Levered Benefits Tip #4: Reevaluating Meeting Frequencies and Formats to Proactively Capture Issues

A regular rhythm of formalized meetings or checkpoints can help maintain the structure for upward management and leveraging value. In general, I have found that there is a reduced need to touch base with self-directed teams compared to traditional teams, as there are far fewer escalations in such teams. However, there are certain needs throughout the organization that do appear, and establishing such meeting rhythms can proactively address ongoing concerns. Here is a sample set of such rhythms:

- **Interim meetings for close monitoring** – This is appropriate when the manager and team have a greater dependence on the leader, possibly as they're still stabilizing their situation. This level of frequency is usually a transient phase.

- **Biweekly or monthly manager coaching** – This frequency is spread out long enough for the manager and team to have enough room to formulate their own plans, but frequent enough to touch base with the manager and coach them on any issues.

- **Monthly "open-floor" or "state-of-the-union" address with a key leader** – It is natural for people to have concerns that they want to bring up. Sometimes, certain things are best clarified by a key leader. Without a platform for them to share such concerns, it can lead to confusion, stalemates throughout teams, or passive-aggressive resentment. A monthly "open-floor" or "state-of-the-union" address is a great way to capture such concerns proactively and create clarity.

- **Quarterly strategy meetings** – This is a good frequency to reassess strategic efforts and co-plan strategies. It gives enough time for sufficient data accumulation to evaluate success of current efforts, and it's frequent enough so people don't forget about the strategy.

- **Annual overarching strategy meetings** – It is good to take a step back and reassess the overall strategic direction of the organization and get on the same page. In the case of a larger organization's spread over multiple locations, it may be worthwhile to consider gathering together in one place in the form of a strategy retreat.

It's also important to recognize that sometimes it's not about the quantity of meetings, but the quality:

- **Reevaluate the quality of the meetings** – If the quality of your meetings is questionable, then focus on having better meetings! There are plenty of external resources that teach you how to have better meetings.

- **Reevaluate the necessity of the meetings** – Some meetings are overkill, take too long, or are unnecessary. This creates a mentality of, *Oh no, not another time-wasting meeting.* Therefore, meetings should be shortened, restructured, or removed.

Capturing Levered Benefits Tip #5: Reevaluating How We Reinforce Our Strategic Alignment

Setting a strategic direction and getting the rest of the organization on board with the strategy are two different skillsets. What's the point of fabricating a brilliant strategy if we can't get people on board with it? Ask yourself the following:

Does everyone know which direction the organization is going?
Does everyone know what the company represents?
Does everyone know what it means to be part of the organization?
Is everyone really working toward that goal?

Getting on the same page on this can be extremely challenging. This is much more than setting the missions, vision, and values of an organization or handing a strategic plan to the teams. This takes a much more deliberate and continuous effort to achieve strategic alignment. Without this, we will fail to leverage strategy, which can be a tremendous source of value. We will spend the entirety of Part V on this topic, but here is an overview:

- **Build strategy skills within the people** – Use situational moments to build strategy skills within people. Get managers and teams involved with strategic planning to build their skills and take ownership. Co-planning strategies and initiatives yield multiple benefits when properly done. First, it achieves alignment and gets everyone on the same page. Second, it also creates opportunities to develop thinking skills within teams and managers. Third, it improves team members' engagement and ability to execute the plan.

- **Involve people within strategy** – People are cautious when it comes to sharing their ideas because they may get shot down, or inadvertently end up overcommitting and "stepping on their boss's toes," thereby putting the security of their job in question. Recognize that such fears exist and make a conscious effort to maintain the safety of the environment for strategy discussions. This must be navigated while balancing the work demands from current strategic goals and developing strategy skills.

Receiving ideas from people is a lot more delicate than meets the eye. It requires a fine balance between encouraging idea generation while simultaneously quality assuring the ideas and using those moments to develop thinking. This is a refined skill that may require training. It may be important to reassess whether leaders have the will to participate in this process.

Some are hesitant with open innovation, because it might open up a can of worms of unrefined ideas that can lead to mutual disappointment for all parties. However, it's important to remember that you have to give trust to get trust. If you really developed self-directed teams, and you have the skills to receive ideas well, the risk will be greatly mitigated.

- **Create an ecosystem where team-led strategy can thrive** – Reevaluate the organizational policies and processes, and whether they are conducive to enabling team-level strategies. Is there sufficient margin, transparency, developmental opportunities, and access to resources? Are we over-centralizing strategic planning in an excessively top-down manner? Is it time to take a chance by getting team-level involvement with strategies? These factors can play a big role in whether we are successful in achieving organizational strategic alignment.

- **Create clarity with the organizational strategy** – Organizational strategies are either too complex or lack substance. Some organizations are not very clear on their enterprise-level strategies. This lack of clarity can lead to confusion or internal bickering regarding the direction of the organization. To ensure that teams are going in the same general direction, it's important to be clear and transparent regarding this.

Playing a Bigger Game

Once you've established a self-directed team, you'll be able to sleep better and enjoy your days, feeling like the business isn't running you anymore. Then, you can play a bigger game through the art of leveraging self-directed teams.

To properly utilize this leverage, you must understand that a manager is someone who oversees a single, self-directed team, contributors are team members with a collaboration-focused mentality, and leaders are positioned outside of the self-directed team, with the capacity to oversee and leverage value from multiple teams.

You must understand how levered benefits of self-directed teams work, so you can identify and subsequently harness them. This includes knowing the value of synergy between interdependent teams, transferring ownership in processes, bottom-up innovation, ownership and sustainability in expansion, and strategic direction. Harnessing this involves enabling upward rather than downward management, continuously developing managers and teams, and reevaluating how we communicate and conduct meetings, meeting frequencies and formats, and how we reinforce strategic alignment.

This puts your organization in a powerful position. But to maintain that, you must also learn to protect self-directed teams, as they don't live in a vacuum. In Chapter 6, we'll look at why it's important to protect self-directed teams by approaching culture at an enterprise level, and what to look out for.

PROTECTING THE SELF-DIRECTED TEAM

Imagine you're a middle manager in a large corporation. You care about this corporation as they gave you an opportunity when you really needed it, and you've even been promoted to manage a team due to your stellar performance. It's an okay place to work, although definitely not ideal. You can see areas where collaboration could use improvement.

You somehow came across culture strategy and learned how it could make a transformative impact. You saw how it could improve productivity and also make a positive impact on people's lives. You learned the skills involved and implemented them into your team. They weren't thrilled with this, but you were committed to making it work.

Months go by, and it seems like the culture strategy is taking root within your team. You worked really hard to get to this point. You overcame great struggles to get buy-in from the team. They resisted at first, but you got over the hurdles. They've come such a long way, developed so much, gained confidence, and engaged like never before. You've built a self-directed team and opened additional bandwidth for more responsibilities and opportunities. Your team is now extraordinary and capable of handling anything. You're extremely proud of them.

However, rather than celebrating, the rest of the company notices that you're not doing things the same way as them, and they begin to complain. They want to see you in the grind, working *in* the tasks, rather than developing people. The company doesn't recognize or reward your efforts. In fact, others claim that you had a good team to begin with, without noticing the sweat, blood, and tears that were involved in developing them. Then, you notice that your boss takes credit for your efforts.

When your team coordinates with other departments, they're told to relax, that they're making them look bad. Either that, or other teams absolutely refuse to collaborate or think about what's best for the organization.

You get the sense that this is not sustainable, and you recognize continuous cultural dysfunction. You actually see the company making harmful decisions to the organization, customers, and employees. But no one seems to care. You try to bring it up professionally and tactfully, but you're told to just get in line.

You get disheartened, give up, and carry on with business as usual. As time goes on, people who know the true story begin talking about your skills outside the company. They noticed the positive impact you're making. Another company, one that focuses on culture, contacts you seeing a possible fit and is eager to utilize your skills. You're conflicted because you've been with your company for a long time. However, it seems like they're not interested in getting to the root of their issues. You decide it's time to move on. It's a shame this had to happen.

There's a Limit to How Much Dysfunction a Self-Directed Team Will Tolerate

This is a common occurrence when trying to initiate culture strategy with uncoordinated increments. For culture strategy to truly work, it's not simply about what happens within a team. It's also about how the team interfaces with the rest of the organization. Without evaluating those interfaces at an enterprise level, you may inadvertently build an unsustainable situation.

In the above story, the manager and team were able to make a positive impact, but it was oppressed through unhealthy interfaces. The team will likely tolerate this dynamic for a while. But there's a limit to that, and they will leave if it's continuously unaddressed. That's an awful shame because the manager may be great at building self-directed teams and developing other managers and leaders. These skills often go unnoticed as they are usually not associated with critical events that capture the attention of the rest of the organization. So, it gets swept under the rug.

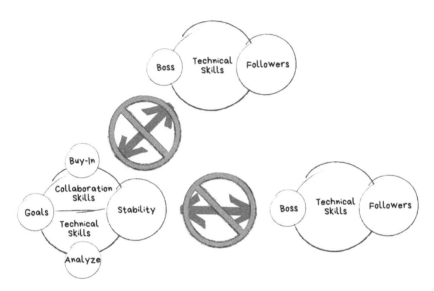

6.1. The Importance of Team Interfaces: Teams Don't Work in Isolated Silos

We're used to having clear-cut organizational structures with designated, functional managers to report to. These structures are used to promote order. Though it is important to maintain structure within an organization, it's also important to recognize that structure may have the unintended side effect of promoting an isolated silo mentality.

The truth of the matter is that we can't work in isolated silos anymore. That won't work in today's market environment where there's a greater need for adaptability. In many instances now, we actually have to work in a cross-functional manner.

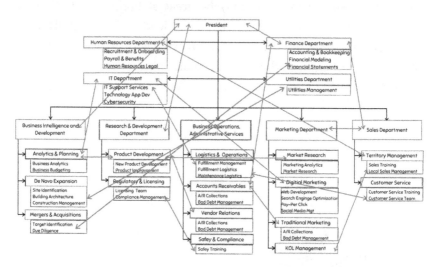

Sample visualization of cross-collaboration within an organization

Let's explore some ways this can occur:

- **Projects** – Temporary initiatives that pull people from different, functional teams.

- **Coordinating everyday tasks** – Teams have to interact with different teams and departments on a regular basis, including IT, HR, marketing, finance, and so on. If collaboration is poor, a lot of tension and issues arise between the teams.

- **Coordinating planning** – Whether it be for planning growth, strategy, projects, or operations, this usually takes a holistic view and multiple perspectives from different arms of the business.

- **Cross-functional teams** – Some organizations have designated teams with cross-functional members for more holistic problem solving.

If we adopt an isolated-silo mentality, then people take on an unhealthy mindset. There will be an unwillingness to help each other. This can open up an unhealthy amount of politics, bureaucracy, playing "hot potato," or even "playing chicken" with a critical issue. A lot of glitches and problems will occur between these interfaces.

This can be a problem, because more and more companies (your competitors) are focusing on improving these interfaces by investing in culture. Traditional companies who do not follow suit will be outcompeted by those who are good at capturing value from these interfaces.

If We Don't Approach the Interfaces at an Enterprise Level, We Will Lose Out on a Lot of Value

We live in such an oversaturated world. Everything is automated and systemized now. Profit margins are extremely thin. Any business value that can be captured with minimal collaboration has already been grabbed.

Today, opportunity is more visible in the in-between functions, where different worlds join together. There are more opportunities here because these areas actually require strong collaboration, something that traditional companies struggle to achieve. This is the value that many disruptive, progressive companies specialize in capitalizing on.

Building an intentionally strong culture can strategically capture this value. Since this value is captured between team interfaces, we need to intentionally approach culture strategy at an enterprise level, rather than in isolated silos.

If We Don't Approach Interfaces at an Enterprise Level, Momentum Will Be Killed

At the beginning of this chapter, we illustrated that the momentum of building and capturing value from self-directed teams needs to be an enterprise-level effort. We can illustrate this by looking at why many acquisitions of innovative companies by traditional corporations fail.

As these progressive companies find ways to outcompete and disrupt traditional industries, it is not uncommon to see them bought out by traditional corporations. However, many of those acquisitions end up failing. The question is, "Why?"

Unfortunately, the importance of the interface between said companies is often overlooked. The difference in cultures means the two companies have completely different processes for completing tasks. Traditional corporations often create stringent rules that disrupt the upward management and flexibility that the innovative company is used to.

This May Be Difficult to See from the Vantage Point of Senior Leadership

From the senior leadership perspective, you can easily overlook the fact that you have unhealthy interfaces, whether between merging companies or individual teams within a single organization. Let's explore why:

- **You're not there to see day-to-day events** – As a senior leader, you don't see the everyday occurrences, so it's difficult to notice unhealthy interfaces and how value is created. It's difficult to tell whether a team is getting things done through a self-directed infrastructure or not.

- **Data doesn't capture this** – As a senior leader, you've become accustomed to monitoring performance through data, but these interfaces don't appear in the data!

- **Your best source of information is your managers** – When you have the right dynamic with your managers, you can keep close tabs on teams from a culture and interface standpoint. However, if you don't have a deep partnership mentality with your managers, you won't get the full picture. This means you need to work on your relationships with them.

- **You don't know what to look for** – Perhaps you're not accustomed to culture strategy, don't know how to recognize it, or don't understand it. You need to learn more about it.

- **You're overworked as it is** – You overlooked unhealthy interfaces because everything escalates to you, and you're always overloaded. Even when managers bring something to you, it gets drowned out by the noise of everything else. This is usually indicative of an unhealthy culture, so it should be a signal to make time and aim for change.

Unhealthy interfaces can happen under the radar very easily. It takes a conscious effort to truly recognize them. It's very difficult to monitor this with data. However, it's possible to keep your fingers on the pulse using better touch-base checkpoints and through healthier relationship dynamics with your managers.

These interfaces are far more impactful than many realize. You must treat them with the due consideration required for successful integration. Otherwise, you will be faced with situations where the momentum of culture strategy is lost and its potential value improperly harnessed.

6.2. People Play a Role in These Interfaces

We all play a role in these interfaces. Culture strategy requires a coordinated effort that involves enterprise-level planning. This is because it involves reworking the infrastructure of an organization at all levels and functions.

We can't put culture strategy on an isolated team by sending them to a leadership class or training event and expect everything to materialize. Too often, companies place culture as a lower priority, as it is more difficult to visualize an immediate gain. Such abdication of responsibility on this strategy results in a failed effort.

Even as the concept of culture gets more attention in today's society, it's treated like an isolated team-level or HR initiative. Unfortunately, that doesn't create the exponential value that is possible. It results in momentum that dies out through unhealthy interfaces. Culture strategy truly needs to get the whole organization on board, involving reevaluation of its roots and foundation.

By now, you've probably realized that this requires buy-in at all levels. There are relevant topics involving the senior leadership, middle management, department, and team levels. Substantial changes in thought processes will need to occur. Let's explore how these people play a role in these interfaces:

- **Senior leaders** – Senior leaders play a significant role in these interfaces as they have influence over the organizational strategy, centralized functions, resource allocation, and organizational policies. These decisions can set the tone on many interfaces within the organization. When these functions are not conducive for culture strategy, it can create an unsustainable situation.

- **Department heads** – Department heads share the responsibilities of centralized functions via specialized roles. Therefore, they can also influence many of the centralized functions, similar to senior leaders. They should also look out for relevance regarding conduciveness to culture.

- **Middle managers** – Middle managers have regular access to their teams and play the largest role in their team members' experience with the company. They should be the beacons for culture strategy by coaching and developing people and building self-directed teams. They should also promote and referee collaborative problem solving among team interfaces.

- **Contributors** – Contributors interact with different teams throughout the organization for various reasons. When they do not play their part and work toward the common goal, it can create unhealthy friction that is deleterious to the organizational culture.

6.3. Policies Play a Role in These Interfaces

Processes play an important role for scaling and replicating functions. They create predictability and organization in a chaotic world by acting as guardrails. Designing and approving these processes is a large responsibility, as it can have a ripple effect throughout the organization. Let's look at two different approaches for designing processes: traditional and culture-conducive.

Traditional Mindset for Processes

When approaching processes with a traditional mindset, the priority is to stabilize disorder. Usually, this is applicable when achieving initial stabilization associated with startups, scaling, or introducing new capabilities. This can be a good interim solution, as the needs in those circumstances include providing direction to people with appropriate guardrails.

It is not uncommon to see such processes with a high emphasis on the following characteristics:

- **Accuracy** – Large volume and highly detailed amount of information and steps.
- **Expertise** – Highly specialized knowledge and expertise applied.
- **Stabilization** – Creating order from chaos through top-down hierarchy and unilateral directives.

This gets the job done in stabilizing the initial chaos and providing direction amidst the uncertainty. However, it is usually not a good long-term solution because it has the following side effects:

- Rigidity
- Inhibited development
- Inhibited collaboration
- Inhibited adaptiveness
- Inhibited innovation

This can be disruptive to the implementation and sustainability of culture strategy. To design policies that maximize the impact we gain from culture strategy, we need to shift the way we design processes.

The traditional mindset for processes worked in the past. Companies met their objectives then. All their competitors were doing it the same way, so rigidity did not harm their market share. However, times are different now. The market has shifted and it now demands more innovative, adaptable, or personalized solutions. This is difficult to achieve with the traditional mindset for processes, as it has an inherent collateral effect of diminishing the establishment of culture strategy.

Culture-Conducive Mindset for Processes

When processes are designed without culture in mind, they can actually cause unhealthy interfaces throughout the organization. In reference to the tree analogy in Chapter 2, culture strategy should be the main trunk, and all other processes should be its branches. They have to integrate with the culture strategy. They should work with it rather than compete against it. That's why processes must be designed as such—to not disrupt the culture flow.

Poor alignment with organizational processes and policies can result in culture strategy failing to penetrate the necessary depths and relevant layers of the organization. When positioned appropriately, processes can promote culture strategy by encouraging healthy interfaces between departments and teams.

This means we cannot haphazardly design processes. We need to take into consideration whether such processes are culture-conducive. Our processes need to encourage culture, with an emphasis on proactiveness, innovation, engagement, and purpose. To accomplish this, there needs to be a paradigm shift in the priorities of our characteristics to:

- **Simple and clear** – Rather than overkilling processes with information, procedures, and data, simplify them to maximize resonance and clarity. This helps build transparency and alignment.

- **Guidelines** – As long as the processes do not entail extremely high risks or danger (in which case, the processes should be very rigid), use guidelines rather than strict policies. Guardrails are still in place, but loosened up in appropriate areas. This gives people space to try things out, customize solutions, and develop themselves.

- **Adaptability** – To maximize self-direction, we need processes with less red tape in the areas we wish to enable upward management. This creates breathing room for innovation and situational problem solving.

This approach positions the policies to support self-directed teams, which maximizes our leverage of them. This is an act of doubling down and maximizing the propagation of culture strategy.

Final Thoughts on Protecting Self-Directed Teams

As we saw at the beginning of this chapter, middle managers attempting to create self-directed teams can get disheartened and give up when they're not supported at an enterprise level. There's a limit to how much dysfunction they—and their team—will tolerate. This is because teams don't work in isolated silos. Today, many teams must work in a cross-functional manner, and this is difficult when self-directed teams must interface with traditional ones.

It's important to address this challenge because these interfaces are where we find value. There is more opportunity available in the spaces between functions, where different worlds join together. This is where traditional companies struggle, as they often lack strong internal collaboration. Companies comprised of self-directed teams can find great value here.

However, it's easy for senior leaders to overlook unhealthy interfaces in their organization. It truly takes an enterprise-level approach to properly address these issues. Processes play a role in these interfaces, as do people, including senior leaders, department heads, middle managers, and contributors, and policies also play a role. To identify and improve these interfaces, we need a culture-conducive mindset for processes that have simple, clear, and adaptable guidelines.

We know what we need to establish and protect culture strategy in our organizations. But how do we facilitate a transition into the kind of teams and processes that support this? What if we face resistance? How do we get buy-in? How do we actually make this work? That is what we'll explore in Part III.

FACILITATING THIS TRANSITION

CHAPTER 7

SHOCKER, THERE'S RESISTANCE!

Anticipating the Landscape of Buy-In and Resistance

The first time I managed a culture change, I was excited about the prospects, eager to implement this win-win situation for my team, provide better services, and grow. I thought everyone else would be as eager to jump on board. Apparently, that was not the case!

I still remember it. I scheduled a time to make the announcement. I prepared and practiced what I would say. I was going to focus on how these efforts would allow us to grow, provide better services, and create growth opportunities for the team on a personal and professional level. I gathered everyone to announce the upcoming initiatives. I thought people would be right on board.

That was not what happened. Rather, I found that only a third of the room seemed eager and just as excited as I was. Another third looked like they couldn't care less either way. The final third actually looked angry and upset!

I couldn't understand it because the win-win prospects were so clear to me. I couldn't understand why people would possibly object to these changes. Since I couldn't understand them, I wasn't prepared to handle their resistance.

It meant my first experience with culture change management was very painful. That's why I want to share my story—to let others know what they may be getting themselves into, to anticipate the various challenges they may face, and to discuss tools that can mitigate the potential risks.

Honestly, facilitating culture change was one of the most painful experiences I had as a business leader. The resistance for this type of change was a lot stronger than I anticipated. There were relationships that didn't work out. This included key employees I'd built deep relationships with, and strong performers I'd put my trust in to prop up the performance of the business.

The thing is, when people cannot buy into the vision of culture strategy, it usually doesn't work out. I wanted to give people the benefit of the doubt. I believed they would see the potential win-win if I helped them see it. Indeed, we did help most through this transition and we reaped the benefits of culture strategy.

However, the root of resistance for some can be so strong that it may involve climbing a mountain too steep to climb. Even if you try to maintain the relationship, it usually leads to passive-aggressive discontent, mutual frustration, and eventual parting of ways. When a key relationship is not meant to work out, you have to prepare for interim operational issues, especially if it involves a key person who is holding up performance or relationships.

7.1. Why Do People Resist Culture Change?

Personally, I'm someone who gets excited with the prospect of change because it involves a new adventure, opportunities, fun challenges to overcome, and new experiences. However, I quickly learned that most people do not share that sentiment. In general, most people don't like change. The truth is that the majority of people are resistant to change.

They're quicker to visualize all the risks and problems rather than the opportunity, even when opportunity clearly outweighs the risks. Once people get used to something, they tend to resist everything else.

It's shocking to see how much effort people will take to maintain their status quo, rather than look toward the future for opportunity. From a bird's-eye perspective, this can look irrational. However, the risk of resistance can be real. Therefore, it's important to recognize the psychology of change, so we are better prepared to manage this resistance.

Change triggers a wide range of emotions within people. These can include emotions associated with resistance such as:

- **Fear** – This can be scary

- **Denial** – Disbelief

- **Anger** – Feeling threatened

The root of those emotions can be due to concerns with the possibility of:

- **Feeling exposed** – This is a concern that change may expose unhealthy performance issues that would have otherwise stayed buried under the rug.

- **Fear of loss** – People are highly protective of what they already have. There can be concerns that change may remove current benefits and shed light on unsustainable perks that people secretly have.

- **Unknown** – People are scared or threatened by what they do not understand.

- **Loss of control** – This is the concern that change will threaten the foundation of a person's world or control.

It's important to help people through these emotions to gain acceptance. There are two main attitudes of acceptance:

- **I accept it** – This occurs when we make an effort to gain acceptance through buy-in and education.

- **It's going to happen anyway, so I might as well get on board** – Some do not get on board until they see more and more people buying in due to momentum picking up. Some people wait until they see that before they get on board.

Once you gain acceptance, it's important to integrate these people well. Answer the following questions for them:

- **Where do I fit in?** – Provide clarity on their role in the overall vision.

- **What actions do I take?** – Give clarity on their involvement in the overall vision.

A well-facilitated change process can greatly reduce the risk associated with resistance and can successfully integrate team members into the vision.

Culture Change Involves a Deeper-Level Change

Culture change resistance is very unique, as it involves a deeper-level change within people. This is more complicated than a process change. Process changes are usually simpler because they do not involve transitions in deeper core beliefs and paradigm shifts.

In short, culture change involves institutionalizing a higher standard of collaboration, management, leadership, and strategy. This requires deeper realizations and epiphanies at an organization-wide level. It involves more than simply adding or changing items on a to-do list. It is about learning to work in a new wavelength. In addition, success depends on buy-in at all levels of the organization, and how people and teams interface with each other. This can also involve organizational process changes that are deeply rooted within the organization.

All this greatly adds to the complexity and challenges in facilitating this form of change. To have a smoother culture change, it's important to understand why people resist culture change.

Deeper-Level Change

As mentioned before, culture change is more involved than a process change, which makes it a steeper mountain to climb. It relates to deeper core beliefs that are often associated with upbringing, past life experiences, and cultural background.

For instance, if someone is from a Traditional Competitive culture, they may be accustomed to a clear, hierarchal structure that has to do with experience or age. The concept of true collaboration rather than authority can seem preposterous. It isn't easy for them because this is more deeply rooted than work itself.

It's not as simple as adjusting a set of tasks. Rather, it requires looking at things through a different lens and with a deeper root cause analysis of situations and paradigm shifts in thinking. It requires managing at a completely different wavelength, learning a brand new set of skills, and maintaining a flexible and solution mentality.

Developing these skills will definitely push people outside of their comfort zones more than other types of change. That's why people will need to learn to be comfortable being uncomfortable. Many of these skills will be discussed in Part IV of the book.

Trouble Understanding It

It can be difficult to get people on the same page and get them to see the value of culture strategy because it is a complex topic. Oftentimes, it takes several layers of paradigm shifts to fully comprehend the topic, therefore making this an uphill battle.

Culture strategy involves many business functions working in a coordinated manner to successfully create this change. Multiple departments, teams across horizontal levels, and even vertical levels of hierarchy need to understand how they can support the culture ecosystem. It can be difficult to understand these roles, as it will likely require reassessing already existing processes that may be deeply rooted within the business.

Now, this doesn't mean that everyone needs to be an expert in understanding the intricacies of culture strategy. However, they do need to understand the general concept and how their role can play a part in it.

"Oh, It's Just Soft Skills."

Much of culture strategy involves the institutionalization of collaboration, engagement, motivation, management, leadership, and strategy. Therefore, many people are quick to judge it by saying, "Oh, it's just soft skills."

Personally, I do not like the term "soft skills." It causes many to underestimate the value and complexities associated with those skills. The funniest thing is that the very people who tend to think in this manner are those who could use improvement.

For example, most people think they are great communicators. However, most people need improvement in communication. Communication isn't simply about being able to make friends and get along with colleagues. It's so much more. If you really want to put yourself to the test, try turning around a dysfunctional team that has high conflict and is completely misaligned and falling apart. If that doesn't sound like something you are confident in doing yet, you likely need to refine these skills.

Skeptical of Relevance

Sometimes, people are skeptical of culture strategy, either because they don't see the relevance or because there is a high degree of distrust of senior leadership pushing strategic initiatives.

In the former, the situation is quite similar to when people do not understand it; therefore, an effective buy-in message, education, and change management tools can help. In the latter, there can be an underlying dysfunction leading to the thought, *This is just a gimmick that senior leadership is trying. It has nothing to do with me, and they won't notice if I don't play my part.*

Perhaps various culture initiatives have been tried before and failed due to improper management. Other times, senior leadership may have tried multiple strategic initiatives that never resolved the real issues. This can include empty promises, multiple attempts at restructuring the organization, changing processes, moving people around, and even layoffs. In such cases, it isn't surprising to see people become numb to dysfunction and skeptical of almost anything.

"My Position Is Threatened."

It is true that successful culture strategy exposes many unhealthy things that were previously buried. It uncovers so much because it's no longer simply data and processes doing the monitoring. Now, there are engaged, bought-in, collaborative people identifying gaps and problem solving around them.

If people were burying things or taking advantage of gaps in the systems, they might realize their position may be at risk. Such situations are unsustainable and may need to be rebalanced when uncovered. Once people become accustomed to unsustainable perks, they may do whatever they can to protect them. This can lead to unpleasant transitions. Sometimes, a grace period of "coming clean" can help mitigate the risk. Other times, unfortunately, it doesn't work out.

How Hoarding Behavior Damages Culture

Sometimes, people will engage in protectionist mindsets that lead to *hoarding* behavior, which can significantly interfere with culture strategy. This is when managers hoard aspects of the job that the organization needs to protect their position. Examples include knowledge, staff, or job hoarding, which blocks collaboration, development, and sustainability of culture.

Hoarding behavior can be extremely harmful to the success and impact of the culture strategy. Let's look at some of these examples:

- **Job hoarding** – This is when a manager who is not bought in to the strategy is desperately holding on to their job. This may be done by not playing their part in developing others to make it look like the team is dependent on them.

- **Knowledge hoarding** – Culture strategy depends on cross-pollination of ideas and solutions. When knowledge of solutions is hoarded, it inhibits development of the organizational "brain trust" and strategic allocation of such knowledge assets to maximize results.

- **Staff hoarding** – Managers have regular access to their team members and may have a gauge on their skill level and potential. Sometimes, managers try to hide and hoard their best team members, and they even take credit for their work. This can block access to key talent for development or critical allocation for organization growth. Collectively, this can create a disengaging environment within the organization.

Hoarding and other types of resistance are real and can interfere with true culture strategy. Resistance can manifest anywhere in various vertical and horizontal layers of the organization. Some resistors will even try to engage in a prolonged battle of passive-aggressiveness to encourage the leader to give up on the vision. Therefore, it's a worthwhile endeavor to try to understand and recognize the resistance, so you can identify steps to overcome it.

As buy-in is a key component to this strategy, it can be extremely helpful to identify buy-in champions, who can popularize almost anything and make the process fun. Strategically allocating these people can assist in facilitating such a change.

7.2. The Buy-In Landscape Is Time and Momentum Dependent

When I embarked on my first culture change, I had an unrealistic expectation that everyone would be bought in and excited right away. Obviously, that wasn't the case, and I was disappointed about that. As time went on and I stuck with the program, many people who initially resisted began buying in to the strategy. I was thrilled to see that, and I became extremely curious to model this phenomenon.

The closest thing that I came across that mirrors this is the Product Life Cycle Model. Simply put, achieving buy-in to culture change parallels the Product Life Cycle—a frame that demonstrates that product adoption is time and momentum dependent based on different categories of people and has separate recommendations for them. This helps rationalize the varying degrees of support along the different stages of culture change.

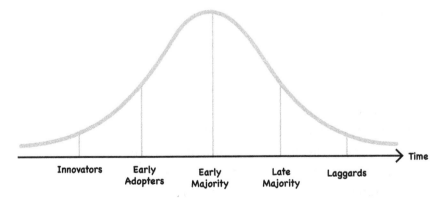

Time dependency of buy-in from Innovators, Early Adopters, Early Majority, Late Majority, and Laggards

Innovators and Early Adopters

Just like with sending a product to market, there will be people who are Innovators and Early Adopters. They see the benefits of culture change early on and are eager to get on board. They're likely to be at the forefront of things, see the benefits early, and can help evangelize the momentum.

Recognize them, capture their support, and partner with them to maximize the momentum and capture the buy-in from the Majority.

Early and Late Majority

Typically, the majority of the people tend to wait to see if others get on board before they choose to do the same. Seeing others join in gives them peace of mind that this initiative is here to stay and is a beneficial movement. Rather than joining in early, they like to "play it safe" by joining only after seeing others safely do so first. In fact, once momentum has picked up, continuous resistance would be a riskier move for them, as they are likely to be the odd one out.

It's important to be steadfast as you continue to get buy-in from the Majority. Continue to develop an effective communication message and educate them on the beneficial prospects. Strategic partnerships with the Innovators and Early Adopters can definitely help get the Majority on board.

Laggards

Unfortunately, there are those who are Laggards and will resist even after the Majority have bought in. They can be stuck in their ways and refuse the necessary changes to get on board. By getting to know their concerns at a deeper level, you may win some over in the tail end of the buy-in process. However, there can be instances where it does not work out.

Sometimes, Laggards resist because they can identify significant obstacles to implementation. In those cases, alliances can be made to recruit their involvement in the planning of the culture change to anticipate and mitigate those risks. This can sometimes smoothen the implementation by getting buy-in from some Laggards while refining detailed planning.

If that can't be done, it is important to closely monitor whether they are spreading toxic resistance through negative gossip, causing the Majority to resist. If this is happening, it may be prudent to deal with this swiftly through management feedback or keeping them busy with other tasks. In the worst situations, it may involve isolation or parting ways.

Overall, you must choose to strategically allocate your energy. It may be wiser to spend the greater amount of your efforts to maximize support and momentum from the Innovators and Early Adopters, so that the Majority can be captured. Then, a reasonable effort should be made to understand and address the concerns of the resistors. This is more efficient than getting tied down physically and mentally by the resisting Laggards. Meanwhile, continuous and steady efforts should be made to effectively communicate and educate the value to the Majority and Laggards to maximize buy-in along the process.

7.3. Identifying Key Stakeholders

When evaluating stakeholders in the buy-in process, there is another important factor to consider: their influence. People can have varying amounts of influence that can make or break culture strategy. This can be through varying forms including:

- **Positional influence** – Represents authority over a large portion of constituents.

- **Functional influence** – Represents key functions, decision-making roles, and business performance.

- **Unofficial influence** – Represents a large portion of constituents without formal authority.

This can definitely add delicate complexity to the buy-in process because highly influential people can resist this effort and cause significant issues. Therefore, it's prudent to maneuver strategically in such a political landscape.

During culture change, it is possible for individuals with *low positional influence* to gain influence by unofficially evangelizing the culture change, or spreading toxicity through gossip.

Below is a diagram and description of the various types of individuals and what to do with them.

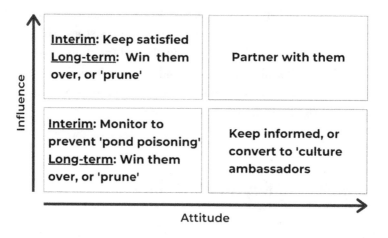

2x2 box diagram: influence and attitude

- **High attitude and high influence** – This is a straightforward situation. You should partner with these people to maximize their impact.

- **High attitude and low influence** – This is also a straightforward situation. You should educate, inform, and facilitate this group's buy-in and integration. However, more value can be extrapolated by converting them into evangelists within the organization and partnering with them, as they can have access to people you normally do not have access to.

- **Low attitude and high influence** – These individuals have the influence to derail the culture change, so it's necessary to be diplomatic and keep them satisfied. However, this usually does not work out long term, and will still need efforts in getting buy-in, or you may have to "prune" them from the organization when it is safe to do so.

- **Low attitude and low influence** – These individuals may initially have a low influence to derail the culture change, but anyone can "poison the pond" and ruin things for everyone. Therefore, it's prudent to monitor this and deal with such people swiftly. Meanwhile, continue to try to get their buy-in. If you cannot, it may become necessary to "prune" them from the organization.

Making Difficult Decisions: Cleaning Up Shop with People Who Do Not Buy In

Sometimes, even with your best efforts, you can't win people over. Ultimately, if you really want culture strategy to take root, you may have to say goodbye to people who do not buy in, as long-term resistors can "poison the pond."

This definitely shouldn't be your initial plan, as you should try to get buy-in first. The better your buy-in skills, the less you have to do this. However, despite your best efforts, if you really can't make buy-in work, it usually won't work out in the long term. There are two main categories of people who don't buy in:

- **Low competence and not bought in** – When people are not competently performing their job duties and are not bought in, it's a much easier decision to let them go because they don't add significant value to the organization. It's fairly easy for both parties to see that it may not be a good long-term fit.

The harder decision is when you've built a deep relationship and been through challenging times with this person. When someone like that is not bought in to the organization vision, unfortunately the relationship doesn't tend to hold out long term.

- **High competence and not bought in** – It's much more difficult to make a decision with a rock star performer who has a long history and deep relationship with the company. These are often top performers who are exceeding job expectations.

  Sometimes, their performance is so strong that they adopt a mentality that they are invincible, believing they have special rights and privileges, which can be harmful to the culture of the organization. This can manifest in ways including treating others with disrespect, unhealthy conflicts, lack of adherence to organizational policy (they believe that they are exempt from it), or job/knowledge/staff hoarding, thereby disrupting the flow of internal talent development.

  This is such a difficult decision, as a leader needs to weigh the pros and cons of keeping them to prop up the business performance versus the business impact of the damage to the culture. It is advisable to rip off the bandage and remove the competent resistors because no single person is more valuable than the rest of the team's potential combined. The long-term damage they are causing to the culture is far greater than the short-term value they are bringing in.

Whatever category a resistor falls into, it is difficult for a leader to admit the situation and bite the bullet for the greater long-term goal. It takes strong character to recognize that the damage that a resistor creates in the culture far outweighs the value they create as an individual. No one is more important than the rest of the team combined.

At times, it can feel like people are irreplaceable, but everyone is replaceable. Sometimes this can be difficult to see when we develop a scarcity mentality. When we adopt a more abundant mentality, it can provide peace of mind when having to make such difficult decisions. Spreading this mentality also grounds unsustainable expectations from people within the organization.

Oftentimes, the frustration is mutually felt, and it is not surprising to see long-term resistors leave on their own accord. If painful goodbyes or "pruning" are part of this culture change process, bear in mind that it's for the greater good and there's light at the end of tunnel. It can be challenging, but it will get better.

With these insights, you can be empathetic to the deeper level change that buy-in requires of some people, and you can better understand their resistance. Knowing how the buy-in process mimics the product life cycle, you can understand the momentum of buy-in and identify key stakeholders who can influence that momentum.

I hope that with this knowledge, you won't be surprised, as I was, when everyone is not as eager to jump on board with the culture change as you are. You can save yourself the disappointment I felt during my first culture change experience, and you can proactively address people's resistance, wherever they fall in the buy-in momentum process. You may face the difficult decision of "pruning" some Laggards, but the people who remain can then fully buy in to the culture change, with everyone playing their part. In the next chapter, we deal with what that looks like and how you can make it happen.

CHAPTER 8

EVERYONE NEEDS TO PLAY THEIR PART

Tools for Getting Their Buy-In

Culture change can be a bumpy ride. It's definitely not for the faint of heart. Nor is it for someone who wishes to please others or maintain the status quo. At the same time, it requires a genuine heart for people.

This is for a leader who is ready to make transformative changes within the organization, one who is ready to take a stand for what needs to be done. It requires refined leadership skills to accomplish this culture strategy. Even in the topic of change management, there is a difference between transformative change and incremental change.

- **Incremental changes** usually involve smaller steps or increments. The nature of the change is smaller or involves a simpler process change, or it's a larger change spread out over a longer timeframe.

- **Transformative changes** usually involve a deeper level of change and have the potential to "rock the boat" or challenge the status quo. There needs to be a willingness to accept risk and overcome large hurdles along with confidence in garnering the necessary support.

Real culture change involves transformative change. Though it may be possible to introduce such changes incrementally, the process will likely be drawn out to an extended number of years, mitigating the gains you would otherwise experience.

That's why culture change can be very challenging. It is usually transformative in nature and it is difficult. It's extremely operator and technique sensitive in nature. That's also why it's worthwhile to invest and develop the skills necessary to achieve the buy-in required for this transformative change. This chapter focuses on these tools.

8.1. Tools to Overcome Resistance

Ask yourself:

> Are you ready to make a transformative change?
> Are you prepared to make a real difference?
> Will you do what it takes to make this happen?
> Are you prepared to live by example?

Hopefully, by now it is evident that everyone needs to play their part in culture strategy. It should also be clear that buy-in is a key component to making this strategy work, and that getting it may not be a walk in the park.

If you go in blind, it's going to hurt. A difficult culture change can be one of the most challenging things to experience as a business leader. Remember, if it were easy, it wouldn't be worth doing. So, it's better to start the culture change process prepared. There are tools that we can use to greatly mitigate the risks. After learning such tools, you can have a smoother ride.

Take a Look in the Mirror: Are You Credible?

The credibility of the leader pushing for culture change can significantly impact the success of the initiative. It can be the difference between every effort being blocked and every door being opened. So, what makes someone more credible than others? Credibility is made up of three different factors:

- **Expertise** – Has the leader done something like this before? Do they really know whether this will create value? If they've never done this before, whose expertise is the leader leveraging? Is there a subject matter expert guiding the effort?

- **Track History** – Does the leader have a track history of living and breathing these concepts? Do they personally deliver results by developing their team? Do they create a motivating environment that involves coaching and mentoring? Can they produce large-scale results? Do they live by example?

- **Relationship** – Has the leader built trusting relationships with people at relevant levels of the organization? Will the leader be able to gather support from all directions?

A leader who does not have credibility may find culture change an extremely difficult path to walk. Therefore, it's important to realize that the leader's everyday actions continuously build credibility to support this effort. It's not simply isolated to the culture initiative.

Does Everyone See the Gap? Using Diagnostics for Awareness

Resistance can occur for any number of reasons. Most of the time, reasons for resistance are subjective. Other times, leaders are blindly optimistic regarding the health of their organization's current culture.

To gain clarity on the current situation, assessments can add an air of objectivity and bring awareness. However, diagnostics can be a tricky thing in culture change because they're not a one-size-fits-all thing. Different organizations have different pain points and reasons for considering culture strategy. In general, though, Employee Engagement

Assessments can be used to gather some data. Common themes with these assessments include:

Employee Engagement
I look forward to going to work every day.
I would recommend this company to a family member or friend.
I look at my work team as friends.

Innovation and Situational Adaptation
I feel like I have a voice on my team.
I feel like my ideas are listened to.
It does not take a long time for a new process or policy to be approved.

Organizational Alignment
I can walk over to another department and ask questions.
I know how the work I do daily impacts the organization's mission.

Access to Resources
When there is an emergency, I can get access to relevant resources quickly.
The resources I need are readily available to me.

Developmental Culture
My company has a learning and growth mentality.
I have opportunities to move up in the organization.

Customer Service
A significant percentage of customers stay in a loyalty program or are long-term customers.
Customers recommend my company to friends, family, and colleagues.

Growth Mindset
My company is willing to look in new directions and explore
new ideas.

This can add objectivity and provides benchmarking that can be applied throughout the organization. Other times, customized metrics can be identified and benchmarked to evaluate a particular component of the organization as it relates to culture.

Sometimes, they can include other metrics, including those from HR, customer service, marketing, and other key areas vital to the company's culture. Some examples include retention rate, cost per hire, training expense per employee, succession planning-related metrics, and more. Some companies already have an abundance of data, whereas others need to build their data-gathering capabilities. The data doesn't capture every element of culture strategy, as that would be impossible, but it does allow us to introduce objectivity to a highly subjective topic.

It's important to note that there may be a need to overcome false data with assessments, because sometimes its data can paint a rosier picture than reality. Interestingly, organizations experiencing culture dysfunction are often blind to it due to false optimism. Even when data is gathered, it can paint a false picture for many reasons. The most common are:

- **Intimidating boss syndrome** – The data can be false when there is an overall atmosphere of fearing the boss. If there is a sense that the responses may be used against the participants, they will likely choose the safe route of providing over-optimistic responses to keep the boss happy. To get over this, there needs to be an overall sense of safety within the answers. The methodology of gathering the information can influence this.

- **Poor verbiage on the questionnaire** – Poorly written questions lead to poor data. Writing quality questions with clear verbiage is a lot more technique sensitive than most people realize. Questionnaire verbiage (and even design) can have psychological influences on responses. Developing quality questions that engage the core of the issue is important in gathering true data.

- **Lack of follow-through** – Many organizations gather a tremendous amount of data and do nothing with it. If people get accustomed to gathering data and doing nothing about it, then it loses meaning. Therefore, it's important to have good follow-through action afterward. When people see results from this process, they're more likely to be engaged with it.

If an organization is experiencing this, it may be worthwhile considering good, external facilitators and focus groups to overcome some of these hurdles. An unbiased, third-party perspective may be a good way to bridge the gap of false data.

Truly Understanding Why You're Doing This

The more you understand and believe in the value of culture change, the more convincing you'll be. That's why it's important to be genuine. *Don't be fake!*

People know when you really don't understand why you're doing this. They know when you're simply patronizing them. It will be in your tone, in your body language, and in other subtle cues.

Know what you're trying to do. Don't aimlessly try to hype things up. Understand how value is created. Understanding the concepts of this book is a great place to get to grips with the depth of culture strategy. Live it by example. Show others how exponential value gets created. When people see it materialize, they will be more likely to jump on board.

Connect with People Emotionally

Too often, we design a strategic announcement that focuses on how this new effort is great for the organization. Let's face it: most people don't care. It's important to accept this, and not deny it. If we are in constant denial, we can't get around it. People won't buy in to something if we don't address the following for them:

WIIFM – What's in it for me?

This is predominantly an emotional process, rather than a logical one. This requires connecting with people at a genuine level. And we can't be patronizing about it either. People can sense when we're being fake. Your message needs to be communicated with:

- The right message,
- In the right place, and
- At the right time.

When this is off, people will have their guard up and resist. Therefore, it's important to be cognizant of these factors when getting your buy-in.

Crafting an Effective Communication Message

When crafting an effective communication message, you must see things from your audience's angle:

- Their world
- Their personality
- Their situation
- Their perspective
- Their technical background

By being genuinely curious, you can usually uncover their source of resistance and aim to address it. You can better understand what's on their mind and prepare your message. Ask yourself:

What in this change may be threatening?
What do they need to envision?

Personality can also play a big role in interpreting any message. It's worthwhile to customize your message so it resonates with different types of personalities. Crafting a message that encompasses a range of concerns is wise to mitigate risk and optimize success. That's because they usually care about different things!

- **Goal Pushers** – What needs to be done by when?
- **Analyzers** – Why are we doing this?
- **Enthusiasts** – Who is doing what?
- **Stabilizers** – What is not changing? And what is changing? (This is the main concern for the majority of people.)

It's important to recognize that the fourth item, "What is not changing? And what is changing?" is usually the largest concern that needs to be addressed. For the majority, change elicits a nervous response that triggers thoughts such as, *Will I keep my job? Am I in trouble? Are we doing everything differently? Do I need to learn my job all over again? Am I moving?* People focus on these thoughts rather than the benefits. It's wise to proactively address these concerns rather than keeping people in the dark.

Sometimes, terminology can be a major factor for distrust or confusion. People can have varying technical, educational, and training backgrounds. By understanding how they talk and adopting their verbiage, a large distance barrier can be removed. Therefore, it can be worthwhile learning this to build trust.

Focus on Awareness, Desire, or Knowledge

Overall, this is an education and buy-in focused message. We're not forcing this on people with directives and hierarchy. That means that we have to get people to want to do this without using authority. Don't shove everything down their throat at once. Know whether you need to focus on awareness, desire, or knowledge.

There's *a lot* of content within culture change. It can be overwhelming to introduce all that information at once. It's important to recognize that *attention is a limited resource.*

By delivering information in bite-sized pieces, it becomes possible to facilitate a smoother buy-in process. The overall message can be broken down into smaller pieces based on the current needs of the culture change.

- **Build awareness and urgency** – This includes promoting awareness of the current situation. People are usually not aware that their culture may have dysfunction. (It's surreal what people can get numb and used to.) They are also not aware that there are alternatives, and that culture strategy can create value, sustainability, and continued market relevance. Subsequently, we may need to create a sense of urgency to foster a drive for action.

- **Create genuine desire for change** – After creating awareness, we need to create a desire for change, so people want to do this. It is obvious that there will be change. Some people can be very uncomfortable with that, so we really need to express the positive aspects of this change. Culture strategy has the potential to create forward momentum for the organization by keeping it market competitive and relevant by leveraging win-win situations. People can potentially benefit through career advancement opportunities, greater autonomy, flexibility, self-expression, being a part of something greater than them, and much more.

- **Educate with knowledge** – Lastly, we need to educate people with knowledge of culture strategy because living this strategy can be very different from what they are accustomed to. They need to know how they play a role in this strategy. This can involve announcements and training, but it is much more than that. This requires living these principles on a day-to-day basis. Therefore, knowledge needs to be integrated with situational feedback, meetings, and reviews. If you don't have access to everyone because of the size of the organization, then other managers and leaders must be coached to live culture change as well.

Culture strategy involves getting results through buy-in, rather than authority. Therefore, it is worthwhile to develop skills in achieving results with a buy-in focus. Even when this initiative is occurring top-down, a paradigm shift from an authority focus to a buy-in focus needs to occur.

8.2. Understanding Different Types of Stakeholders

Interestingly, the push for culture change can come from different directions. It can be initiated from:

- Senior leadership,
- Middle management,
- The board of directors and then put on senior leadership,
- Senior leadership and then put on middle management, or
- A particular department.

The obstacles for buy-in can depend on where the push for culture change is initiated and who needs to be influenced. Obviously, the originator of the push is usually bought in, but that person may have challenges getting buy-in from other parts of the organization. Therefore, it's worthwhile to understand the typical thought processes at various levels, so you can anticipate and proactively address their concerns.

Getting Buy-In from Senior Leadership

Senior leadership buy-in is a key component to implementing culture strategy. If it is initiated by them, then this is usually not an issue. However, if it's initiated from the bottom up, there is a tendency for senior leadership to abdicate the ownership of culture change to the initial instigator. That's a significant challenge because lower layers of the organization often don't have the authority to initiate culture change across the organization. Additionally, momentum is adversely affected when it is visible that senior leadership has not bought in to this strategy.

If it is initiated by senior leadership but farmed out to lower layers or treated like a lower priority (like completing a check on a to-do list), then it has the same effect as not being bought in. This can happen due to various reasons, including the initiative being a directive from a board of directors (without being bought in) or picking it up from other opinion leaders without truly understanding what's involved.

What You Need Senior Leadership to Do:

- **Live it by example** – Senior leadership needs to live the culture strategy by demonstrating real results through a people-development-focused mentality. They also need to harness the levered value from self-directed teams, develop other managers/leaders, and build an ecosystem of strategy throughout the organization. If they are not accustomed to doing things in this manner, it may also require development of new skills.

- **Possess the courage of a transformational leader** – Senior leaders need to be willing to confront resistors and make difficult decisions when necessary. This takes true character, a willingness to stand up for what needs to be done, and the ability to embrace the calculated risks required.

- **Treat it like the core strategy, rather than a tab in a "to-do list"** – Senior leaders need to be willing to reevaluate the central strategy and priorities using culture as a focus. This may reprioritize how resources are allocated for a unified, strategic push.

Why Senior Leadership May Resist:

- **Can't see the relevance** – Often, senior leadership has a goal-oriented and analytical mindset, and they disregard people-focused efforts as something to minimize their complaints and "simply keep them happy." This can be due to lack of understanding of how people and culture-related initiatives can create exponential value. Other times, it's because they prioritize short-term objectives over long-term growth focus. (Culture strategy is a long-haul strategy.)

- **Stuck in their ways** – Some senior leaders can't get accustomed to collaboration and self-directed, bottom-up management. Imagine a senior leader who believes there are certain privileges that should be granted to them based on their position, but now is expected to win people over with skills involving influence, buy-in, and getting to know them and their motivators, so they can develop them. It is a new set of skills that could go against their past experiences and beliefs, and may potentially expose vulnerabilities or skill deficiencies that would weaken their position. This can shake their ingrained beliefs of how things should be run.

- **Fear of loss of control** – Culture strategy involves capitalizing on the value of human capital and trust. If senior leaders are accustomed to dysfunctional cultures, they may have a real distrust for other people. They may believe, *If I give them an inch, they're going to take a mile.* They may be concerned with exposing the vulnerabilities of their position, influence, and developing new skillsets. The inability to get over this mentality can be extremely disruptive to culture strategy taking root.

Why Senior Leadership Should Do It:

- **Organic, sustainable, innovative, and exponential growth** – It may not be immediately visible, but if this strategy takes root, it actually yields greater productivity than any other effort. If they are the resistors, then the key may be to get them to understand by communicating from the business point of view. Subjective claims will likely be interpreted as baseless claims. Therefore, it would be more prudent to utilize data, financials, results from assessments, demonstration of ownership, business proposals, comparable evidence, and subject matter experts' help to support the claim. It can also help to demonstrate proof-of-concept with real results from an isolated team within the organization to gain the credibility to spread the values across the organization.

- **Recapture balance in their lives** – It's not uncommon for senior leaders to be overworked overachievers. Sometimes, that comes at the cost of their personal lives. Culture strategy creates an infrastructure to achieve greater heights without sacrificing their personal lives.

- **Regain a purpose in their career** – At the end of the day, many senior leaders often want to leave their imprint on the world. They want to be a part of something bigger than themselves. Culture strategy offers that through the potential impact that it can make.

Getting Buy-In from Department Heads

Historically, many teams and departments were able to get by while working as isolated silos. In today's business environment, this is not effective as there is a greater need for unified and adaptable problem solving. Different departments must be able to come together under a unified strategy and be willing to collaborate.

What You Need Department Heads to Do:

- **Reassess their current processes and policies as they relate to culture strategy** – Many departmental processes may be archaic, outdated, and irrelevant to culture strategy. In fact, they can interfere with it, so it's important to reassess them.

- **Understand their role in the overall strategy and buy in to that strategy** – Culture strategy may involve rebalancing the influence and prioritization of various departments. Department heads must be willing to look at the overall strategy and accept their role in it.

- **Collaborate with the rest of the organization** – Department heads also need to represent the values of culture strategy within their own teams and when they interact with the rest of the organization. They need to encourage their teams to do the same.

Why Department Heads May Resist:

- **Processes are deeply rooted and department heads are unwilling to reassess the status quo** – There may be a mindset that deeply rooted organizational processes and policies are untouchable. A mentality of, "That's just the way we do things" can significantly interfere with the adoption of newer processes. Also, there may be a reluctance to manage the change associated with such process updates.

- **Unwilling to accept their role in the overall strategy** – During the rebalancing of priorities of various departments based on the strategy, some will gain more access to resources, and others will lose some. Department heads may resist if their department is deemed a lower priority, especially if it involves a decrease in resources or their own personal benefits.

- Unwilling to collaborate with the rest of the organization – Many departments may have become accustomed to working in isolated silos, and they may resist the newer collaboration requirements.

Why Department Heads Should Do It:

- **Improved and relevant processes** – By improving processes, their department will be more relevant to the organization. There will be a reduced number of headaches from dealing with fires within their team and between teams.

- **May create additional innovative opportunities for their department** – Culture strategy may create opportunities for the department to grow further with the organization. This is the case even if resources are initially reduced. With an exponential growth company, there will be a growing need for the functions of various departments.

- **Regain purpose, team spirit, and the feeling that the organization has your back** – Being a part of an organization with a purpose and having an active role in it is more satisfying than having constant dog-eat-dog political battles among departments. It's nice when the company has your back. Even if your department drops the ball, rather than jumping on it as ammunition for political endeavors, the organization supports you. It gives a nice feeling of peace of mind.

Getting Buy-In from Middle Management

Buy-in from middle management is key because they have access to the majority of the people within the organization. Not only that, direct managers have the greatest role and influence on the experience of an employee. If the manager is not bought in, then the culture strategy will fail to impact their entire team. Therefore, it's important to strike a partnership with middle management to spread the culture strategy.

What You Need Middle Management to Do:

- **Dig deeper and reassess their ways** – If a middle manager is not accustomed to managing through a people-developmental focus, it may require several paradigm shifts to transition their ways to methods conducive to culture strategy. This can require digging deeper and reassessing their ways, which may be uncomfortable.

- **Be the beacon for culture within their team** – As middle managers have regular access to people that senior leaders do not, they become the face of the organization for their team. It's important to represent the culture by living it in their everyday actions. It also requires them to be a coach and have a collaboration mentality to create self-directed teams.

- **Collaborate with the rest of the organization** – Middle managers need to be willing to collaborate with other teams and promote that mentality within their team.

Why Middle Management May Resist:

- **"It's just another senior leadership gimmick"** – Sometimes, organizations have a track record of unsuccessful attempts at creating value. This can include failed attempts at restructuring the organization, strategies, process changes, leadership changes, and even layoffs. Middle management can often notice when the ground-level issues are not being dealt with. This can dishearten the mindset of middle managers and create distrust. They may adopt a mindset that this is just another gimmick that won't work.

- **Stuck in their ways** – Just like senior leaders, middle managers may also be accustomed to preconceived beliefs of management that are deeply rooted in their upbringing, cultural background, previous experience, and habits. They may not be willing to adapt to managing collaborative teams, as they may have an overdependence on hierarchy and authority. This can be harmful because it may breed mentalities such as, "They should feel lucky to even have a job," which can result in demotivated teams. Then, they will likely be stuck with traditional teams and struggle to reach a self-directed team status.

- **Hoarding** – Culture strategy has the potential to uncover unhealthy behavior. It can uncover self-serving protectionist behavior that is harmful to culture strategy. Middle managers may be aware of this and concerned about the security of their position. They may have been hoarding knowledge, staff, or their job. They may have participated in causing the culture to be dysfunctional themselves. They may have concerns that they will be exposed and they'll subsequently resist the culture strategy.

Why Middle Management Should Do It:

- **Good for the team** – In general, middle managers have a greater tendency to care for the needs of their team. In such cases, culture strategy is a great way to create value for their team members, as it can usually lead to greater autonomy, fulfillment, personal growth, flexibility, perks, and professional opportunities.

- **Transparent opportunities** – Culture strategy promotes transparency for growth opportunities throughout the organization. If a middle manager demonstrates aptitude and interest, they are more likely to be developed as a leader, as there is a greater preference for promoting leaders internally rather than through external hires.

- **Regain a purpose** – A sense of purpose goes a long way. It creates engagement and greater satisfaction in their career and life. Middle managers have the opportunity to find their purpose and calling through partnered efforts with the organization.

Getting Buy-In from Team Contributors

Team contributors represent the largest share of people within an organization. Buy-in from team members is necessary as the bulk of work, collaboration, and problem solving needs to come from them. Partnership with middle managers is essential in accomplishing this, as they have direct and regular access to their own team members. However, it is important that senior leaders are also living the culture strategy by example, as people will take notice of that. Additionally, communication that focuses on connecting with the people and carefully crafting WIIFM messages can definitely help with the buy-in process.

What You Need Team Contributors to Do:

- **Embrace self-management, ownership, and engagement** – Team contributors need to take ownership of their role. They must be engaged rather than treating the job with a "clock-in, clock-out" mentality. They should be clear and confident communicators without being aggressive or passive, demonstrate self-management, and be emotionally strong, especially in trying times. They should also be open to coaching and feedback.

- **Improve thinking skills** – They must understand how their role affects the bigger picture. We want them to look upon the horizon, think ahead, problem solve, and think critically and analytically. We don't want them to be scared to strategize.

- **Collaborate** – Contributors should be excellent team members who are willing to collaborate, have each other's backs, and not cause drama. They should learn to communicate in a clear manner, and understand the communication preferences of different people and adapt accordingly. This way, they won't ruin the culture for others.

Why Team Contributors May Resist:

- **Just want to be told what to do, don't want to take ownership** – Interestingly, there are contributors who prefer a role with less autonomy and growth opportunities. They're so used to being told what to do that they find that thinking for themselves or taking ownership is too uncomfortable.

- **Don't want to improve self** – Some people are not interested in developing themselves. Sometimes, they cannot accept change. Other times, they're not willing to jump through the hoops of learning new skills. Sometimes they can't accept that they're the ones who can use improvement because they can't see their own blind spots.

- **Don't want to collaborate** – Contributors can resist collaborating for multiple reasons. Collaboration requires true, empathic listening without jumping to conclusions. Often, people struggle with that because they have a habit of blaming others. Sometimes, adapting their communication to different types of people is too stressful for them, and they are unwilling to build those skills.

Why Team Contributors Should Do It:

- **Improve themselves** – I've received feedback on multiple occasions that the lessons they learned in becoming a part of the culture strategy are applicable to and have improved their personal lives as well. The quality of their personal relationships and control over their own lives improve as a result of developing these skills.

- **Perks** – Organizations with strong cultures have healthier work environments with a sense of purpose, dignity, mutual respect, flexibility, autonomy, and potential for growth. These perks can go a long way and often are more compelling retention mechanisms than other benefits.

- **Team spirit and camaraderie** –If you count up the hours, we actually spend more time with our "work families" than our own families. People ought to be at a job that makes them happy. Life is too short to be unhappy at a job. When people choose to be with a team that makes them happy, a sense of team spirit and camaraderie develops. It strengthens the pride in being a part of such a team. There's fulfillment in being a part of a team where people grow and make an impact together.

These are not absolutes but trends I've noticed within these groups. Bear in mind that each group can have their own personalities and nuances, so they should be assessed situationally.

It's important to get buy-in from all parties. Unfortunately, people who do not buy in usually do not work out long term. The methods of culture strategy can go against their instincts so much that people who do not buy in typically leave voluntarily, as they are so bothered to their very core by such differences. If they remain and choose to be disruptive to the culture, it may be necessary to part ways with them.

8.3. The Importance of Regular Communication to Reinforce the Culture

Getting buy-in doesn't happen with a one-off announcement. To nurture the momentum of culture strategy, communication needs to repeatedly be reinforced. Creating a culture is like trying to create a brand internally. It often requires four to twenty touch points before something becomes recognized as a brand. That's why it is beneficial to be intentional about this.

Organize Communication Structure

Throughout the course of our busy work and responsibilities, it's easy to forget to regularly reinforce culture strategy without structured communication. Structured communication plans can help us stay organized. However, developing a communication plan is not a one-size-fits-all solution. It's customized based on the priorities of the organization. That's why a prescriptive approach in building a communication plan is not effective, but it is better to have guidelines to adapt to your specific situation. Communication needs to occur multiple times, through multiple media, using multiple channels, throughout multiple directions. Some of these considerations are:

- Involving sponsors, a core implementation team, and targets – It's important to involve the right people. Sponsors are especially important as they can provide the approval, authority, funds, and resources you need to move this forward. The core implementation team, if there is one, needs to be in frequent communication to organize and implement their efforts. We also need to get buy-in and achieve behavior changes with our target people, which will involve multiple touch points and communication in multiple directions—up, down, horizontal, and cross-functional across the organization.

- Integrating a communication plan into the organization – Communication and meetings must occur at appropriate frequencies and intervals. It may be necessary to evaluate any existing communication structures and their schedules. If they exist, it may be wise to integrate culture strategy efforts into those channels, because it's easier to do that than create new ones. If there are redundant channels that are wasting people's time, it may be worth removing them. If there are critical communication channels that are missing, it may be beneficial to create them.

- **Diversifying your communication method** – Communication should be a diversified effort rather than having all your eggs in one basket. That's why culture strategy should be reinforced through multiple means including informal encounters, hallway or breakroom chats, one-on-ones, team meetings, management meetings, organization-wide media, strategy meetings, and more.

Improve the Quality of Communication

Not only should we have a well-structured communication and meeting plan, we must also evaluate their effectiveness. This involves the quality of our communication. Here are some considerations:

- **Evaluate the effectiveness of our meetings** – It's important to have effective meetings and communication formats. It begins with including the right stakeholders with the appropriate expertise, influence, and perspectives. It involves using planning sessions as opportunities to create alignment among multiple parties through a co-planning process. We must also be efficient because if we waste people's time with meetings, they will lose their meaning.

- **Focus on connection, engagement, and buy-in** – Remember, it's not the structured process that makes or breaks this. This isn't just a logistics exercise. We need to get quality involvement, which requires focusing on connection, engagement, and buy-in. So, even if the meeting rhythms are in place, they need to be done in a quality manner.

- **Acknowledge that we all play a part in this** – We need to hold everyone to a higher standard of collaboration, self-management, and thinking. Facilitators must demonstrate superior facilitation skills by being better organized and setting the right tone. People must bring their A game into discussions in a manner that is conducive for collaboration.

- **Live it in our everyday moments, even outside our meetings** – As a leader, you need to reinforce culture strategy beyond meetings. You need to be an example and set the tone of the culture. You will likely need to coach others to do it, too. When you live it in your everyday moments, you will create a ripple effect by setting an example with your demeanor and communication.

With improved communication, we can help everyone play their part in getting buy-in. However, this starts with you. Your expertise, track history, and relationships will determine if you are a credible champion of culture change for your organization. Beyond your own credibility, you can use diagnostics to increase awareness around the need for change—as long as you are aware and avoid the traps of false data. It's also essential to connect with people emotionally, crafting a communication plan that speaks to WIIFM (What's in it for me)? An effective communication plan should use the verbiage of Goal Pushers, Analyzers, Enthusiasts, and Stabilizers, and deliver information in bite-sized pieces.

We've seen that this information and the push for culture change can come from senior leadership, middle management, the board of directors, a particular department, or others. The obstacles you face will depend on where the push is initiated and what the thought processes are for the various stakeholders. With these insights, you can encourage culture change through reinforcing regular, high-quality communication.

CHAPTER 9

KEY ITEMS IN ENTERPRISE-LEVEL CULTURE CHANGE

When some people ask me about culture strategy, they want to size up the scope of culture change. Now, that can be challenging to answer because it is different case-by-case, and not everything is done at once. Some initiatives only make sense after you reach a certain scale. Other initiatives are not relevant for certain companies. And still others make sense during later phases of culture change. Furthermore, some items are dependent on which chronological phase of culture change we are in, which will be discussed in the next chapter.

Despite that, some people still want an overview of the key items involved in culture strategy. As long as we understand that we need to evaluate situations on a case-by-case basis, rather than following a steadfast rule, I am happy to provide an overview of the key items typically involved with culture strategy.

This chapter can be a lot. The content may come at you fast. This is not meant to be an in-depth discussion but more of an overview, so you can get a relative idea of the scope of what needs to be done. We'll go over many of the concepts in greater detail throughout the rest of the book. If everything doesn't soak in, it's okay. We'll be going over many of the concepts again.

We discussed the foundational theory behind culture strategy in Parts I and II. We spent the two previous chapters talking about resistance and tools for managing culture change. Now, we're going to shift our discussion to what we're actually changing. This chapter sets an overview for some of the key items that need to be accomplished to successfully enact culture change.

Key Cross-Functional Initiatives

As you read this chapter, you'll quickly realize that many of these initiatives need to be approached from a cross-functional standpoint. To truly develop and sustain culture strategy, different departments must move in the same direction rather than acting as individual silos. There are many initiatives that involve support from cross-functional teams and departments. If we do not approach this with a cross-functional standpoint or get buy-in from those who have such influence, there will be tremendous blocks and misalignment that will impede the success of the culture strategy. This will hinder the sustainability of the culture due to compromised collaboration interfaces.

This requires buy-in from people with high authority, and it usually requires support from senior leaders to influence the different departments to align with the culture strategy. This often requires:

- Initiation or backing from the CEO
- A culture strategy steering committee that provides the appropriate authority and governance
- An enterprise-level strategy that creates clarity on priorities and unites the different functions of the business
- Acknowledgment of culture strategy as a high priority within the enterprise-level strategy

To accomplish this, various paradigm shifts may need to occur from various cross-functional departments. This may include:

- **Alignment with operations** – Operational processes should maintain order, but not constrain the individual's situational problem solving and development. This is accomplished with processes that focus on clarity, flexibility, and adaptability.

- **Alignment with finance** – The finance department must account for the initial and ongoing expenditures to create and sustain the culture. It is important to align the compensation and reward structure so it is congruent with culture strategy. The finance department should align with the rest of the organization with an adaptive financing approach to account for situational adaptation of resource allocation (for example, funding) for teams, which may be proposed in a bottom-up management direction.

- **Alignment with human resources** – Human resources can play a large role in culture strategy through its strategic recruitment, onboarding, succession planning, and training/coaching resource support. Depending on the influence of the department within the organization, this may occur as a prominent or supporting role.

- **Alignment with strategy** – The value of strategies can be maximized by leveraging culture through a focus of having an ecosystem where strategies at all levels can thrive while maintaining alignment, which maximizes innovation and adaptability throughout the organization. This is opposed to the traditional top-down approach, which decreases ownership and engagement.

- **And more.**

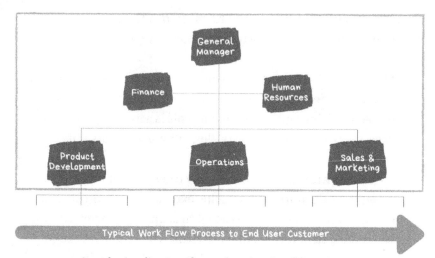

Sample visualization of cross-functions in an organization

Once the various departments and teams are aligned with the culture strategy, it will optimize the collaboration interfaces among the different teams throughout the organization.

9.1. Investing in the Value of People

We need to adopt the mindset to view people and culture as assets and investments rather than expenses. Sometimes, this can be difficult for senior leadership who are accustomed to reading financial statements. If you look at a typical financial statement, people do not appear as assets. They appear as expenses for payroll. But the truth of culture strategy is that you're investing in people infrastructure, which is clearly an asset, but not usually recorded as such.

Why else would large companies pay top dollar for smaller, innovative companies that aren't justified by their current revenue? Sure, we can claim that it's based on possible future cash flows, or synergistic value from the merge. But often, they're buying the culture and the future value it can create. It is common to see large companies acquire innovative companies for their culture, then destroy them with how they integrate and interface with them. Often, they overlook the fact that they are buying the culture and fail to preserve it. It almost makes you wonder why they bought it.

As such, it makes sense for companies to invest in their own people, build their own culture, and treat them as assets. This requires a paradigm shift in the way of thinking for senior leadership, especially financial officers.

Call It a Higher Standard, Higher Baseline, or Requirement

Culture strategy works by institutionalizing a higher standard of engagement, collaboration, management, and leadership skills. However, there may be a tendency for people to downplay its impact or relevance. It's amazing how creative people can get when they resist learning such skills. They say things like:

- "Oh, it's just soft skills."
- "I'm already good at communication."
- "Management and leadership training? Been there, done that."
- "We have a real job to do."
- And the list goes on.

That's why I prefer to use the terms *higher standard*, *higher baseline*, or *requirement* when describing these skills. Interestingly, the very people who resist the most are often the people who need it the most. They try to underplay culture. Other times, people try to abuse the perks of being in a culture-focused company without playing their part, which is obviously unsustainable. Calling it a *standard*, *baseline*, or *requirement* emphasizes its importance and gets people on the same page. This helps negate resistance or abuse.

A Higher Standard of Universal Collaboration Skills

This is a valuable investment to increase the degree of collaboration within teams and the organization. Collaboration skills are essential for a team to mature into a self-directed team. They reduce overall conflict, stimulate better problem solving, increase ownership, maintain culture alignment, and may spark the interest of a possible successor leader. By building baseline skills, such as emotional intelligence, understanding differences in personality preferences, communication, conflict management, and so on, value can be created in many forms. These skills become even more critical for teams that frequently encounter change. In addition, teams within modern organizations do not work in silos, and value is often lost when there is poor collaboration at the interface between them.

Unfortunately, this is often ignored or undervalued, especially in technical functions and senior leadership teams. The value of these efforts is difficult to quantify and measure. These considerations are also emotions-based, which could appear to be "fluffy" topics. People tend to have trouble seeing the return on investment—even when executed properly—because results appear in the long term rather than the short term, and value appears organically in unpredictable avenues. In fact, value gets credited typically to the immediately preceding action that led to the result, and people do not realize that improved coordination led to that value-creating action. However, if you make an intentional effort to pay attention from the vantage point of the leader, you'll clearly notice the decreased number of unfortunate incidents and escalating situations. You'll also see an increased momentum of team-driven growth and problem solving, which creates a ripple effect of value.

Culture-Conducive Management Development

Managers are important in organizations because they have access to a larger number of people than senior leadership. They're the ones representing culture in their teams, facilitating self-directed team development, and coaching and developing collaboration skills within team contributors. In fact, managers play the largest role in the employee experience for their direct reports. Without development of managers within the organization, the culture will not penetrate to the majority of people.

Emphasizing a higher baseline of management skills that are conducive to culture strategy can standardize essential skills within your managers including delegation, coaching, overseeing team dynamics, and tactics. Many organizations lack a quality management development and standardization program. Managers often get promoted into their positions because they demonstrated strong performance as a contributor, and not necessarily because they have good management skills. This results in them having to learn to manage on the job. It is typical to see an unpredictable range of management skills within organizations without standardization of a quality management development program.

Culture-Conducive Leadership Development

Investing in the leaders of an organization is critical because they set the tone and overall direction for the organization. Without quality leadership development that is conducive to culture strategy, the wrong tone can be created and go unchallenged. Without knowing it, leaders may end up creating a dysfunctional culture and disrupting self-directed team development and collaboration.

Leadership skills that are conducive to culture strategy will foster growth through an emphasis on developing other managers/leaders, leveraging self-directed teams, and maintaining a strategy ecosystem that fosters problem solving at all levels. Without this, leaders may end up shooting down any ideas that are brought forth, inadvertently creating a hierarchal culture where situational adaptation, proactive thinking, and engagement are killed.

Do It Yourself (DIY) versus Building a Formal People Development Program

Now, the question that arises is: how do we develop the people? Like many things in life, the answer is: it depends. A transformative leader has a large reach and can influence the development of a large number of people by developing other managers and leaders to do the same. They have a ripple effect of developing people throughout the organization. Usually, smaller companies can focus on building these skills within their main leader(s), so those people can develop others within their organization. It's simpler and more cost-effective.

- If you understand this strategy and can apply this as a leader, you can likely develop other people yourself.

- If you aren't crystal clear and are not sure how to apply this strategy, but believe that you could develop your people if that gap was filled, then you may personally benefit from leadership coaching or an advisory with culture strategy in mind.

- If you see the value in this and are willing to support it, but you simply don't have the time to develop others yourself or lack the team to push it forward, then it may be worth seeking a partnered approach with consultants or coaches.

The scope of this effort may be large enough that there needs to be adjunctive support with a formal and structured development program to augment this.

- If you have a more complicated situation due to having a larger scale organization, multiple layers of approvals, cross-functions, and degrees of resistance, then a more formal and structured developmental program may be necessary.

Considerations When Building Formal People Development Programs

Formal people development programs don't replace the need for improved leadership skills or allow leaders to abdicate the responsibility of developing people to those programs. These are supportive programs to help bear the weight of this effort, and still need to be represented by the leadership and management of the organization. Creating such programs may add to the complexities and cost, but they may be necessary in some situations.

Though it is the manager's responsibility to develop their team members, we can develop supportive programs that can aid in filling skill gaps. This can come in the form of training or coaching programs. They should be designed to develop the skills for their job, but also for culture alignment. This involves skills in collaboration, management, leadership, and strategy. This is not meant to substitute the coaching relationship between the manager and trainee.

Many companies lack a quality people development program because it tends to be either ignored, under-emphasized, poorly managed, or ineffective due to lack of buy-in. Often, it's placed as a lower priority and is the first item to receive budget cuts during economic hardships. Furthermore, a people development program is often ineffective because it was poorly designed. It's important to remember that *this is a content initiative, more than a logistics initiative.*

When people treat this solely as a logistics exercise, it will fail. Logistics is a secondary concern for people development programs. More important considerations include:

- Who's the audience?
- How do they think?
- What would resonate with them?
- Is it relevant?
- Is there buy-in? If not, how do we get it?

It is important to partner with key managers in the development of the training program, as they have an understanding of their people's needs, their availabilities for training, and the type of instructor and message that will resonate with them. The training content and instructor must connect with the trainees at a deep level. Otherwise, participants will keep a closed mind and resist it, which means they won't make the necessary realizations and apply the lessons in their jobs. That would make the program ineffective.

It's important to evaluate the quality of the training. Different trainers have different styles, and their instructional design needs to match and resonate with the intended audience. Therefore, it's important to consider:

- Does it make sense to build this internally or partner with external vendors?
- Who's the right person to deliver the message?
- Will they understand and resonate with the intended audience?

Then, we can consider the logistics:

- How do we coordinate the program with participant availability?
- Do we have sufficient team margin to do that without sacrificing important business functions?
- It not, how do we create it?

Then, we need to consider backing it up on a daily basis. A people development program is much more than training. It needs to be synchronized with coaching and on-the-job application. Otherwise, it won't bear fruit. That's why it's important to develop a culture of coaching within the organization. Ask yourself:

- Do we have good managers and leaders with a coaching mindset who can reinforce these concepts on an everyday basis?
- Are they positioned properly?
- How do we spread that mindset across the organization?

Frankly, these considerations are more important than logistics. Otherwise, resistance or a lack of penetration will result. Too often, a people development program fails due to it being treated like a logistics exercise.

9.2. Setting the Right Tone

It's important to set the right tone within the organization. This is the intangible force that subconsciously influences the perceived norms of acceptable and unacceptable behavior throughout the organization. This is what reinforces culture on a continuous basis.

It's important to set the right tone *proactively*. Here are key items that can influence the tone in the organization.

- Understanding the talent landscape
- Recruitment and hiring
- Onboarding for culture alignment
- Continuous culture alignment
- Refereeing culture

Alignment with Talent Needs and Desires

By better understanding the talent landscape along with their needs and desires, the organization is better prepared to offer packages that are highly attractive for the recruitment of external talent and retention of existing talent. Sometimes the needs are health benefits, loan repayment programs, or other vehicles. Sometimes, they prioritize a healthy, fun, and engaging work environment. This is one of the reasons why some creative offerings have come about, such as having cool slides, games, and complimentary lunch buffets, though it is important to remember that it's not the essence of capturing this capability.

Nontraditional Perks

Culture strategy has the potential to create nontraditional perks for the employees. Many of these perks can go a long way for the company, and they can sometimes create exceptional value for employees. This is in contrast to traditional perks, such as health benefits, pensions, and so on.

In today's landscape, more and more companies are beginning to offer nontraditional perks to be more competitive in attracting and retaining talent. At the same time, many of those initiatives can boost the productivity of the company when rolled out properly, simultaneous to improved engagement. Here are some possible examples:

- Remote work capabilities,
- Flexibility,
- Diversity and inclusion,
- Autonomy: upward management,
- Sense of dignity and respect,
- Sense of purpose,
- Team spirit,
- "Wow!" perks: regular sponsored food, amenities, and services,
- And more.

Many of those perks require maturation of the culture strategy and mutual trust as they are double-edged swords. They give exposure for employees to take advantage of the system. I've seen many instances where companies tried to roll out such perks, but it turned out to be a counterproductive effort.

Therefore, it's prudent to roll out nontraditional perks the right way. This requires understanding the current maturation state of the culture, appreciating the technique-sensitive nature of the initiative, and rolling the initiative out properly.

This can create a tremendous amount of value for organizations and employees when done right. Morale and engagement can improve the bottom line. In addition, it can negate the costs of new hires, training, and the opportunity cost of integrating them into their new position, which can take up to six months. If we have a high turnover problem, we never fully reach a high-functional status. That is costly!

Hire for Culture Fit: Recruitment

Recruitment for talent is not simply putting up a job posting and receiving applications. The recruitment strategy needs to have offers that align with the talent needs and desires based upon the current talent market conditions, as well as strategically aiming for both active and passive (not actively looking) candidates. The search needs to find talent based on the needs of the hiring managers, so that the recruiter is better positioned to recruit and maximize the possibility of a good fit. Criteria should include potential fit for culture alignment and not just technical skills.

In addition, unlike how most people think, culture alignment is an ongoing process that doesn't end within the first few months. Culture alignment is perpetual for the duration of an employee's career within the organization. It needs continuous reinforcement through vehicles such as monthly one-on-ones with their managers, team meetings, and quarterly and annual strategy meetings, which are typically non-HR events.

Initial Alignment: Onboarding for Culture

When new hires join the organization, they will come with a lot of preconceived notions and beliefs of acceptable and unacceptable behavior. This needs to be proactively aligned with culture strategy to minimize miscommunication, mutual frustration, and work-related problems.

Onboarding is not the same as orientation. In fact, onboarding is more involved and impactful than orientation. Whereas orientation involves procedures to get employees into the system of the organization through HR's formal, legal, and logistical considerations, onboarding is about integrating the employee to the team and organization. This involves training, providing resources that employees need to learn about their role and culture alignment. In fact, onboarding can be a powerful tool to aid in maximizing culture alignment.

Understand the difference between onboarding and orientation.

A purposeful onboarding program can help manage the expectations of the organization's culture. Many managers treat onboarding as if it's the same thing as orientation, and they put the entire responsibility on the HR department. However, it's an integral step that is essential for alignment within the organization's culture, often requiring a part-nered effort between the business functions and HR to truly succeed. Managers have a key role in ensuring that onboarding resonates with their team and successfully aligns culture expectations.

Continuous Alignment

Culture alignment is not simply a short-term occurrence completed at the initial hire stage. Culture alignment needs to occur on a longer-term basis, even for the entire duration of the employee's career. There are several ways to reinforce culture alignment on an ongoing manner. These include:

- **Coaching within feedback** – Whether it's a formal coaching session (for example, biweekly meetings or monthly one-on-ones) or reinforcements from everyday events, providing feedback with a coaching focus is a great way to maintain the culture of people development.

- **Facilitating within meetings** – Meetings are a regular component of an employee's job. By utilizing a facilitation approach rather than a directive one, you create opportunities for alignment through greater engagement, buy-in, ownership, and value reinforcement.

- **Partnering within performance reviews** – Even performance reviews should be utilized as alignment opportunities. As a rule of thumb, if there are any surprises during a performance review, there is a misalignment somewhere.

- **Aligning communication channels with senior leaders** – Organizations with stronger cultures are well-connected between their leadership and people. As an organization grows in size, this may be harder to accomplish. Therefore it's common to see efforts such as "state-of-the-union" addresses, regular company-wide email updates, and so on. This can help promote culture alignment on an ongoing basis.

Managers and leaders play a key role in reinforcing culture throughout the course of employees' careers. That's why they are integral roles to partner with, to ensure the success of the culture strategy.

Referee Culture: Protecting the Culture

Refereeing the culture is a vital element in culture creation and maintenance. Once the culture has been put in place, results can appear in an organic and scalable manner. Since it's such a valuable creation, the leader has to protect the culture with everything they've got.

The importance of maintaining the culture can be highlighted from the words of Stanley Bergman, CEO of Henry Schein, who was awarded 2017 CEO of the Year by *Chief Executive Magazine*.

> "I meet with our investors frequently, and they always ask the same question: What keeps you awake at night? My answer is always the same: I sleep very well. What's most on my mind is making sure the culture of Henry Schein remains strong."

This statement really highlights the strategic importance of culture reinforcement. When a leader prioritizes their time, energy, and effort on culture, the results organically follow in a manner to outcompete the market. However, in general, negative sentiment that is harmful to culture tends to spread faster than positive sentiment. Therefore, an intentional effort needs to be made to protect this culture.

On top of that, it may take people an intentional effort to live up to the standards of culture strategy. There will be a tendency for regression without proper reinforcement. When left unattended, people tend to project their own standards upon others, without understanding the strengths of different perspectives and collaboration. This can lead to unhealthy conflicts, low probability of success for synergy, protectionism, aggressive behavior, and a lack of engagement, motivation, ownership, and more.

Most people feel extremely uncomfortable and vulnerable when they open their mind and adapt to different types of people. There's a natural tendency for people to seek the path of least resistance, which often entails congregating around similar individuals. In such circumstances, they don't develop the skills to adapt to different people. Therefore, people tend to have unhealthy interactions when this culture is not reinforced properly. In such cases, people will not develop the necessary collaboration, management, and leadership for culture strategy to thrive.

There are particular types of behavior that must be confronted with constructive and potentially firm feedback. These include:

- Unhealthy conflict (this is time sensitive and should be dealt with immediately),
- Not demonstrating engagement,
- Excessively needing to be told what to do,
- Not demonstrating accountability and ownership,
- Refusing to adapt communication styles to different people,
- Managers and leaders refusing to develop a coaching mentality with their team,
- Managers and leaders overutilizing hierarchy,
- Job, staff, or knowledge hoarding,

- Managers and leaders excessively shooting down others' ideas rather than refining and developing them,
- And more.

These behaviors are a form of resistance that can disrupt the culture. It demonstrates that they are not buying into the practice of a higher standard of collaboration, management, and leadership. If we hesitate on such matters, the tone of the culture can be poisoned rather quickly. This is because culture can be impacted by rumor spreading, loss of confidence in leadership in addressing the issues, and a perception of an unhealthy work environment. Swift action can mitigate the damage from such matters and protect the culture of the organization. Leaders should  keep a feel on the pulse of the organizational culture and be prepared to confront mishaps when they occur. If they don't do anything about it, they have just made such behaviors acceptable.

9.3. Approaching Our Work Differently

There are organizations that have structured their day-to-day operational processes through documentation, specialization, standardization, and data accumulation. This can create order from chaos. It benefits the organization through specialization, standardization, and even data accumulation. However, it's important to recognize that these structured processes can have a collateral effect if they are too rigid. This can have an adverse impact on the culture of the organization.

In a paradigm where day-to-day operational processes are conducive to culture strategy, structured and documented processes are still used, but they also leave room for adaptability, collaboration, and team-level strategy. This gives breathing room for coaching and developing optimized work styles. Innovation is encouraged, especially at the interface with stakeholders and customers as teams have ground-level knowledge that higher-level leaders are not privy to. Data acquisition is predominantly automated and streamlined. Manual data gathering is greatly simplified and focused on critical information only, so it doesn't interfere with the employees' actual jobs.

Adaptable Processes Provide Structure with Room to Breathe

It's difficult for culture strategy to take root with rigid processes. We still want to encourage documented processes to aid in maintaining structure and streamlining training. However, they should be designed as guidance more than rules or inflexible procedures such as rigid checklists. We want some degree of standardization, but not rigid enough to get in the way of individual self-expression, development, and engagement. This is done by cleaning up the complexities of processes by simplifying procedures and maximizing resonance.

Of course, there are exceptions to this, especially when such processes are to maintain safety in dangerous environments, or when team development is still in its early stages and contributors hunger for directives.

Coaching and Facilitation to Create Self-Directed Teams

Rather than having the traditional team dynamic with a boss and followers, we foster the creation of self-directed teams through a coaching and facilitative approach. By exercising good management skills, we develop our contributors to become well-balanced collaborators who work together toward a common goal. To accomplish this, we need to ensure we have buy-in from our managers with this approach, and that they have the skills to do it this way. This creates a path for the continuous building of a people infrastructure.

Enable Situational Adaptation and Innovation

Rather than an over-focus on standardization and rigid procedures, we can create value in unexpected ways through enabling situational adaptation and innovation. This can be extremely valuable, as it gives teams the opportunity to adapt to their customers, local considerations, and ground-level information. This is not something that can be captured effectively through detailed scripts and checklists. There's no way for us to design processes that can replicate this value, especially as we are not physically there, have less visibility, and are blind to many of the considerations.

Adopt a Partnership Mentality

Work and collaboration should be done with a partnership mentality. This is possible when we succeed in getting engagement and work with self-directed teams. This can enable bottom-up management from team members to managers, and managers to senior leaders. When people have sufficient skills and exhibit ownership, they can size up the obstacles in front of them, identify gaps in resources, and partner with their manager to acquire those necessary resources. This mentality also works when collaborating with different layers of the organization. This approach is much more effective than the traditional top-down mentality.

This requires readily deployable resources and support. Are resources in your organization readily deployable? If we truly succeed in achieving partnership mentalities and a competent upward-management dynamic, we need to ensure that resources are readily deployable. Otherwise, it will create a black hole for overcoming obstacles. On top of that question, dig further and ask yourself:

- If an issue is critical and time sensitive, can resources be provided quickly?
- If the same resources are being asked for repetitively, is there a chronic resource issue that needs to be reevaluated?

Recognize that newer or crisis-related initiatives tend to have more frequent and customized resource deployment needs, as there are substantial unknowns that are being progressively figured out as we move forward. This interface should be evaluated when optimizing the environment to enable culture strategy.

Simplified and Streamlined Data Management to Maximize Resonance

Data is a critical tool that can provide transparency and benchmarking for the organization. Without data, senior leaders have challenges in getting objective information and understanding the team performance throughout the organization. However, this can be taken too far by creating an excessive burden of data accumulation and overcomplicated reports that few can understand.

Care should be taken to overcome these interferences. We achieve this by avoiding excessive manual data-gathering tasks so people can focus on the functional tasks that really matter. Whenever possible, it is wise to consider streamlining data accumulation, which can often be done by leveraging technology. A lot of data can be acquired automatically and passively through this route. Once data is collected, it should be processed with simplified reports. This maximizes resonance, so we can make data transparent and include reports within our collaborative discussions.

If you are going to gather it, use it! People do not take data seriously if you spend a lot of time, energy, and resources to gather it but don't use it. Integrate it within your collaborative discussions to diagnose issues and plan accordingly. If you don't do this, people will lose respect for data and won't take data collection seriously.

Transparency and Trust: Greater Alignment and Engagement

Transparency is an important concept as it creates alignment throughout the organization and can improve engagement. When employees have transparency with data and understand the direction the organization is going, it is easier for them to stay engaged with the process. This is not to say that confidential information should be made public, as the appropriate specificity of the topic should be evaluated on a case-by-case situation. Transparency is an interesting topic because I've seen different forms of reservations regarding it. These include:

- **Some leaders view transparency as a risk** – Some leaders tend to view transparency as risk exposure, because employees could use the transparent information against them. This can actually be a sign of a dysfunctional culture.

- **Some leaders have underdeveloped buy-in skills that are necessary for transparency** – When leaders choose to be transparent, more vulnerability points are exposed. This actually needs to be reconciled through greater communication and buy-in skills from the leader. However, when leaders have not developed these skills, they may have challenges when creating a transparent organization. This is often the case when strategic planners are in charge of key decisions. They may focus on the planning component with a lack of focus on communication for buy-in. This can often lead to misalignment, lack of transparency, and confusion.

- **Some leaders are in denial** – They believe they are transparent when they are actually not. I've also seen that some leaders consciously believe in transparency but have subconscious reservations deep within. Sometimes, such individuals have actually convinced themselves they are transparent when they really aren't.

At the end of the day, transparency can increase risk exposure if mishandled. Therefore, there's a need for good buy-in skills to create a mutually trusting environment that neutralizes the risk. It takes great leadership to overcome these barriers and capitalize on the value of trust. However, trust does not come easy.

People from dysfunctional cultures have the mentality,
"If I give them an inch, they will take a mile."

It takes great leadership to break this cycle. It takes a great deal of vulnerability, vision, hope, and skill to decide to trust and earn others' trust.

If you do not believe that people can be resourceful and
trustworthy with information, they never will be.
You have to give trust to get trust.

When we successfully create a transparent and mutually trusting environment, it sets up the potential for so much more. People demonstrate greater ownership and proactive thinking, which can be translated to more advanced forms of productivity.

Intentionally Creating Margin: Setting Up Development and Strategy for Success

Much of the value creation from culture strategy comes from people development, coaching, facilitation, planning, alignment, and even "white space" (the spare time for strategic thinking). This takes time and effort! In today's cutthroat market environment, many companies are already working at full capacity to maintain efficiency. If that's the case, when do they have time to do this?

That's where it's important to introduce margin. This is the additional bandwidth that people have to proactively work on value-creating efforts in a strategic manner. However, this doesn't come for free. We have to create time for this, and we can do so in various ways, including:

- Allocating separate resources, budget, and schedules for strategies and projects.

- Increasing operational capacity, possibly with additional hiring. This may also help stabilize teams to deal with absences or turnovers.
- Identifying and improving current inefficiencies and misalignment (process inefficiencies, strategy misalignment, improved time management, and so on). Removing inefficiencies creates time.

If we don't allocate time and resources in preparation for the initiatives associated with culture strategy, it will be difficult to implement it. If we attempt to force culture strategy implementation within the organization without such preparation, it may have a collateral effect on the business. The following may occur:

- Sacrifice of existing business functions due to overload
- Settling for a slower pace of culture development
- Unsustainable situations with staff

The decision to potentially increase financial budgets can be difficult. If we want to feel comfortable allocating resources for culture strategy, we need to be confident that we can create more value than the associated expenses. Rest assured, if we implement culture strategy correctly, it will create exponentially more value than the expense.

9.4. Culture-Conducive Financial Management

Different companies have different types of finance functions to support their needs. Some only have basic financial functions that are passive and work behind the scenes. Such functions include basic accounting, budgeting, and compliance considerations. Other companies have more robust financial functions that play an active role in strategies. They may have financial modeling capabilities to analyze and make future projections. In such cases, financial considerations play a larger role in goal setting, screening strategies, providing budgets, and governance.

As you can imagine, these financial decisions can have a large impact on the propagation and sustenance of culture strategy. As they are back-end functions, they are often overlooked in their relevance to culture, but they are equally essential. This includes decisions on budgeting, making resources readily deployable, compensation, rewards, benefits, and more. It's important to evaluate this because rigid financial management can be a major reason why culture strategies fail.

Often, larger corporations have a robust financial department that has a large influence on the governance and strategic direction of the organization. This is because it provides the structure and objectivity that it needs to maintain a scaled enterprise. In addition, many such companies realize that it creates rigidity within their organization, and thus they source for ways to be innovative through acquisitions.

However, rigid finance management is a major reason why traditional corporations' acquisition of innovative companies often fails. To succeed, there is a need to cultivate working relationships that are more collaborative or bottom-up driven. Rigid financial management often creates excessively top-down directives that disable innovation. There are countless stories of large corporations that acquire innovative companies with great cultures but fail at integration because they end up killing their culture. To successfully integrate these companies, they may need a mindset shift to manage decisions, goals, and budgets differently than they may be used to.

Create a Budget for Culture

Culture strategy doesn't materialize simply through sheer will and trying harder. Just like any other strategy, it needs to pull in resources, whether it be manpower or dollars. Without setting aside a budget for this endeavor, it will likely fail. Budgeting for culture strategy needs to account for the associated expenses with the mindset that this is a long-term, intangible investment. It must account for the initial and ongoing expenditures to create and sustain the culture. Such budgeting includes:

- Training, coaching, consulting, and subject matter experts as needed,
- Creating margin within teams, possibly through additional hiring,
- Equalizing compensation structure (if applicable),
- And more.

To justify this, we need to understand the return on investment (ROI) of culture strategy. When successful, it can generate a much higher ROI than other initiatives. However, as this is a long-term initiative, it will require patience.

Make Resources Readily Deployable

The financial management of the business must be prepared to align itself for an adaptive, bottom-up workflow. When the baseline skills of the people within the organization are sufficiently built and mutual trust is established, it becomes increasingly possible to have bottom-up proposals and budget requests. In fact, such readily deployable resources enable teams to optimize their success and adaptability. Enabling this from a financial management standpoint requires a flexible, strategic, and open mindset. It also means that budgets may be adapted as initiatives move forward and new information presents itself. This may involve maintaining a higher reserve balance for "rainy days" that is capable of quick deployment, maintaining mutually trusting work relations, and having a good eye for evaluating efficacies of initiatives when assessing internal budgets or proposals.

Provide Rewards and Recognition for the Right Things to Align Incentives

It's important to reevaluate the rewards and recognition structure of the organization and whether they align with culture strategy. Often, people are only rewarded for hitting goals or for their display of technical expertise. We must also recognize when people play their part in culture strategy, such as coaching or developing self-directed teams. These are essential behaviors that propagate the culture and create sustainable situations. Otherwise, people will get the message that it's not important to the organization, and they will push for goals and technical expertise only. In fact, they may push it at any cost and at the expense of other people, which can harm the culture of the organization.

Have a Clear and Competitive Compensation Structure

Having a market-competitive compensation structure is important to sustain the culture strategy. This isn't about having the highest offers, either. The largest value proposition of culture strategy to employees is usually nonmonetary (for example, purpose, team spirit, respect, and autonomy). However, if the compensation structure is below market rate, it can have an adverse impact on retention, and it is important to consider equalizing it. It may even be wise to consider creating a standardized compensation structure and sharing it with employees, as it would add to the transparency in the organization.

9.5. Developing the Leaders of Tomorrow

Within organizations that promote a strong culture, it is important to purposefully develop the leaders of tomorrow. This is critical for the company to continuously grow and sustain itself, as the company needs competent leadership talent. This benefits the organization in multiple ways, including:

- **Smoothening transitions during management/leadership changes** – These transitions have the potential to create abrupt changes and issues. When knowledge, process, and relationship handovers are poorly managed, it can create problems and volatility within the organization that can move it backwards. Therefore, prudent transitions can help better stabilize the company, so that more emphasis can be on growth.

- **Continuously engaging growth-minded individuals** – The performance and growth of the company is highly dependent on your engaged and growth-minded individuals. It becomes easier to engage them when there is organizational growth and subsequent professional growth prospects for the talent.

- **Increasing the success rate of management/leadership positioning** – Poorly positioned managers/leaders are perhaps the single greatest cause of failure in reaching objectives or strategic goals. Interestingly, many people recognize this but do very little to proactively address it. Purposeful leadership development can help bridge this gap.

Preference Switch to Promoting from within Rather Than Hiring Externally

There needs to be a mindset shift toward a preference for internal promotions rather than external hires. Of course, this won't always be the case, as sometimes we need to bring in external capabilities that do not yet exist within the organization, or existing internal leadership candidates are still underdeveloped. However, an overall preference change can create a seismic shift in how we approach culture.

This is an integral piece in optimizing motivation and engagement, thereby promoting sustainability of the culture, as this type of culture is predicated on developing people who have a growth mindset. When individuals have developed and demonstrated leadership skills, they may look for opportunities for upward mobility. If that is unavailable, they can get bored or disgruntled, and may leave the organization.

Therefore, this mindset takes a proactive stance in maintaining a motivating environment for growth-minded people by filling leadership positions from within.

Partner to Create a Development Plan

The best way to approach developmental plans is through a partnership effort with the individual. This involves a shared ownership that can gear efforts for mutual alignment. This approach creates a shared responsibility that is customized and geared toward their aspirations, interests, and talents. Better maneuvering of resource allocation and training opportunities is possible with this approach. This also creates a proactive mentality to align such efforts with the goals of the organization and possibly ground their expectations in reality. (Sometimes people have unrealistic expectations due to an overestimation of their abilities.) Such conversations can be captured during one-on-one coaching sessions and performance reviews.

Develop a Clear Career Path

For some organizations, especially larger ones, building a clear career path within the organization can be helpful in creating transparency. This transparency can minimize confusion and misleading situations that can cause bad aftertastes when expectations are not managed well. On top of that, this clarity can strengthen the engagement level for the growth of the organization, which is essential to building a scalable and organic growth strategy.

The career path must not neglect rewarding leadership skills, and it must not focus only on rewarding goals or technical expertise. This creates a form of transparency that allows employees to make intentional efforts to develop leadership skills, which maintains a growth pattern that continuously builds people infrastructure in a scalable manner.

Smooth Management/Leadership Transitions

When promoting from within, a void is created within the organization that needs to be filled, and this needs to be managed as well. The transition must be coordinated based on timing, expectations, knowledge transfer, and relationship transfer. There is the added benefit that this reduces the burden of cultural and organizational alignment needs. Internal promotees are already accustomed to the organizational culture, whereas external hires have a higher risk of being a bad match for the position and organization.

This requires a mindset of always building a strong leadership bench team. Not only does it strengthen the people infrastructure by mitigating risks of leadership turnover, but it provides a steady supply of leadership to fill openings created during growth initiatives. It increases the success rate of such positioning because these candidates are already familiar with the existing culture, processes, and relationships. Here are a few approaches to developing the bench team and smoothening transitions:

- Leadership pairing to learn all the components of managing/ leading. Some companies do this for approximately six months with a one-year post-transition, on-call pairing.
- Transfer relationships and knowledge of processes with smooth handovers.
- Leadership development programs.
- Rotations, stretch projects, and transfers.

In Scaled Situations, Consider Organized Succession Planning Programs

Eventually, as an organization continues to grow, leadership development becomes increasingly important so that the company can keep up with a rapid growth rate. This can be done with a succession planning program. Unfortunately, most organizations have a nonexistent succession planning program, or it lacks standardization and is not set up for scalable growth. A successful succession planning program can provide systematic and scalable leadership development solutions while filling leadership positions through internally developed candidates.

Standardizing Identification of High Potentials

Hopefully by now, I have made the point that we should build a culture of promoting leaders from within whenever possible. This requires searching through every corner of the organization for *high potentials* (HiPo's). People who demonstrate leadership aptitude and interest are very tough to come by. Many organizations have differing views on descriptions of high potentials, so let's get on the same page with their description.

High Potential (HiPo)

Who, really, are the HiPo's? Are they your strongest performers? Are they the most knowledgeable people? Actually, there's a lower correlation between being the strongest performer and most knowledgeable contributor and success as a leader. There is a greater correlation between the ability to build people and teams and success as a leader.

This might come as a surprise to people who are accustomed to Traditional Hierarchal cultures. Often, people are promoted due to being the strongest contributor. Unfortunately, this actually has very little correlation to the ability to build people and teams. If we promote those who don't develop people and teams, they become a blocker for organizational growth, as they inhibit the creation of self-directed teams and the development of future leaders. This often leads to culture dysfunction and protectionist behavior that includes job, knowledge, or staff hoarding.

Once HiPo's are identified, we must ask ourselves whether they are given opportunities. We may find out they are blocked because opportunities are given to others. Other times, they are blocked because they were not given opportunities to be developed or coached. Sometimes, this can happen due to a middle manager demonstrating hoarding behavior. In this regard, there are three categories of HiPo's:

- **Confirmed HiPo rock star** – Confirmed HiPo's have already demonstrated great performance and enormous potential, and you should immediately give them additional opportunities, or they may get bored or disgruntled and leave. They have the skills or potential to build teams in almost any situation and are extremely resourceful in reaching goals even outside their field of technical expertise.

- **Undeveloped or unproven HiPo** – These people have very high potential, but their performance is mediocre. This often occurs when they haven't been developed, coached, or trained yet (possibly being too new to the organization), or because the opportunity that engages them hasn't presented itself yet (consider engaging them with a stretch project). Monitor this person closely as they may be your next HiPo rock star.

- **Blocked HiPo** – If a HiPo has high potential but their performance is unimpressive, this may be the result of having a poor manager who does not engage, train, or coach them, or provide opportunities. They may be creating demotivating environments through actions like taking credit, being extremely hierarchal, or breaking trust. This is a reminder for leaders to have checkpoints for managers to buy-in to the organizational culture because blocking this person's potential harms the organization.

Unfortunately, many don't identify or define HiPo's in this manner. This is in contrast to how many Traditional Hierarchal companies often choose their future leaders. They often select them based on individual performance or technical expertise. However, this may be suboptimal positioning. Let's explore how such candidates would be better fitted within an organization.

Strong Performers or Subject Matter Experts (SMEs)

These individuals are extremely skilled at their job, have a track record of reaching goals, or are extremely knowledgeable in a particular subject matter. However, they are not as skilled in developing other people and teams. They have demonstrated high performance, but they tend to have lower potential for leadership skills. They struggle to build self-directed teams and develop other people, and they may resort to using force and hierarchy on a regular basis. Oftentimes, they fit in the following categories:

- **Medium Potential (they can possibly handle one more level)** – Strong performers or SMEs who exhibit medium potential may be able to handle one higher level of leadership responsibility. They won't be able to handle a second increased level of leadership responsibility unless they have a significant life experience that creates a large paradigm shift, unlocking a high-potential ability to build self-directed teams and people.

- **Low Potential (ground them to reality)** – In the event there are strong performers or SMEs with a low potential, there is a possibility they have unrealistic expectations of their own potential. It is important to ground their expectations to reality because giving into their desires will likely result in mutual frustration and an unsustainable situation. In reality, most of them don't want to deal with people and the team dynamic aspects of leadership. They would be happier as a strong performer or subject matter expert.

A common mistake of Traditional Hierarchal companies is to bring up the wrong individuals, which further deepens their culture dysfunction. It's better to build the right culture and pick the right leaders to represent it.

To dive deeper into this topic, look into the McKinsey 9-Box Grid as it relates to performance and potential, which is a widely used HR tool for employee development and succession planning. It includes more granular descriptions of types of people and appropriate recommendations for them.

Partnering with Middle Management

Many of the items discussed in this section require partnerships with managers because they have regular access to their team members that you do not. As identifying HiPo's and developing their leadership potential is a critical component of culture strategy, it is important to maintain mutual trust with middle managers who are often the gatekeepers to accessing, identifying, developing, and providing opportunities to HiPo's. However, let's face it, managers may have reservations in playing this role due to fears of weakening the security of their position. That's why it's important to maintain transparency in the strategy, mutual trust, and a partnership mentality.

These efforts are important to minimize job, staff, or knowledge hoarding from middle managers that would block the identification and development of HiPo's. They would create a very damaging environment to the growth of the organization. If managers partake in such protectionist behavior, it can lead to culture dysfunction. Therefore, it's important to alleviate their concerns by building a fair and mutual understanding between management and the company. The following themes can help with this:

- The organization invests in the manager's marketability, while the manager invests in the organization's infrastructure.

- Managers build infrastructure by sharing knowledge, documenting processes, coaching, and identifying and grooming other managers/leaders.

- The organization invests in the manager's marketability by coaching, training, and developing the manager's repertoire of skills.

Some may still resist the culture and may not buy in to it. Such individuals are usually motivated by fear or ego. They maintain their position by hoarding their job, knowledge, or staff. Unfortunately, they may not be a good fit with the organization.

There are techniques like the 360 Assessments to evaluate managers from multiple directions that may help maintain transparency and monitor for unhealthy management habits. It accomplishes this by gathering perspectives from subordinates, colleagues, supervisors, and self. Despite the existence of such tools, it is very important to establish transparency and trust with your managers because even this tool may yield misleading information.

9.6. Evolving the Way We Approach Strategy

Strategy is a unique topic because there are usually two spectrums of challenges for different organizations. On one side, there are some organizations that do not have a clear strategy, vision, or direction. This results in employees who are unclear which direction they are going, due to a lack of direction and forward thinking. It may even occur when there are too many directions and rapid changes to the strategy that are occurring.

- Unclear vision and direction – People don't know what the overall vision is. Either there is no forward momentum, or it was never communicated.

- "Flavor of the month" strategy – This occurs due to leaders shifting directions too frequently, which is as confusing as having no vision.

On the other hand, there are companies with elaborate strategic plans, but they have issues getting the organization on board. A common mistake is treating strategy as something meant only for the "higher-ups" or the "big wigs" of the organization. Creating strategic plans in an isolated manner can result in misalignment, and a lack of ownership, engagement, motivation, morale, and adaptability.

- **Misalignment** – When strategy is completely centralized by senior leaders with no involvement from peripheral teams, it can result in little to no alignment. Creating clear, enterprise-level strategies and decentralizing certain aspects to teams can improve alignment, engagement, and even the quality of execution.

- **Unilateral and long-winded strategic plan** – In some organizations, few understand or are even aware of the strategy of the organization. Often, it is the result of long-winded strategic plans with little emphasis on co-creation, buy-in, and situational reinforcement.

Maximizing Position and Clarity of an Enterprise-Level Strategy

A clearly defined enterprise-level strategy that maximizes value from strategic positioning can set the path for the organization to win. At the same time, the enterprise-level strategy should be purpose driven to maximize resonance, as it will be the *guiding light* for the rest of the organization and applied throughout multiple layers of the organization. This will maximize market positioning and purpose-driven engagement.

Many organizations already have an enterprise-level strategy with a core mission, vision, and values. However, there tends to be a gap of understanding that exists between senior leaders and the rest of the organization. This creates a great deal of misalignment. Ask yourself how many people within the organization know and truly understand the strategy. How many of them actually live and breathe it? Does it penetrate throughout the various divisions, departments, and teams?

If the people within the organization are not on the same page, it can result in a great amount of inefficiencies. So, how do we get on the same page? How do we accomplish this? Enterprise-level strategies are extremely complex and aren't made available for easy consumption by a larger number of people. We need to reconcile this by:

- Simplifying and breaking down the strategy
- Communicating the strategy with crisp clarity

Build Strategy Capabilities within Teams

Not only do we need to focus on optimizing strategy from a top-down direction, but we also need to optimize it from the bottom up. That means peripheral teams need to develop their baseline, strategic capabilities to synchronize with the enterprise-level strategy in the middle. This involves developing strategy skills at the team level, which is an entirely different approach.

- **Developing team-level strategic thinking** – Developing the strategic capabilities of teams creates tremendous value within an organization, but this is more involved than meets the eye. It first begins with ensuring maturation of the culture and development of self-directed teams. This becomes the foundation to develop the strategic skills of the teams and managers. Without this, you may be dealing with an excessive amount of bad proposals, unrefined ideas, distrust, and lack of ownership. It may be exceptionally difficult to juggle this while simultaneously managing the goals and objectives of the team.

  Developing strategic skills within teams can be very challenging. It involves thinking about the future, which involves an abstract and futuristic mindset. The majority of the population does not naturally think in this way, and it may be difficult to develop these skills in others. It's also important to recognize that most people view participation in strategic thinking as scary and risky. Therefore, it involves a combination of coaching, facilitation, and setting the right environment to let it thrive.

- **Developing and bridging the essential hard skills of strategy at the team level** – Strategy involves more than a mindset. There are hard skills associated with it as well. For example, strategic planning can sound like a higher-level skillset, but there are ways to implement simpler versions of strategic planning at the team levels. The more we develop and bridge these capabilities, the more we can allow strategy to penetrate almost every layer of the organization.

  Although it may seem extremely challenging to get teams involved with this, it becomes more feasible when we've adequately developed the culture, people, and thinking skills. We accomplish this by getting teams involved with the planning through a facilitated co-creation process. This improves engagement, adaptive problem solving, innovation, and quality of execution. This needs continuous situational reinforcement during training, coaching, and facilitative planning sessions.

In essence, by developing the strategic thinking capabilities within people, we are also promoting proactive and innovative thinking. Nowadays, it seems like everyone talks about proactive and innovative thinking. Everyone wants to enable this but they struggle to do so because they are unsure how. It can be beneficial to recognize that this actually goes by many names. When we see that it's the same thing as enabling strategy throughout all levels of the organization, we can make a better organized effort in enabling this.

Proactive Thinking = Innovative Thinking = Strategic Thinking

This can create an enormous amount of value in the performance of teams, as they become more competent in identifying challenges and addressing situations proactively. It reduces issues that arise and improves the value delivered to stakeholders. This also helps maintain strategic alignment throughout the organization. It is opposed to performing the same daily routines, without ever questioning why we do things the way we do. That approach would lack situational adaptation. Such teams are usually delivering lower value and plagued with a large number of issues.

Maximize the Interface between Enterprise-Level Strategy and Team-Level Strategies

By now, I hope the point has been made on the importance of a well-positioned and clear enterprise-level strategy, along with improving baseline strategic skills within teams. Now, we can focus our efforts on maximizing the environment for team-level strategies and maximizing strategic alignment. This emphasizes the importance of:

- **Ecosystem of team-level strategies** – This involves being strategic with strategy through an alignment focus. Many strategies fail due to misalignment between enterprise-level strategies, planning, and execution. A paradigm shift to focus on alignment allows us to merge the best of those worlds and capture more value. This keeps the organization together and moving in the same direction.

  To accomplish this, we need to double down on the ecosystem. This involves a combined approach in prioritizing strategic skill development, transparency, team involvement, alignment, and promoting an environment where team-level strategies can thrive while maintaining alignment with the overall vision of the organization.

- **Balancing strategies** – As we have to juggle multiple strategies throughout the organization, it becomes increasingly essential to create clarity on the overall strategic priorities, and allocate resources based on those priorities. Otherwise, the organization may end up with an uncoordinated collage of unrelated, short-term initiatives that lack returns. Proper alignment with strategies among different teams, departments, and divisions united under an overarching, enterprise-level strategy can create synergistic value and a larger impact. This involves referencing the enterprise-level strategy when team-level strategies are created and maintaining a holistic outlook throughout the process.

Ultimately, when we apply these strategic approaches, it keeps everyone moving in the same direction. This creates a great amount of synergistic value and eliminates inefficiencies. If this section didn't make sense so far, don't worry. We will be discussing this further in Part V of the book.

For now, though, I hope this chapter has given you a sense of the scope of culture change in your organization. Remember, you need to evaluate your situation and apply these guidelines as needed, rather than following them as steadfast rules.

The key items to successfully enact culture change include investing in the value of people, setting the right tone, approaching work differently, culture-conducive financial management, developing the leaders of tomorrow, and evolving the way we approach strategy.

To determine which items are most applicable to you, you must first know which phase of culture change you are currently in, and what the next steps are. That's what we'll discuss next.

THE SIX PHASES IN ENTERPRISE-LEVEL CULTURE CHANGE

Many people are unclear about where to start and what to do about culture strategy. That's because they don't know what stage of the culture change process they are in. Different companies are in a variety of stages of culture development, whether they are aware of it or not. Some are further along the process without their conscious realization. Others are stuck in earlier steps.

When people ask me about culture strategy, the first thing I do is ask about their situation. What are their current issues and challenges? This helps identify what stage of the process they are in. By understanding the current stage of the culture development process, it becomes clear how to identify the current priorities.

This alone can create tremendous value, as it can highlight and shift the priorities of the organization. If we don't do this right, we will end up misdiagnosing the situation and providing the wrong treatment. This can end up with an effect of sweeping things under the rug and it misses treating the root cause. During this time, you won't be aware that this is even happening.

You can't hit a target if you don't know what it is.

Therefore, let's be prudent, investigate accordingly, diagnose properly, and deliver the correct treatment.

The Six Phases of Culture Change

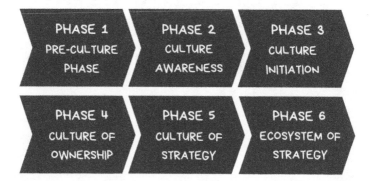

In this chapter, we're taking many of the concepts that we've already talked about, and we're putting them into perspective based upon phases and recommended sequences. The phases of culture development are:

- **Phase One: Pre-Culture** – Initial stabilization of the business, preparing to transition.

- **Phase Two: Culture Awareness** – Diagnostics and extreme clarity.

- **Phase Three: Culture Initiation** – Beginning the process, getting buy-in, and living it.

- **Phase Four: Culture of Ownership** – Transferring ownership of processes and refining them.

- **Phase Five: Culture of Strategy** – Bridging the strategy chasm and enabling strategy at all levels.

- **Phase Six: Ecosystem of Strategy** – Making a strategic impact at all fronts.

Identify which phase you are in and follow the steps sequentially. Subsequent phases hinge on what was developed in the previous phases. Therefore, it's important to be honest with yourself and not overestimate the current status of your culture. Otherwise, you may end up building upon things that don't exist.

Common Mistake: Companies Skipping Fundamental Steps or Trying to Introduce Strategy at All Levels Too Soon

All companies have unique circumstances. Most of them are under a lot of pressure to reach targets and goals to stay afloat. As a result, they have introduced efforts in a haphazard manner. This may have involved unsuccessful culture and people development efforts, which resulted in an incomplete maturation of the culture within the organization.

Additionally, I commonly see companies skip developing the culture. They prematurely try to introduce proactive and innovative thinking at all levels, which should come at later phases of the culture change. Then, they struggle and are perplexed. They find themselves asking:

"Why aren't people innovating? Why aren't they engaged?"

Well, strategic thinking should be introduced *after* the core culture strategy has taken root. That's what happens when we skip steps.

"But we have real goals to hit! Culture strategy looks like it may take a long time."

That's why this must be assessed on a case-by-case basis. Sometimes, we have no choice but to address it from multiple angles at the same time due to business demands, but we can still recognize the need to further develop the culture. This will enable us to shift priorities and allocate additional resources to the development of the culture. In this way, we can develop the culture simultaneously to reaching goals. This can bridge the need to meet current deadlines while building the infrastructure for a free-flowing strategy ecosystem.

If such cutthroat demands do not exist, it may be worthwhile to fully allow the effect of the phases to soak in before moving onto the next phase. This will allow maximum penetration of culture strategy within the organization.

10.1. Phase One: Pre-Culture

Honestly, when I first opened my business, culture was the last thing on my mind. I was still in the first phase of this process. When you're in this early phase, the sheer volume of tasks that creep up on a daily basis and the multitude of decisions that need to be made can be overwhelming. Your mind never really has a chance to switch off. All this is needed to keep things afloat to survive and break even! In this phase of the business, it's important to recognize the challenges of:

- **Newer organizations** – Anyone who has built a business from ground up, or built a new division or department from scratch, will understand how chaotic that world is. There is limited understanding of processes that keep the business afloat. They have yet to figure out what will capture the market or satisfy stakeholder needs. The network of synchronized relationships that keep the business running has yet to be established. Business objectives may or may not be met, which means we may have yet to get in the green.

- **Organizations with prolonged unstable conditions** – This phase is not limited to new organizations. It can include older organizations that actually live here in a continuous chaotic state. People are still struggling just to keep things afloat. In such situations, it can be extremely exhausting for both the leaders and team members. If the organization remains in this state for an extended period of time, it can lead to burnout.

During this phase, a *directive* leadership style may often be needed to keep up with the rapidly evolving challenges within an early stage or chaotic business. This can be a trialing period for many. There is often a high degree of turnover and confusion over expectations and processes. There's often confusion on what will even work! Your existing challenges may be dependent on your experience level as a leader:

- **For newer leaders** – This may be a soul-searching time period. This requires getting to know and harnessing your strengths along with understanding and covering up for your weaknesses. Due to the challenges associated with this phase, you're forced to put your life priorities in perspective and get to know what's truly important. Suddenly, things that used to be important no longer seem that way when contrasted with these challenges and other competing priorities. All this is often required for the initial stabilization of the organization.

- **For seasoned leaders** – This may be an important self-reflective period. You may be so accustomed to chaos and dysfunction that you think it's the norm and you become numb to it. This can be difficult to acknowledge, as it often requires questioning the questions you ask. It also requires reassessing the current foundation of how the world works, in search for a stronger understanding that yields greater results. This can be an uncomfortable and vulnerable process.

Despite such internal challenges, during such times we still have to be proactive and establish the initial set of processes, market positioning, and team dynamic. We need to focus on:

- **Establishing initial systems and processes** – This can include training, consulting, acquisition of capabilities, bootstrapping (learning from experience with force of will), and more. If possible (depending on the team dynamic and business health), it is wise to get the team involved with this process. This will increase ownership and minimize challenges with transferring ownership of the systems. However, evaluate this on a case-by-case basis, as sometimes it can introduce undue risks if a healthy team dynamic has yet to be established.

- **Establishing initial agreements and expectations** – It is important to establish the initial stabilization of relationship dynamics. Whenever possible, try and get the right set of people who could eventually establish a healthy team dynamic and bring in necessary skillsets. This is to lay up for a smoother process when introducing culture strategy and establishing a self-directed team status. However, sometimes we don't have such flexibilities. An additional focus must be made on establishing clear agreements, an initial set of team goals, and individualized team member goals.

- **Confirming that it works** – Just because you introduce processes and set expectations doesn't mean it'll work! Will you be able to break even and remain profitable? Does it meet customer or stakeholder expectations? Does it stabilize the situation, stay afloat, and keep the doors open?

If a business is still stabilizing chaos to stay afloat, implementing a culture change may not be its initial priority, unless you know how to implement it while simultaneously dealing with the initial chaos. This may be quite a handful to manage, but once we establish initial stability, we can begin preparing for the next phase. We do this by:

- **Creating intentional margin** – If we're barely keeping our heads above water and have no margin, then we will have trouble implementing a culture change. At first glance, it may even seem impossible to create bandwidth if we've become accustomed to chaos. Overcoming this requires a very intentional effort in creating margin, which can involve proactive time management, delegation, self-management, removing inefficiencies, and possibly setting aside an additional budget for new hires. Once we have this, we can better lay up to the next phase.

10.2. Phase Two: Culture Awareness

For an existing stable business that is considering a culture change, this phase will likely be the first step. It's time to put all the culture change management tools introduced in previous chapters into practice! The priorities of this phase are to:

- Create awareness of the need for culture transformation.
- Create a desire for the culture transformation.

I remember the first time I did this. I was nervous. I didn't know how people would take it, and I didn't know what would happen. However, I was in a situation where I had no choice but to buck up and do it because my business really needed a transformation. This can be an uncertain time, but it's a necessary one to get the process started.

Build a Case

First, get to know why you want to do this, the impact that it can create, and what it means to you. This requires gaining extreme clarity on culture strategy. By gaining a stronger understanding of it, you will have a more compelling case for buy-in.

- Learn about the business rationale of culture strategy.
- Learn how people would have to play their parts.

Depending on your role in the organization, it may be necessary to build a case to get approval for this strategy. If you are the owner or the most senior leader, that may not be necessary. Sometimes, the need for this change is self-evident, and everyone is already on board. Other times, it may be helpful to build a case to promote awareness, especially for larger organizations with more buy-in hurdles. This may involve:

- Gaining a deeper understanding of the current situation and its pain points
- Identifying desired benefits
- Diagnostics and assessments to provide an objective analysis
- Proof of concepts and demonstration of business value
- Getting to know the political climate of the organization
- Understanding your intended audience and how they make decisions

Truly Understanding Your Audience

Get to know the audience at a deeper level. Understand the people who need to buy in to this strategy.

- Who are you talking to?
- What does their world look like?
- Are they already amenable to culture strategy? Will it be relatively easy to get their buy-in?
- Have people lost hope and become accustomed to dysfunction? Will they be resistant?
- Can you anticipate who will support and resist this?
- What are their reasons for resistance?

Understanding your audience will help you anticipate potential resistance and craft a message that will better resonate with them. In addition, it will help size up the scope of the culture change. For some organizations, it may be a simpler process to manage the change because there are less chasms to bridge. Other times, organizations can have deeper issues with people who have become so accustomed to dysfunction that this will be an extremely challenging and painful process.

Preparing Your Plan of Attack

Some leaders who are leading culture changes get confused on whether they need to build an implementation team for this effort. They ask themselves:

- Do I do it myself?
- Do I build a team?

This really depends on the scope of the culture change. In general, I recommend the simplest plan that involves the path of least resistance. This tends to maintain the greatest chance of success and keeps expenses low. If we make it more complicated than it needs to be, it can get overwhelming.

In smaller companies and simpler situations, it's usually better to have a key leader who is highly motivated and engaged in this initiative to facilitate the culture change within their organization. A well-positioned leader who has a strong understanding of existing functions can have a ripple effect of influence throughout the organization. If the leader is unsure of what to do, they should seek training, coaching, or advisory.

However, there may be circumstances where that's not reasonable, due to added complexities, which can be due to having a larger company size, scope, complicated processes, and resistance associated with the initiative. In such situations, it may be necessary to break it down to various teams for specific functions, such as:

- **Governance or sponsorship board** – Team of sponsorship who can provide the necessary authority, resources, and support.

- **Implementation team** – Team to coordinate the tasks associated with the strategy.

- **Targets and advocates** – Targets you need to get buy-in and achieve behavior changes from.

If these intricacies exist, it may be worthwhile to bring in a consultant who understands how to navigate them. An expert advisor for the core implementation team can go a long way.

Structured Communications Plan

After getting a sense of the buy-in landscape and understanding the relevant teams, targets, and audience, it is important to maintain regular communications with them. Begin assessing:

- How will you monitor the progress?
- How will you keep in contact with them? What channel?
- How frequently?
- What will be the agenda?

Remember, this will require much more than a simple one-off announcement. There will need to be strategic reinforcements with the right people using the right channels with the right message at the right timing.

Introducing the Culture Strategy

It's time to introduce culture strategy with the organization. Choose your delivery channel, block out time, prepare your message, and share it with the audience.

This is often done as an introduction of a strategic initiative. It usually entails an announcement to build awareness of the culture situation, and sharing or revisiting the mission, vision, and values of the organization. Here are some ways to do this:

- **Craft the enterprise-level strategy** – Relevant for smaller companies that don't have an enterprise-level strategy yet.

- **Revise the enterprise-level strategy** – Relevant when there is an ineffective enterprise-level strategy that is due for a revision.

- **Craft a separate strategic initiative** – This is applicable for larger and more complex organizations where it's necessary to superimpose culture strategy into the existing infrastructure.

Be prepared to customize the message to their concerns. Describe what it means to them, including the potential growth opportunities. A common mistake is to fixate on how great it will be for the organization. Let's face it, most people usually don't get excited about organizational growth unless they see how it benefits them. I've come to learn the hard way that most people don't care about that. In general, it's wise to touch on the following points, as it covers concerns from multiple perspectives:

- Who needs to do what by when?
- Why are we doing this?
- Who is doing what?
- What's changing and what's not changing?

This can be a confusing and sensitive time for people within the organization because everything can seem uncertain. Even though it may seem that everyone would be interested because of the win-win value proposition that it can create, that's often not the case. I find that many people still resist change because they tend to be creatures of habit. There may be questions and concerns. Encourage them, prepare to address them, and create availability for people to voice concerns on a one-on-one basis with you offline.

Make this initiative about the people. If there is a culture dysfunction, they will likely be skeptical and have their guard up. Be transparent and encourage people to bring up concerns or talk with you privately.

Emphasize re-humanization of the workplace.

People will size you up to see whether you're serious about this. They want to know whether this effort is here to stay. They will also size up whether you really do care about the people aspect of the organization.

10.3. Phase Three: Culture Initiation

Now that we've had a chance to get the message out there in Phase Two, it's important to transition to Phase Three by making sure we apply it in our everyday work environment. At this point, people are still unsure and not convinced that this is a real thing that's here to stay.

This is the time to show everyone that you're serious about culture strategy. When I first did this, people were skeptical. It wasn't until people saw it being lived on an everyday basis that people believed this was real and actually happening.

This is a *critical* period in culture change because:

This is a battle for the minds of the people.

The battle is between the norms of the old way and the new proposed way. The best way to win this is to start living it! We accomplish this by integrating concepts of culture strategy within our daily lives. This includes applying people development within our everyday moments. The main objectives for this phase are:

- Initiate and stabilize the culture.
- Create the frame for culture and people development to propagate and sustain.

As a result of this, people will take notice. Momentum will be built, and more and more people will buy in to the strategy. This is because they realize:

- **This is real, not just talk** – As we integrate the values within our everyday actions, people realize that everyone needs to play their part and get with the program. That includes them! When they realize that, then they make the connection that these new standards are real and here to stay. It's time to reevaluate how we've been doing things.

- **This is going to be refereed** – When people fail to live up to the values of culture strategy, those deviations are consistently being refereed. When people witness the continuous reinforcement of these values, they recognize that this initiative is really happening.

- **Actually, this really is better for us!** – More people start to realize that there are significant advantages this movement can have on their lives. They recognize that they are treated with dignity and given more autonomy and opportunity for personal and professional growth. They embrace the team spirit in making an impact together, and they regain purpose by being a part of something bigger than them.

- **It's going to happen anyway, I might as well get on board** – Even when people still aren't fully bought in, as more and more people are won over, people tend to conform and get on board.

Live It

We can live this by demonstrating and integrating people development into our daily lives. This involves the application and institutionalization of:

- **Deeper root cause lens** – This involves putting a larger emphasis on seeing things through the deeper root cause lens (people development and collaboration focus) rather than the visible root cause lens (task focus).

- **People development focus** – We accomplish this through the right mix of coaching, facilitation, and so on. This is about using everyday moments as an opportunity to develop people.

- **Self-directed teams** – This is about converting our traditional teams (overdependence on authority and technical skills) to self-directed teams (using collaboration to create synergy). This involves a balanced set of perspectives and reconciliation of tension points.

Ultimately, this will involve:

- Improving universal collaboration standards
- Improving management standards
- Improving leadership standards

When we set this bar higher throughout the organization, it becomes the new norm of the organization. More of this is discussed in Part IV of the book. Depending on our access to people within the organization, we can do this by:

- **Coaching your direct reports within your team** – Use everyday moments to coach your direct reports.

- **Using facilitative meetings within your team** – This involves using good facilitation techniques in meetings with your teams to foster their own problem solving.

- **Coaching managers who report to you** – Managers have access to people that you might not. If you live and breathe it, they will learn it from you. Incorporate management coaching with your one-on-one meetings with them.

- **Fostering cross-pollination between the managers/teams that report to you** – Through synergistic facilitation between managers of different teams, it becomes possible to create an environment of cross-pollination, similar to the effect of having a mastermind for similar responsibilities.

- **Using facilitative meetings with departments that report to you** – Cross-functional facilitation between managers of different departments creates the potential to synergistically collaborate on how they can live the culture and support the organizational strategy.

- **Using mass communication channels and technology to regularly reach a broader audience** – With a theme similar to a "state-of-the-union" address, you can utilize larger group presentations or other media that reach a larger number of people to mobilize and update the majority of people.

Remember, it is not only about whether you do these items, but it is about doing them with the right intent. Just because we utilize these methods, it doesn't mean culture strategy will penetrate. The quality of the connections with people matters.

Open and Adaptive Communication

It's also important to note that as you progress along culture change, new information will present itself. Therefore, it's important to maintain an open communication channel to capture relevant information.

It's important to have an open-door policy. People may approach you, and you will get to know their concerns at a deeper level. This can be an opportunity for you to refine plans to address those concerns.

You may get a better understanding of who are the true Early Adopters (through real action and follow-through rather than talk) and who really are the Resistors. It's important to keep a flexible mentality with the communication plan to adapt to new scenarios and maximize the impact.

Manage the Momentum

Managing the momentum of buy-in is important for culture change, as this is a critical period to spark and maintain said momentum. As time moves on, it becomes increasingly clearer who the true Early Adopters, Resistors, and Majority are. Managing them in a strategic manner will maximize the development and sustenance of the buy-in momentum. You have a limited supply of time and energy, so you must be wise on how you allocate them throughout the buy-in process to maximize results.

Build Partnerships with Early Adopters

This is the most efficient utilization of your time and energy. Maximize their involvement through partnerships. Coach and empower them to live and breathe culture strategy, so they can be a beacon within their sphere of influence.

- **Early Adopters with influence** – If they have sufficient influence, codevelop initiatives and programs to better implement culture strategy.

- **Early Adopters with minimal influence** – Sometimes, early adopters with little positional authority can actually develop a larger influence by becoming an opinion leader within their team or surroundings. This may even uncover latent HiPo's that were being underutilized.

- **Fake Early Adopters (all talk, but no action)** – When you're in a position of authority, there may be a tendency for people to tell you what you want to hear. That doesn't mean they really support you and the cause. As time moves along, this should become increasingly evident, and a heart-to-heart conversation to get to know their real motives may be due.

Win Over and Educate the Majority

The Majority consists of the largest pool of constituents within an organization. Ultimately, they must be won over for culture strategy to truly be established as the new norm. It's important to have a feel of the pulse of the mindset of the Majority. Is the momentum picking up steam and winning the Majority over?

- **Concerned Majority** – You can win some of them over by understanding their concerns and addressing them.

- **"Play it safe" Majority** – Other times, they may be "playing it safe" by watching others "cross over" and seeing how it works out for them. After seeing others do it first, they believe that it is safe and join in.

It's important to continue to provide clarity to the Majority as more and more of them are won over. They will start thinking, "OK, I'm in, how do I play my part?"

- **What does it mean to be bought in?** – Be clear on what it means to buy in to culture strategy. This isn't about being fluffy and seeing whether people nod their head, smile, and agree with you. It means becoming engaged, demonstrating ownership, collaborating, being a proactive problem solver, playing their part in self-directed teams, and so on.

- **As people are won over, educate them on how to play their part** – As people are being won over, they will want greater clarity on what it means to play their part. You can fill those knowledge gaps through adequate coaching, training, and partnered efforts with culture champions who support this initiative.

Manage Resistors

Resistors can come in multiple forms. Management of Resistors will depend on the type of Resistors they are. Some Resistors can give valuable feedback, some are simply resistant to change, and some can actually be quite dangerous. We must be prepared to deal with them strategically.

- **Resistors with valid concerns** – Sometimes, there are Resistors because they can identify real and valid concerns that would become actual blockers to this initiative if left unaddressed. In such situations, it's wise to genuinely hear them out, and create a partnered effort to overcome such obstacles. In this manner, we can proactively identify and resolve issues, and at the same time get their buy-in for addressing their concerns.

- **Passive Resistors** – Some Resistors are extremely late to buy in to anything. They're highly resistant to any form of change. It may be wise to monitor them closely to ensure that they don't become *Toxic Resistors*. There is a chance that they may buy in at the tail end of the culture change initiative.

- **Toxic Resistors** – Some Resistors can actually be quite dangerous and actively cause harm to the initiative. They may be engaging in behaviors that are disruptive to culture strategy. It can happen from people with various positional authorities to safeguard or hide unhealthy activities or hoard jobs, staff, or knowledge. Even without a positional authority, it is possible to do this by spreading negative gossip and rumors. It is important to identify this swiftly and address it quickly, otherwise we are sending a message to the organization that we are condoning such behavior.

Mitigating Larger Risks

Bear in mind that you may need to be on high alert in this phase due to potentially large risks associated with resistance. This is because key people may be the resistors of culture strategy, and can hold various business functions as hostage. Therefore, you may need to be prepared to mitigate such risks.

- **Look for the win-win first** – I always recommend finding a win-win solution before implementing any forceful solution. Usually, there is a way to identify such solutions if we dig deep enough.

- **Mitigate larger toxicity risks** – Sometimes, it's simply not possible to stabilize the situation with certain people, and it may require a more drastic solution, including putting your foot down with a hard stance, isolating their influence from others, or parting ways.

- **Mitigate functional gaps** – If we need to part ways, depending on the situation, we may need to find fast solutions to fill any functional gaps from the voids that may be created. This is another reason why it is wise to have some margin by intentionally having your teams slightly above capacity. This greatly mitigates the functional risk of any possible turnover.

Referee Culture

Be prepared to referee the culture, as there will undoubtedly be many instances where the standards are not being upheld. This is very important to do when dysfunctional issues arise that are not conducive to culture strategy. Those are the moments that often define what becomes the new set of norms. People are watching to see if you let dysfunctional behavior go. If you don't referee this, you've just condoned the dysfunctional behavior. More about those norms will be discussed in Part IV.

Develop Supporting Programs

Culture alignment and higher standards of collaboration, management, and leadership are key components of this strategy. This can be a lot of weight to bear. Therefore it can make sense to develop, codevelop, or improve supporting programs that can aid in successfully implementing culture strategy. Here are some examples:

- **People development program** – A people development program should have the aim to increase the standards of collaboration, management, and leadership in the organization. This involves a combination of training, coaching, on-the-job application, career development, and programs to broaden work experience (for example, rotations, stretch projects, business case proposals).

- **Culture alignment-focused onboarding** – An onboarding program that has a key focus on culture alignment can be a tremendous supporting asset that helps integrate new hires. This doesn't just involve orientation logistics.

- **Internal communications** – An internal communications program can regularly update people regarding the bigger picture and even share accomplishments of other teams and departments. Not only can this help with alignment, but it improves organizational camaraderie.

On the surface, these programs may look like an isolated human resources function. However, it usually requires a partnership and collaboration mentality with multiple departments to achieve the results that we want. It's important to understand that the employee experience and their development are all-encompassing efforts.

10.4. Phase Four: Culture of Ownership

In this phase, many of the initiatives from the previous phase carry over. However, now we give a chance to let the culture marinate within the organization. This allows the culture to permeate every corner of the organization to create an atmosphere of ownership. Furthermore, it gives people the opportunity to reassess the effectiveness of their processes to make refined updates where necessary.

Team-Led Process Refinement

Up to this point, performance has not been fully optimized yet. There are still many detailed issues that are being missed. There are customer management-related situations that could use improvement or further finesse. There are operational kinks that can be managed and coordinated better.

That being said, people are beginning to have a better understanding of their own role, their team's role, and the expectations of relevant stakeholders. This knowledge allows them to deliver better results, as there are improvements in managing stakeholder expectations (for example, expectations from customers, internal stakeholders, senior leaders, board of directors, and so on.)

Throughout all of this, there will still be unfortunate incidents that need to be addressed. It is important to respond to these incidents with good feedback and coaching techniques, meanwhile continuing to referee the culture. It is also an opportunity to identify and fill training and skill gaps, while reinforcing the importance of good coordination to solve problems. Persistence is vital in this phase.

Eventually, people will begin to recognize a need to update and make further improvements to existing processes, systems, roles, and responsibilities. It's good to empower them to reevaluate, codevelop, and refine the following:

- Business processes that deliver better results
- Clearer team goals that everyone understands
- Clearer individual goals to better understand their role

Participation in improving these processes can further increase engagement, ownership, and motivation levels. As people get involved in this, it's important to empower them to problem solve. This can be done by encouraging:

- **Proactive problem solving** – Encourage people to conceptualize solutions. This further increases their ownership.

- **Bottom-up management** – Get rid of the notion that the solutions need to come from the boss.

- **A safe environment** – There may be reservations to proposing ideas due to fears of being shot down or overstepping boundaries. You have to make the process safe.

- **Continuous coaching** – Great coaching is paramount to refine and develop ideas proposed by the people. Especially in the beginning, many ideas may be unrefined. Coaching helps develop and filter the ideas.

- **More transparency and access to process modification** – People can't take ownership if they don't have access to important knowledge or haven't been empowered to modify processes. When mutual trust is established, be sure to give this to them.

Cross-Functional Tweaking

To truly unlock the potential for culture strategy, there may also be a need for:

> **Reassessment of organizational policies and cross-functional processes** – There may be archaic or insufficient processes that are not conducive to culture. This can lead to unhealthy interfaces throughout the organization, which can result in disruption of the culture strategy.

This may involve reevaluation of deeply rooted procedures within the organization. Oftentimes, this is not easy to do, as they may be deeply entrenched into the functions of the organization. Therefore, you may encounter a great deal of resistance regarding this, due to concerns that currently existing functions will be compromised.

However, by now, there may be a momentum of buy-in because the value of culture strategy should be more tangible. People should be seeing the fruits of their efforts, and a sense of mutual trust is being established. Archaic and rigid processes were often implemented to stabilize a chaotic and distrusting situation in the past. With more mutual trust, there can be more openness to reassess existing cross-functional processes. This can pave the path to redevelop the systems in a strategic manner that maximizes culture. This can also be applied to various departments to achieve:

> **Alignment between cross-functional departments** – Different functions (for example, finance, human resources, legal, IT, and so on) interface with teams, and they can either support or disrupt the flow of culture strategy. When we achieve greater alignment between these functions, we can create an environment that is more conducive for this strategy.

This will greatly clean up the unhealthy interfaces that exist between teams throughout the organization. This can ensure the continuity and sustainability of growth through culture strategy.

A New Normal: Get Used to This New Flow

Eventually, people become accustomed to this culture as better coordination and performance becomes the new norm. They are bought in to this culture strategy to the point that they even begin to self-reinforce the culture. They take ownership of the processes that were transferred to them.

This can be a liberating phase, as you may get your first sense of freedom. This is where less things escalate to you, trust is being established, teams have your back and are holding their own. People are starting to get the hang of how this new culture works. They are beginning to understand that coordinating leads to synergy and can achieve goals better. They are connecting the dots on how culture, communication, and leadership relate to their tasks.

Additionally, our aim is to have the teams and people surpass the leader's skills in their respective expertise. This is possible if we've adequately developed our culture and people infrastructure, along with transferring ownership of processes to them. This should free up the leader's bandwidth and allow them to place a greater emphasis on leveraging higher-ticket value.

10.5. Phase Five: Culture of Strategy

It's ripe to introduce team-level strategies throughout the organization. We accomplish this by challenging the organization to be forward thinking, innovative, and proactive. This further optimizes processes, customer or stakeholder interfaces, and the ability to overcome challenges they face. This creates a tremendous amount of value as it promotes:

- **Holistic perspectives** – This encourages teams to see their roles from a broader viewpoint and anticipate factors that are outside their day-to-day considerations.

- **Innovative problem solving** – Pertinent and innovative solutions can originate from anywhere in the organization. These are solutions that would otherwise never have been considered if problem solving was centralized.

- **Collaboration and alignment throughout the organization** – This helps get the whole organization on the same page.

The people infrastructure built from the previous phases is critical for the success of this phase. This makes it ripe for developing strategic capabilities within teams. It puts the team in a proactive stance rather than a reactive stance by focusing on the endgame.

Strategy requires a great deal of mutual trust and vulnerability. If you've developed the infrastructure from the previous phases, this phase shouldn't be too hard. If you find this phase to be extremely difficult, it is likely because there are deeper issues that haven't been properly dealt with from the previous phases. In such cases, it's important to revisit the previous phases and invest more in the people infrastructure.

Vision Breakdown: A More Granular Version of the Vision

By now, we should have already shared the vision statement with the organization (through the enterprise-level mission, vision, values [MVV] or a different strategy initiative) in a previous phase. However, what does it mean? A vision is a highly complicated group of thoughts, and without a breakdown it can end up as a poster on a wall or simply a catchphrase. Other times, it gets severely misinterpreted.

If it hasn't been done already, now is a good time to offer a breakdown of the vision into phases and strategic goals to help people in the organization digest it. This helps them visualize how they play a role, organizes their thoughts, and opens up dialogues with relevant people. It gives them something to work toward and helps them be strategic themselves. By now, they should exhibit the improved collaboration skills that are necessary to productively coordinate and work toward a vision. This will also involve promoting strategic thinking at team levels.

Set the Tone: Promoting Team-Level Strategies

We have to get clear on what strategy is. One of the issues with the word "strategy" is that everyone has a different definition of it and how it should be done. That's why it's important to set the stage on what it is and how it should be done. In this phase, we approach strategy with a focus on building an environment of *team-level strategies*.

This means that it's creating strategy at all levels of the organization. It's not something that's limited to the highest-level executives of an organization with a top-down approach. We all need to get involved in it. Though the highest-level strategies, such as the enterprise-level strategies, should still be centralized and set forth by senior leadership, we have to come together to represent it at our respective levels.

Increasing Baseline Strategy Thinking

For the majority of the population, strategic thinking does not come naturally. There are skill gaps that need to be filled. If left undeveloped, it can lead to chaotic idea proposals, unhealthy collaboration, and mutual frustration. By increasing the baseline strategic-thinking skills, better quality ideas and collaboration can be achieved.

This can be developed through a combination of people development efforts. It can develop the team's ability to recognize issues, imagine a desired future, plan for it, and reach those goals. It includes:

- **Training** – Basic strategic capabilities can be trained.

- **Coaching** – Most people are not accustomed to using this skill. Therefore, it needs to be coached as ideas are proposed, discussed, and refined.

- **Encouraging "white space"** – We have to encourage the utilization of margin for white space. This is time reserved to research external and internal factors, think about possible solutions, and refine them. Otherwise, people won't have the time or energy to think strategically.

We also have to develop the leaders' and managers' ability to receive and develop others' ideas. This is a technique-sensitive skill, which often gets overlooked. This requires:

- **Coaching leaders and managers to develop others' ideas** – Leaders and managers play a critical role in developing people's ideas. They are either promoting an environment that encourages ideas or are killing its momentum. In fact, many leaders and managers who harm this environment are actually unaware of this. It may be necessary to coach or train them to develop ideas within others.

- **Hosting facilitative sessions to guide strategic thinking** – Organized facilitative sessions can draw out and guide strategic thinking within others.

Bridging Essential Strategy Hard Skills with Facilitation

Strategy can be an advanced process. However, it can be made more accessible to everyone by using organized strategic processes to help guide thinking. In essence, this utilizes a series of facilitative sessions to go through the strategic thought processes as a team. This can include:

- **Situational analysis** – External and internal considerations
- **Trend analysis** – Potential trends

- **Strategy** – Possible team-level strategic approaches
- **Balancing priorities** – Understanding holistic priorities
- **Goals** – Defining strategic goals
- **Objectives** – Defining tactical objectives
- **Risk** – Probability, impact, and mitigation plan
- **Budget** – Resource allocation
- **Stakeholders** – Relevant parties and subsequent communications plan
- **Tactics** – Task breakdown
- **Execution** – Coordination, feedback, morale
- **Reporting** – Updates and adaptation
- **Review** – Retrospectives and transitions

This co-creation process can also help get everyone on board with the strategic plan. Too often we see a strategic plan that is created by senior leaders but does not resonate with implementers. This type of segregation between strategic planners from executioners often creates division, misalignment, lack of ownership, lack of engagement, lack of innovation, and lack of situational adaptation.

Through this methodology, strategic plans can be conceptualized at various layers of the organization, reaching down all the way to the team level. This involvement in strategic planning increases ownership, engagement, and situational problem solving. More details on strategic processes will be discussed in Part V.

10.6. Phase Six: Ecosystem of Strategy

This is the pinnacle of leverage that we are trying to achieve, and why many leaders embark upon culture strategy in the first place. In this phase, we use everything that we built in the previous phases to set up and maintain an infrastructure for organic, sustainable, innovative, and exponential growth.

In essence, we are promoting strategies at scale, while moving together as an organization in the same direction. This involves a focus on the ecosystem and maximizing the alignment between centralized strategies and peripheral strategies. With this, we can enable a team-led growth trajectory that is pushed by teams, rather than only coming from the senior leaders. This allows for more leverage, while maintaining the integrity of culture strategy. Let's explore this further.

An Ecosystem to Sustain Multiple Strategies Organically

Now that we've enabled strategic capabilities and innovative problem solving throughout teams in the organization, we shift our focus to maximizing the benefits that we gain from this. This is achieved through a paradigm shift in how we approach strategy by having an ecosystem focus. Rather than a *linear* outlook on strategies, we view it from a *life cycle* management perspective. This allows strategies to form organically and be managed at scale. We achieve this with a focus on:

- Continued team-level strategy involvement and development – We should continue to involve teams within the strategic planning process to maximize engagement and have ongoing strategic capability development.

- Partnerships between relevant parties to promote the ecosystem – To sustain this ecosystem, there needs to be a partnered focus in maintaining transparency, margin, alignment, and resource allocation. This involves being on the same page with senior leaders, departments, managers, and teams, and having supportive cross-functions. Furthermore, this partnership can be used to create a centralized command center for larger numbers of peripheral strategies.

There's always going to be a judgment call to determine how much of the strategic decisions should be centralized and decentralized.

Overall, the more we can safely let go to competent teams, the more we can accomplish. However, this is largely based upon the strategy competencies of the teams, mutual trust, and the existence of a supportive ecosystem. Haphazardly letting go can introduce undue risk and misalignment. That's why we should be building onto this ecosystem on an ongoing basis. This is how we become strategic with strategy and get the organization to look at the long-term horizon together.

Refining Enterprise-Level Strategic Priorities to Magnify Results

The more we understand the enterprise-level strategy, the clearer we can be when we communicate it and align with the rest of the organization. As an organization experiences growth, it is more likely to lose touch with *why* the organization exists in the first place. Therefore, when necessary, it's important to dive deeper and refine the organization's overarching strategy as it relates to being:

- **Opportunity-driven** – Based on the opportunities available in the market trends.
- **Purpose-driven** – Refocusing on the why of the organization to maximize engagement.

With a well-positioned enterprise-level strategy, it becomes easier to penetrate markets and engage people within the organization. There will also be a greater need to maximize alignment by focusing on:

- **Clear communication of the enterprise-level strategy** – Enterprise-level strategies are extremely complex and need to be broken down and communicated in a clear manner, or we lose resonance with the majority of the organization.

- **Clarity on the enterprise-level strategic priorities** – Many organizations already have enterprise-level strategies; however, most of them still lack the understanding on its priorities or what it really means. This can lead to misinterpretation, internal conflicts, and misprioritization.

- **Maximized alignment between enterprise-level and team-level strategies** – This involves ensuring that the various team-level strategies are guided toward the same overall direction and allocating resources accordingly.

When this is not clear, it can lead to a random trajectory of initiatives. Growth can quickly become chaotic with a sporadic and spontaneous pattern. Over time, this can result in a random portfolio of mediocre strategies. In the long run, that can cause the downfall for large companies because mediocre strategies do not perform well in the market. Therefore, let's be proactive to not let that happen. In fact, by doing so, you'll notice that a tremendous amount of value gets created through a ripple effect, even with minor refinements and improved clarity.

Leveraging Team-Led Growth

If the teams can handle strategic initiatives to optimize their own functions, it is time to redirect those capabilities toward growth. This is a great way to get the team(s) on the same page and thinking about growth. Such initiatives would also create unique opportunities for the team to expand their skillset. This is usually accompanied by the opening of new positions, which may also create potential opportunities for people interested in advancing their career.

We can be strategic with our growth by creating synergy through:

- **Vertical growth** – Expansion into additional steps in the value chain.
- **Horizontal growth** – Additional locations, teams, or offices, or acquisition of customer bases.

After conceptualizing this, we may have to consider reassessing our infrastructure, capabilities, networks, resources, and team dynamics. It may become necessary to conceptualize a next-level team that can sustain the next level of growth. This can create new roles in the organization. When this is conceptualized, position preference should lean in favor of internal selections. However, if the required knowledge capabilities do not exist or cannot be developed internally, external selections should be highly considered.

These growth spurts may seem like there's a lot involved, but if you have a team that has your back, the workload and risk are greatly reduced. Overall, you'll notice that team-led growth (as opposed to traditional forms of growth) will have the following benefits:

- Increased success rate of stabilizing expansion efforts
- Sustainability of culture strategy
- Reasonable distribution of work associated with growth initiatives

These growth initiatives act as stretch projects to develop internal talent while simultaneously growing the organization. This can help with the development of advanced skillsets for managers and teams, career advancement opportunities for key individuals, increased engagement, and long-term sustainability of the culture strategy.

This looks very different from the scenario in which a single leader bears the entire weight of the expansion project. If a leader tries to do it by themselves, they may end up collapsing from being overloaded. It really highlights the key points of the saying:

> "If you want to go fast, go alone. If you want to go far,
> go together."
> —African Proverb

In this chapter, we have discussed the six phases in enterprise-level culture change: pre-culture, culture awareness, culture initiation, culture of ownership, culture of strategy, and ecosystem of strategy. In understanding these six phases, you can diagnose your organization's current state properly and deliver the correct treatment. You can target the next phase and the next, in an order that builds one layer of foundation upon another, until you can fully leverage team-led growth and see its value in your company. You can do this together with the rest of the organization joining you in ownership over the expansion. This leads us to the most foundational part of the book: making the difference in everyday moments. If you get this right, everything else just comes together.

PART IV

THE
DIFFERENCE
IS IN
EVERYDAY
MOMENTS

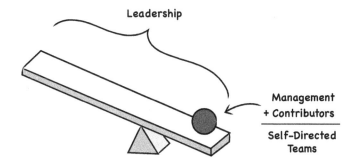

Leadership

Management
+ Contributors

Self-Directed
Teams

CHAPTER 11

LIVING CULTURE AS A MANAGER AND LEADER

I began my experience in management and leadership with a heavy focus on the tasks. Initially, this helped us grow very rapidly as a team, but there came a point where it became unsustainable. I felt as though I was herding cats all day long. It was a very stressful time for me because no one seemed to care as much as I did. I realized that I was bringing my problems home. This was a difficult realization, and when I recognized it, I had to learn to draw the line because I didn't start a business and become a leader to hurt my family. That's when I became committed to looking into transforming my leadership focus and skills.

I studied many different perspectives to understand my situation. Upon several realizations, breakthroughs, and paradigm shifts, it dawned on me that:

Most problems are actually caused by poor communication.

This meant that my view of management and leadership was all wrong! It took a while to see things that way, as it doesn't appear like that at first glance. Once I started seeing things that way, it introduced a brand new way of approaching problems and solutions. Now, there was a path to a more sustainable and scalable way of solving issues.

If you really look at things from this perspective, you can break down almost every task-related issue and isolate the communicational problem. It takes a while to develop this perspective because most people naturally focus on the task component.

This paradigm shift can be applied to almost any situation. Let's look at some examples.

- When someone doesn't do their job, don't jump straight into thinking they're incompetent. Explore the possibility that the expectations weren't clearly defined well enough, or there was insufficient training/coaching support.

- If someone had an escalated conflict with another person, don't immediately reprimand them. Evaluate both sides, whether the person adapted their communication style to the situation, whether there was insufficient training/coaching on collaboration, or whether the expectations for appropriate behavior within the culture were unclear.

- If someone was unwilling to work hard and be a team player, don't jump straight into thinking they were lazy. It is possible there was an insufficient amount of quality coaching. If that's ruled out, then we can consider whether this was a poor fit, or the person shouldn't haven't joined the team in the first place (which is actually a communicational breakdown of setting clear criteria at the time of hiring).

We could actually go on and on with countless problems that can occur in an organization, and isolate where relevant communicational breakdowns occurred. Once this realization is made, the priority shifts to removing communication blockers, developing people's skills in collaboration, and coaching fundamental skills like goal orientation, confidence, logical thinking, teamwork, and so on.

Upon having this paradigm shift, managers can address situations from this angle. Then, they can work toward getting out of the vicious "cat-herding" cycle. This requires approaching issues from a coaching mentality. After a sustained effort, teams can level up and handle problems on their own. In essence, this reaches a self-directed team status.

This takes real management and leadership skills.

This requires a higher standard of management and leadership skills. So, let's go over what that looks like.

Don't Breeze through This Part

Your initial tendency may be to breeze through Part IV. That would be a critical mistake, as this is the *true* infrastructure. The foundation of culture strategy works through the concepts that are covered in this part. If something within the company is not working out, it's likely because we haven't dug deep enough here. If there's any part of the book that may need to be reread over and over again, it's Part IV.

So, open your mind, remain flexible, dig deep, and connect the dots. Contrast the concepts with what goes on in your everyday lives. This requires a different way of viewing what management and leadership really is.

11.1. Using Everyday Moments as Coaching Moments

We all had a person who guided or inspired us in a way that transformed us and maybe even changed our life. It could have been a role model, a coach, or a mentor—in the form of a teacher, parent, relative, friend, boss, or colleague.

Perhaps it was the way they lived life that impressed you. Maybe it was their skill, talents, or ability to get things done. Maybe it was their success and accomplishments. Or maybe it was their philosophy and how they understood things.

All in all, they really helped you shape who you became. They were there for you in both the good times and the bad. They guided you through the tough times and helped you get back on your feet.

Remember the trust and connection that developed? Remember how that felt? Remember how deep that relationship became?

That's who you need to become to be a culture champion, whether it is through management or leadership. You need to encourage the other managers and leaders too.

Coaching needs to be in the manager and leader's DNA.

Putting It Together

Now, I am not suggesting making coaching your profession. However, you do need to develop a coach's mindset to really bring the best out of your people.

This requires drawing on principles discussed in earlier parts of the book.

- **Deeper root cause lens** – Identify the deeper collaboration breakdown rather than pinpointing the immediately preceding task breakdown.

- **No single point of failure** – This keeps us in a solution mentality in identifying multiple points on why issues continuously arise and proactively resolving them. It also prevents us from putting the blame on a "symptom," rather than the true root cause.

- **Use everyday moments as coaching moments** – Rather than a reprimanding approach, a coaching and developmental approach is used. Don't just do this on formal reviews. This should be done on an everyday situational basis.

This doesn't mean you become a softie. It does not mean we let people get away with things. We still need to be clear with the impact of their actions. However, it does mean that we try to identify the skill gap and codevelop a solution whenever possible.

The Heart, Ethics, and Attitude

You need to have a genuine *heart* that gets excited when developing people. To you, their successes are your successes, and you're proud of them. You can't fake this. People can pick up if you're being self-oriented and when you make everything about you.

You also need a set of *ethics* that people are willing to follow.

These might seem self-evident to individuals who have the heart and ethics. But interestingly, this is the hardest thing to train and develop. When someone doesn't care about these things, it's really hard to develop this attribute.

You have to personally live and represent these values too. You can't simply delegate this away without playing your part and expect it to come together. Your *attitude* will set the tone.

- If you're not willing to live and represent this, you're a part of the problem too, and likely one of the resistors.

- As a manager or leader, you're either supporting the culture or harming it. You can't be neutral.

At first glance, all this may sound easy to do, but it's harder than it sounds. Once you contrast these values with the pressures of reaching goals, that's when it starts getting difficult. Balancing goals along with people development can be more challenging than meets the eye. It is definitely possible and requires a journey of self-development to be able to juggle this.

Get Over It

Developing true management and leadership skills is going to push you outside your comfort zone. This requires paradigm shifts. You're going to have to confront many of your insecurities. It's going to feel uncomfortable. So, you're going to have to:

Get comfortable being uncomfortable.

Maintain an *abundance* mentality, rather than a scarcity mentality. If we live life with a "glass-half-empty" approach, and expect that it isn't going to work, a self-fulfilling prophecy will occur.

11.2. Transitioning to Management: From Managing Tasks to Developing People

Interestingly, most companies have no formal training for management, and people are expected to learn on the job. This often leads to subpar management skills, without ever receiving guidance to develop the skills necessary for successful management. This can lead to a fast deterioration of culture by utilizing hierarchy, rather than people development.

For a successful transition from being a contributor to becoming a manager, a major paradigm shift must occur. The job becomes more about producing well-balanced contributors working toward a common goal, rather than producing the results themselves. That means the input of the manager's job is unpolished team members, and the manager's main output is polished, balanced, and competent team members.

- **INPUT** – Unpolished people.
- **OUTPUT** – Polished, balanced, and competent team members.

This is a completely different set of skills from being the strongest contributor (often the prelude to getting promoted to management). Now, the job requires great people skills. The main *control levers* for managers to influence their team involve:

- **Coaching** – This involves connecting, training, motivating, engaging, and providing feedback to team members. It's important to emphasize the importance of developing higher standards of communication, self-management, and thinking skills to become well-rounded contributors.

- **Team dynamics** – This involves managing the team development, tension points, conflicts, engagement levels, and team values, and being the beacon for culture strategy.

- **Tactics** – They must use their business acumen and tactical skills to guide the team to meet goals. This involves observing, organizing, planning, directing, evaluating others' activities, and so on.

These *control levers* will be further discussed in Chapters 12 and 13.

A Great Manager Makes Their Job Obsolete

This may initially sound counterintuitive, but a truly great manager makes their job obsolete.

"What? How?"

This is accomplished by creating self-directed teams through people development and grooming the next manager and leader.

"Why would they do that?"

This actually demonstrates stronger and more valuable management skills!

"Aren't they concerned about losing their job?"

Actually, they shouldn't be! A manager who is capable of doing this can be strategically allocated to the next major initiative. There is one caveat though. Their superior does need to know the value of these skills, as it enables a strategy of succession planning to develop the talent of tomorrow. This creates a continuous stream of internally developed talent that they can choose from when positions open up. This mentality is more prevalent in organizations with a well-developed culture, where there is mutual trust and transparency.

Transition from Team Member

For a team member who is making the transition to management, one of the realizations that the manager must make is that they are:

Accountable for everything and everyone on the team.

This can be quite overwhelming for a newer or unskilled manager who is used to working their role as an individual silo. Even if they wanted to prop things up with their sheer will, there are far too many tasks for them to complete in a sustainable manner. They have to learn to manage their time and collaborate with their team. That means they can't be a one-trick pony.

Managers must learn to reconcile the fact that
they have limited time, energy, and resources
by developing and utilizing their team.

As tasks for the team come their way, managers have the following options to complete them:

- Do it yourself,
- Delegate it, or
- Build a system around it.

It is important for the manager to internalize this, so that they can own their problem-solving thought process on how to best approach the tasks. It also puts them in a situation to be self-aware of their own strengths and weaknesses, and be introspective of their team members' strengths, weaknesses, and motivations. This allows them to conceptualize solutions to synchronize with their team members, by asking themselves:

Is this something that someone else should and can do?

Utilizing team members involves delegation, which can be challenging for some managers because they are accountable for what they delegated, but they're unsure whether they can ensure the quality of the delegated work.

However, in proper management, the job is to produce well-balanced contributors working toward a common goal. More than anything else, you're a trainer and a coach. Because your job is not to simply perform the tasks anymore, that means you need to learn to:

Let go. Relinquish control to seize control.
Give trust to build trust. Trust is a two-way street.

At first, this was extremely uncomfortable for me because I had to let go of the control and the quality of the tasks. In addition, I wouldn't see the results immediately because there was a delayed effect in improving results through developing people. This was because I had to use situations as coaching opportunities, rather than fixing them myself or telling team members exactly what to do.

Remember, letting go does not mean out of sight and out of mind. You need to coach, train, develop, and provide feedback. However, therein lies a new challenge:

People are different from you, and
People are unpredictable.

That means that what worked for you will not necessarily work for your team members. You need to learn how people operate differently and are motivated by different things. This way, you can work on reconciling these differences.

Stabilizing teams, working together, creating synergy, and simultaneously reaching business objectives is part of the learning curve of managers.

Considerate Managers May Be Abused by Their Team!

Some managers have such a caring heart that they allow themselves to get taken advantage of by their own team! They bombard the manager with everything and even reverse delegate to them.

In such situations, the manager must be good at managing their time and energy. They must strike the fine balance of reaching their goals, developing people, and having limited time. Here are some tools they can use:

- Have an open-door policy, but don't become a "punching bag" – If you are being abused, you may need to neutralize this by being less available.

- Establish boundaries – Establish clearer criteria of what is acceptable to escalate.

- "If it's not a big issue, ask me after you do it" – Setting this tone can encourage and empower people to be more confident in their own solutions. Sometimes they need to know that it's safe to try out their solution without repercussions.

- **"If you bring something up, have a possible solution in mind"** – Setting this tone can encourage people to be confident in their own thinking and create opportunities to refine their thinking with their manager if it needs more guidance.

Some People Regret Getting into Management

Some extremely strong contributors find this transition (due to the people management and accountability components) to be so painful that they prefer to remain as a contributor or a subject matter expert (SME). Others may implode from the pressures of management, due to not being able to handle the accountability and responsibility of other people's performance. Embarking upon the journey of learning real management skills is like developing a new set of skills for someone who has never "properly" managed before. It is challenging to motivate someone to learn such skills if they are not internally driven to do so. It may become a painful experience for the manager and their superior. That is also why the *aptitude* and *motivation* of the individual need to be assessed before promoting them to management. This can help minimize painful experiences involving backtracking for both parties.

Transition from Traditional Management

Unfortunately, there are managers who think, "I'm the boss. You have to do what I tell you to do because we pay you, and you're lucky to even have this job." This attitude can be a very toxic way of thinking. For such managers, it's important for them to remember that:

- **This is not a title, it's a responsibility** – Rather than viewing management as a title with privileged authority, it's important to see it as a responsibility. This means that they should know how to get results with buy-in, rather than force and authority.

- **Use the boss card very sparingly** – There may be moments when you will still need to use the "boss card" to rein in the situation, but it should be done sparingly and when all else fails.

- **Don't overuse hierarchy** – If you overuse and abuse it, you will lose out in the long term.

It's really important to understand how the hierarchal manager mentality has a tendency to create a disengaging work environment, which can result in lower overall productivity.

A lot of companies end up with managers with such hierarchal mentalities because they lack an effective and standardized management development program. Oftentimes, managers were promoted due to their high performance, rather than their management skills or potential. Remember, being a strong performer is a very different skillset from being a good manager, which relies heavily on the ability to develop people.

The Mispositioned Subject Matter Expert

Occasionally, there are oddly placed managers who would be better positioned as subject matter experts. Oftentimes, they shy away from people-related issues or push that on others. This quickly degrades to a situation that is disruptive to the organizational culture.

It's possible to empower them to gain the interest in developing such skills, but it is extremely challenging. Their resistance is usually deeply rooted. More often than not, they're much happier being repositioned as a subject matter expert, where they can dive deeper into their expertise and truly shine.

This reduces the people-related aspects of the job for them. However, even as an SME, bear in mind that they still need to be able to have healthy collaboration with others.

The Largest Influence in Shaping Employee Experience

Direct managers have the largest impact on an employee's experience, and we would be losing out on a tremendous amount of value if alignment with managers is not achieved.

Since managers have the largest influence on the employee experience, investing to improve the baseline management skills of the organization can improve overall employee engagement. Companies that have higher employee engagement are recognized as having higher productivity, higher profit, higher customer satisfaction, less turnover, less accidents, and less absenteeism.

People don't leave companies, they leave their managers.

When people leave, they often leave due to their manager rather than the company. Bad managers can be a black hole for employees and create significant engagement and retention problems. Therefore, if we don't get on the same page with our middle managers, culture strategy will fail to penetrate into their direct reports.

11.3. Transitioning to Leadership: Differences between Management and Leadership

Leadership, in an objective nutshell, is all about accomplishing more with less time. This maximizes the impact and efficiency of the leader's time because time becomes the most limiting resource. How else can great CEOs of large multinational organizations or higher-level officials make such a large impact without knowing the ins and outs of every technical field or community that they serve? If we truly dissect the skills that allow them to do it, it comes down to leadership skills.

In essence, leadership skills are more about leveraging the skills of others. This is far more powerful than a do-it-yourself (DIY) or even a management approach. This leverage can maximize the impact that self-directed teams and managers can generate. Leaders' action items are different from managers', which requires another paradigm shift to build a new set of skills. Through this, the leader can make an impact and have a presence of being in multiple areas at once.

The Control Levers Are Different for Leaders

I find that leadership is a highly misunderstood topic. Leadership, just like culture, is often used like a buzzword or exciting topic in today's society. People say that leadership is all about inspiring others. Though it is true that this is important, I believe there's so much more to that because otherwise it would simply be a "cheerleader" job. Then, a lot of people would be qualified for the job, which is simply not the case.

Leaders accomplish their results through leveraging self-directed teams, developing future managers/leaders, and setting the strategic direction of the organization. They also represent the moral tone, values, and heart of the company. Leaders have a different set of tools and techniques to accomplish their results from managers, as the role of a leader is designed to be able to influence multiple teams. These tools include:

- Developing other managers and leaders
- Strategy
- Mobilizing teams from the outside

An additional challenge for leaders is that as their role continues to grow, they increasingly become responsible for leading multiple teams. This may even be in arenas that are outside their field of technical expertise. This creates a limitation because the leader cannot be everywhere at once and know everything. Thus, they must be more effective and impactful with the utilization of their time.

You can't be everywhere at once, and
You can't know everything.

In essence, they have to learn to "clone" themselves. That means they have to maintain the same level of results by the team without physically being there! This includes the same level of team unity, discipline, communication, and coordination that required so much energy and effort to painstakingly develop. They have to do this by developing their successor manager, who would ensure that culture strategy is promoted, nurtured, and refereed.

Developing Other Managers and Leaders

Leaders should be involved in producing other managers and leaders who can develop their own contributors. This is challenging because it involves letting go and trusting the manager/team to notice problems, discuss problems, problem solve around them, organize a plan, and fulfill the plan. This is far more complicated than simply performing tasks. This involves leveraging the skills of teams/managers to enable higher-level problem solving. This may involve significant developmental efforts to get to this point.

Strategy

Once leaders have successfully built this infrastructure, they get to focus on higher-ticket items, such as strategy. This involves identifying and capturing strategic value, which can generate enormous business value. This is one of the strongest forms of leverage that exists, which involves forming a higher-level strategy to set the tone and direction of the organization. Subsequently, to get the organization on board with the strategy, leaders can involve more people with the strategic process. This requires building strategic skills within people and creating an ecosystem that promotes team-level strategy. By making people a part of this process, leaders can maximize strategic alignment and ownership/engagement with the overall strategic direction.

Leaders should look out for identifying potential
strategic value and setting the course to capture this
value by determining the tone and direction.

Mobilizing Teams from the Outside

To truly harness this value, we need to be able to mobilize teams from an outside position of the day-to-day tasks. This is more operator and technique sensitive than many realize. It leverages results from managers and teams through "nonsupervisory" approaches to maximize the results from self-directed teams. This requires delicate care and mutual trust between the leader and managers/teams.

Leaders need to move teams without "messing with their
groove." This involves leveraging their self-direction by
mobilizing them toward a strategic direction, while they solve
their own obstacles.

When a "supervisory" approach is inadvertently employed, the effectiveness of the self-directed teams is compromised. This can ruin the self-directed nature of the teams, which would actually have the team move backward! The leader would be forced to micromanage those teams, which would become an unsustainable situation.

As you can imagine, there needs to be a strong baseline of people infrastructure and self-direction within the organization to pull this off. This also requires a great deal of mutual trust among the leaders, managers, and teams. This is because the leader's role is to influence a team's performance by leveraging their skills to handle complex challenges. This can feel extremely uncomfortable for those who are still developing this skillset to deliver results in this manner because it involves a higher degree of letting go.

Transition from Management to Leadership

The transition from a manager to a leader is just as challenging as transitioning from a contributor to a manager. This requires even more vulnerability, letting go of more control, and a greater degree of trust for the team.

> *Leadership involves a greater degree of*
> *letting go than management.*

This requires another paradigm shift and can be another painful experience to go through. Unfortunately, many who embark upon this path realize they cannot keep up. Just like in management, it's wise to reserve these roles for HiPo's as few other people can keep up. This reduces the likelihood of a painful backtracking experience for both ends.

> *Transitioning from management to leadership is difficult.*

If you succeed in making this transition, you've just enabled a more powerful leverage. More of these skills are discussed in Chapter 14.

Leadership Maximizes Impact

The mechanism of leadership leverages productivity, which is more dependent on influence and relationship dynamics than manual exertion and force of will. In fact, these techniques can be so efficient that it can maximize impact to accomplish more with less. This is how we break the cycle of having to achieve results by investing more time and energy.

Accomplishing more with less – Leaders have a limited amount of time, energy, and bandwidth. There are countless situations that are thrown at them, and they have to deal with them with the maximum efficiency and impact. Otherwise their world would fall apart. Therefore, skilled leaders must be wise in selecting which activities to be involved in to maximize productivity based on their limited amount of time.

Another advantage to these techniques is that the leader can utilize an approach to have teams solve their own problems. That means the leader does not need to know all the technical moving pieces behind the team for it to function. This can greatly increase the sphere of influence of the leader without having to be an expert in everything because that is simply not possible after reaching a certain level of responsibilities.

Leadership can consolidate multiple technical capabilities under one common goal.

In fact, properly employed leadership techniques can consolidate and assimilate several technical capabilities toward a common direction. A leader without all the technical skills and expertise could achieve this because they have a different arsenal of tools that allow them to leverage teams with different capabilities. This can be a more sustainable and impactful approach than trying to become an expert in every technical field.

A Three-Step Transition

There are three types of tasks that make up a manager or leader's schedule:

- Do-It-Yourself (DIY)
- Managing
- Leading

Transitioning from DIY, management, and then to leadership skills is not as clear cut with obvious boundaries as you might imagine. Notice that they can try applying leadership techniques as a single team manager. In fact, when a manager employs these techniques and is successful at it, they may find themselves in a unique situation. They built up the team members and a successor so much that everything runs on its own and without them! This is a fantastic place to be, and that is the embodiment of leadership. If that has truly been achieved, then it might be time to move on to the next challenge that will grow the organization. This is a highly valuable skill and in scarce supply. It's the stepping stone to leading multiple teams and utilizing such skills even more!

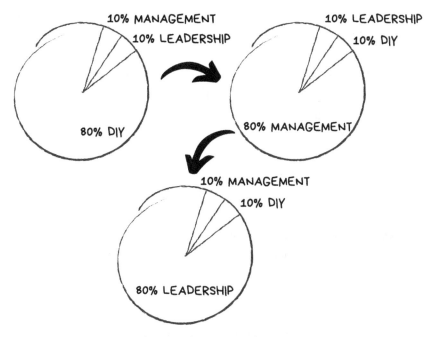

Pie charts of three different types of manager schedules

Overall, these transitions are usually made incrementally as our skills develop. As we progress along this path, our effectiveness and productivity increase. Let's explore these categories further.

- **Do-It-Yourself (DIY) manager** – A less capable or newer manager typically fills their schedule with a lot of DIY actions. The reason for this is that most untrained managers are most comfortable with this type of work. They can ensure the quality of the work at the most consistent level (because they are doing it themselves rather than supervising another person doing it), and they can confirm that it gets done in a timely manner. They can see the results right away, and many people enjoy that type of work as opposed to managing others doing a job (especially if they have not developed proper management skills). However, there is definitely a limitation to this approach. It doesn't create an environment of team growth, and the manager's working capacity to oversee projects is very limited.

- **Management** – A manager who fills most of their schedule with management activities would have made the paradigm shift that greater things can be achieved when they focus on producing well-balanced contributors. They learned to train, audit, give feedback, coach, organize, observe, direct, and hold meetings, and their schedule is filled with these activities. They've also learned to reconcile people-related matters including their motivation, differences in personalities, differences in strengths/weaknesses, conflict management, morale, emotions, and so on. A manager who has learned these skills can competently handle a greater amount of working capacity and can make a larger impact within the organization than the DIY manager.

- **Leadership** – There are those who fill their schedule with leadership activities, and they take developing people to another level by focusing on developing additional managers/leaders. They've brought up the baseline competency of skills within the team(s) to the extent that they are self-directed. Their main emphasis is focusing on strategy and leverage. This is seen from how they coach, facilitate problem solving, and mobilize team(s). They can skillfully leverage the competencies inherent within the team(s) to bring them to a higher level. Such team(s) can exhibit a great amount of adaptability in their customer-facing interfaces and/or innovation, to outcompete their competitors. These people can lead the largest amount of working capacity, sustain continuous growth, and lead multiple teams.

As an interesting side note, managers who apply leadership skills within their team often build them to a level where they feel they're no longer needed. They often get bored of their role and crave the next challenge. This is a great indicator of a HiPo, and it would be wise to consider designing their next challenge within the organization, whether it's to build another team or work on a different project.

Whatever the course your career takes, it is always the everyday moments that make a difference. You can escape the seemingly endless cat-herding approach by improving your management and leaderships skills with stronger communication. If you get this right, everything else just comes together. You become a culture champion. You start coaching in everyday moments with heart, ethics, and attitude. This lets you shift from managing tasks to developing people, transition from a manager to a leader who can maximize impact, and eventually—hopefully—make your own job obsolete so that you can work on the next challenge. However, before we get there, you need to know what you must develop and how you can make your team members accountable.

CHAPTER 12

UNIVERSAL SKILLS
FOR TEAM MEMBERS

Have you ever been a part of a team where everything just gelled well? Where everyone was on-point and the team always got *a lot* done, often exceeding goals?

Interestingly, in those scenarios, it seemed like the team did not have to work too hard to get those results. Everyone knew their role in the team, and they naturally knew what to do. Each person understood the strengths and value that they contributed to the team. They also had each other's backs and covered up for each other's weaknesses. They trusted each other. They were synchronized in this manner, like a well-oiled machine.

They had a purpose. Everyone was growing personally and as a team. When the team won, everyone won. They were excited when the team made achievements. There was a sense of pride in being a member of the team.

That's what it's like being a part of a self-directed team.

Though it may be a no-brainer that everyone wants to be a part of this kind of team, is everyone willing to do what it takes to be a part of one?

To be a part of this, team members need to exhibit
a baseline standard of collaboration.

As the manager, to create this team, you need to hold your team members to these standards.

Universal Skills: Setting a New Baseline Standard of Collaboration

These are actually *universal skills*. They're not just meant for team members. It's for everyone:

- **Contributors** – Team members
- **Managers** – Those who are accountable for a single team
- **Leaders** – Those who are accountable for multiple teams

When the baseline collaboration skills within the organization improve, something magical begins to happen. From the vantage point of a leader, there are fewer conflicts, less escalations that need your attention, organic problem solving, decreased customer-related escalations, and greater stakeholder satisfaction. This frees up the leader from a time and bandwidth consideration to work on other high-ticket activities, which subsequently generates more value.

This enables everything else.

This approach lays the foundation for greater self-direction, adaptability, and innovation, which can translate into greater market competitiveness. These are more complex sets of behaviors that require coordination around information gathering, problem solving, rallying together, and implementing solutions. This becomes more feasible when we have improved collaboration skills throughout the organization.

In addition, these skills improve the sustainability of teams. Otherwise, teams are more likely to implode under internal pressures, conflict, miscommunication, and improper management of stakeholder expectations.

Sometimes, it can be difficult to attribute value creation to increased baseline collaboration skills because they indirectly impact results. They influence people to have better actions, which create better results. So oftentimes, those actions get recognized rather than the improved collaboration skills. But it's important to keep in mind where the origin of the improved results came from.

Contributor Management: At First, Resistance

Adopting the mentality to solve problems through this paradigm shift can be difficult. It requires an approach to achieve results through people development and improving their collaboration. Every incident is an opportunity to get their buy-in on this approach and paradigm. Every moment matters, as they add up and create a momentum for culture strategy.

When I first started this method, I had concerns that people would resist me if I approached situations and problems via a collaboration/people development standpoint. In essence, I'd be putting the accountability back on them through coaching their own problem-solving skills. Obviously, this was not something they were used to. People may wonder, "Why is accountability always put back on them, and why is everything about communication? Don't we have a job to do?" For example, if an issue was brought up regarding another person, I'd respond with, "Interesting, did you communicate with them properly? How did you communicate it? How could you have done it better?"

Initially, people did resist it because it required them to have accountability and they weren't accustomed to it. However, when you persevere with this route long term, people begin to buy in and recognize that it gives them more control over their situations, more control over their lives, more self-expression, and more purpose. I also noticed that a lot of them would take those skills and apply them to their personal lives. On multiple occasions, I received feedback that the quality of their lives got better. It was great to learn that this approach had such a positive ripple effect.

12.1. Communication

Everyone thinks they're a great communicator. But in reality, most people can use improvement in communication. Everyone thinks making friends and getting along with people at work means they're good communicators.

However, communication is much more difficult than that. It involves dealing with competing ideas and perspectives. This includes dealing with different personality types and adapting your communication style to how they absorb information. It includes managing heightened situations and conflict. It involves problem solving around situations where you personally have blind spots. This is much more difficult than meets the eye. This section discusses some of those elements.

Understanding Differences between People

Culture strategy aims to achieve greater competitiveness and productivity via synergy. This requires the celebration of differences in people to create synergistic value. The natural instinct for a manager is to gather a team of similar people due to its simplicity and ease of management (less of a need to adapt to different types of people).

That would lead to a homogenous team. Overall, a homogenous team leads to lower productivity than a well-balanced team. This is because homogenous teams usually share the same weaknesses and blind spots, whether it be in customer service, team cohesion, analysis, or goal orientation.

Achieving a synergistic team can introduce new challenges because different people with very different values must learn to coexist and coordinate. Due to this, there is a higher chance of disagreement, and it therefore requires better management skills to successfully integrate such a team. Let's explore common nuances of different types of people:

The Goal Pusher: "Let's Get It Done."

Why you need them: Introduces goal orientation to the team. Often likes to manage. Often enjoys challenges. Not shy to competition. Resilient. Good at dealing with issues with breadth (many business issues have more breadth than depth). Often craves leadership situations.

How to get their buy-in: Focus on "What needs to be done by when?" Talk big picture goals, then let them figure it out. Challenge them.

How to talk to them: Get to the point. Be direct. Start with the bottom line. Don't beat around the bush. Don't waste their time.

How to engage them: Challenges. Big picture goals. Hitting targets. Loves to be in control.

Typical weaknesses: Overlooks "boring" details. Leaves a "trail of dead bodies" behind as they push for goals. Has challenges in listening. Struggles with buy-in. Often overuses hierarchy. Defaults to moving people with authority rather than influence. Challenges with emotional intelligence or the "human side." Pride and ego.

How to work on those weaknesses: "The devil is in the details." Don't leave a "trail of dead bodies" behind. Train on culture and people-oriented topics. Endorse culture and people-oriented topics from people they respect.

Pet peeves: Details. "Petty" topics. Feelings. Being personal. Excuses.

The Analyzer: "Let's Do It Right."

Why you need them: Introduces logical assessment. Deeper analysis. Careful risk-benefit assessments. Gathers objective data. Filters potentially incorrect information due to hype or persuasion techniques.

Plans ahead. Designs processes and pipelines. Identifies objective findings that may otherwise be missed.

How to get their buy-in: Explain the *why*. Don't suddenly pounce on them for ideas, results, or agreements. Rather, give them space to internalize and process things.

How to talk to them: Follow a logical progression of ideas. Compartmentalize ideas. Use an analytical communication style. Use data/evidence/comparables/historicals. If you need something to move forward, avoid telling them the detail is wrong. Instead, rationalize how it's not the current priority (may need to bring up considerations regarding probability and impact). If they're not committing to any idea, say, "As of now, what can we do?" (they tend to be perfectionists, so it gives them a chance to mitigate being wrong by bringing up variability).

How to engage them: Analyze something. Design a process. Develop their expertise.

Typical weaknesses: Likes to work alone. Most people don't naturally understand their wavelength of analytical language. Misalignment and miscommunication. Gets stuck in the weeds—myopia. Gets fixated on a detail and has trouble moving on.

How to work on those weaknesses: Pull them out of the weeds (being stuck in the details) and help them see the big picture. Prioritization. Be in the moment with people. Stop over-analyzing all the time and connect with the team. Deal with extroverts by helping them talk it through. Train on strategic thinking. Help them remove blockers.

Pet peeves: Doesn't like to be pushed on things that "don't make sense." Emotions. Connecting with people.

The Enthusiast: "Let's Do It Together."

Why you need them: Introduces cohesion, momentum, engagement (makes anything fun). They naturally improve morale. When they're in the mix, everyone knows what's going on, which improves alignment. Usually has extremely creative and out-of-the-box ideas. They can generate hype and excitement regarding a message that needs buy-in. Social awareness and skills.

How to get their buy-in: Answer "Who's doing what?" Make them look good (they love being the center of attention).

How to talk to them: Get to know their personal side. Get excited with them.

How to engage them: Talk ideas through with them (they like to talk things through rather than think things through). Leverage any momentum that's going on. Demonstrate hype, energy, excitement. Share stories with them. Appreciate and recognize them, especially publicly and in front of people. They get motivated and engaged in the midst of a lot of people interactions.

Typical weaknesses: Chases "shiny" objects. Disorganized. Trouble focusing. Doesn't think things through. Trouble following through. Easily distracted. Ups and downs. Takes up too much "airtime" (talks over people). Overuses hype and may come across as unprofessional.

How to work on those weaknesses: Organization tools (schedules, notebooks, etc.). Self-control. May need to slow down and really consider whether their natural response is the best course of action. Mindfulness exercises. Listening. Holding back from talking over others. Focus and follow up on agreements. Finish the job even if it gets boring. Train on goal orientation and logical analysis.

Pet peeves: Weasel wording. People not getting excited with them. Offensive and tactless statements.

The Stabilizer: "Let's Get Along."

Why you need them: Often handles the bulk repetitive tasks of a company. Introduces stability and predictability. Introduces sensitivities to the team. Caring for others. Usually the first to notice when people are unhappy.

How to get their buy-in: When pushing for an initiative, explain "What's changing, what's not changing." Make it safe.

How to talk to them: Ask about their personal life. Care about their life. Show some concern.

How to engage them: Create "safe zones." Lots of situational positive/negative reinforcement. Demonstrate appreciation. Tell them when you're happy with them or not happy with them rather than focusing on the tasks/goals/logic. Be very clear on what you want from them (they love routine instructions and even checklists). Hold their hand and walk them through things. Encourage them.

Typical weaknesses: Assertiveness challenges. Indirect communication (assumes the other person will read their mind). Confidence challenges. Fear of change. Fear of unknown. Fear of disappointing others. Has trouble understanding relevance of goals. Has trouble seeing the big picture—myopia. Has trouble prioritizing.

How to work on those weaknesses: Help them with confidence and assertive communication. Help them with time management, decisiveness, prioritization, and goal orientation.

Pet peeves: Rudeness. Unfairness. Changes.

If you haven't done so already, it may be worth taking assessments with your team to better understand each other. DiSC is one of my favorite frameworks to explain the differences of communication styles and values between various people. Myers Briggs, Strengths Finder, and Kolbe Index-A are among other notable ones. This is not a one-size-fits-all. In fact, people can exhibit a mix of traits. On top of that, people often modify their style to adapt to the expectations of their work. However, people do tend to have a natural profile that they default to.

The four types that were just shared are an applied version of DiSC, which is a great framework. I believe its greatest advantage is in its simplicity. It gives users an opportunity to quickly assess the opposing styles of others so they can easily adapt their communicational style for better connection and engagement. It has multiple applications based upon various situations that guide operators to have smoother and successful communication.

The Platinum Rule

Interestingly, a lot of tension points inadvertently arise out of efforts of being respectful. I know this sounds counterintuitive but bear with me. Often, it's because people are exercising the Golden Rule, "Do unto others as you would have them do unto you."

The problem is that people are different from each other.

This actually causes problems! This may work with people who are very similar to you because they have very little natural tension points with you. However, if you apply this to people who are different from you, they will fail to meet your expectations. In fact, different people inadvertently offend each other all the time. Therefore, it's better to apply the:

Platinum Rule – Do unto others as they want done unto them.

This is much more relevant when dealing with different types of people within teams and organizations. Remember, this is necessary if we want to build self-directed teams. This diffuses tension and keeps us together.

Is this being fake? Some people think that adapting to other people using the Platinum Rule is being fake, but that's not true. It's more like learning to speak another language! Different profile styles have their own "language" and you would be learning to speak their "language." Imagine how many more people you can connect with if you learned how to do this.

Interpersonal Emotional Awareness and Management

Beyond the functional task management of work, there is an intangible and social atmosphere that exists between people and within any environment. The mood can have a range of emotions in the atmosphere including engagement, excitement, happiness, sadness, fear, anger, and more. It's important to be aware of such an atmosphere.

Social awareness – Awareness of the emotional landscape.

This comes naturally for some people, but others struggle with it. Poor awareness of others' emotions and poor management of relationships with others lead to compromised listening skills, collaboration among teams, synergy, and ability to manage and lead others, and to excessive conflict.

Pay attention to what's going on around you. Not just the words, but also the tone and body language of the situation.

Interpersonal emotional awareness gives us hints to how power, influence, and decision-making flow throughout the organization. Harnessing this can be important to move an initiative forward. Some call this maneuvering "politics." This goes beyond understanding the functional authorities and positions within the organization. It's how decisions are really made. It also gets us to become aware of how much influence people wield and what their attitude is regarding various initiatives.

When we understand this, it becomes more about delivering the right message. It's important to not over-focus on the message as how you see it but to focus on understanding other people and communicating in a way that resonates with them.

- **Know your audience** – Know what moves them, speak their language, and make it natural.

- **Sometimes, your instinctive response may not be the best route** – There are times when it's better to hold back to avoid making quick judgments and rushing in with your initial instinct. Your audience may be different from you, and you may need to adapt to resonate with them.

There will be moments when you have opportunities to build a relationship by doing things for them. There is an intangible force that compels people to be there for you because you were there for them. This builds emotional credibility with each other.

> **Depositing in the emotional bank account** – Build up reserves in the emotional bank account—metaphor by Stephen R. Covey. This is where people have your back because you had theirs.

These and many other interpersonal emotional awareness skills will help people interact better and get better results through people.

The Pinnacle of Communication: Collaboration

Collaborative communication involves the effort to yield a *win-win* outcome, while being faced with opposing ideas and perspectives. This yields the most effective and sustainable results when used properly. We should use this approach whenever possible. Here is what is involved:

1. Understand overall team goals
2. Understand your concerns
3. Understand other party's concerns
4. Craft a win-win solution
5. Offer a proposal
6. If a satisfactory agreement has not been reached, repeat the steps until a satisfactory win-win is achieved

This requires good interpersonal communication, thinking, and self-management skills. Unfortunately, many people default into other forms of communication. It's so easy to jump into conclusions and end up doing something else, such as:

- *Competing* with the other person to yield a win-lose outcome.
- *Avoiding* the situation, which will result in a lose-lose outcome.
- *Accommodating*, which may preserve the relationship, but will yield a lose-win outcome.
- *Compromising*, which involves bargaining. This doesn't involve diving deeper into the situation. Both parties compromise, and a suboptimal agreement is made.

These outcomes can lead to compromised results and should be used sparingly. Ask yourself: do you tend to collaborate, or do you default to a different form of communication? How do you become more collaborative?

Unfortunately, you can't be collaborative in every scenario. You'll notice that this is not effective or efficient in certain situations, including when there is:

- **Time urgency** – Collaboration can be time consuming, so if an issue is urgent, this may not be the best approach.

- **An unhealthy culture and distrust** – If the other end refuses to meet you in the middle, this may not be as effective. However, it's always good to give the benefit of the doubt first.

- **A dangerous situation** – If it's not safe to collaborate, it may be necessary to take control or avoid the situation.

- **A petty situation** – If the situation is petty and a waste of time, it may not be worth collaborating on it.

But whenever possible, try to problem solve collaboratively. For more information, dive deeper in the Conflict Management Framework by Thomas Kilmann.

Get on the Same Page on Assertive Communication

It is important for an organization to get on the same page on the definition of assertive communication. This is very different from passive or aggressive communication. Assertive communication involves a sharing of rights between parties that involves direct communication in a professional matter. This becomes the foundation for collaborative communication.

Passive versus Assertive versus Aggressive

The greatest challenge associated with assertiveness training is that people have different definitions of assertive communication.

At times, passive people have a perception that assertive behavior is aggressive behavior because they and the people close to them would perceive it this way. Because of that, they find it very difficult to apply assertive communication. They feel like they are being rude and aggressive. There may be cultural influences, upbringing, or deeper-lying issues that may be creating this resistance.

Conversely, aggressive individuals may think that they are being assertive, but are in fact being aggressive. They may have had a more competition-focused upbringing or belong to such a community where aggressive behavior is perceived as assertive. They may have trouble understanding how people can get offended by their communication style.

Either way, it requires a lot of effort to recognize this and address it. These are often deeply rooted values, which can take a great deal of introspection to recognize and adapt.

Ownership of Communication Delivery

Communication doesn't just involve the words that you speak. In fact, a great deal of miscommunication often results when we over-focus on words only. There is more communicated through our tone and body language.

- *Words* communicate 7 percent of the message.
- *Tone* communicates 38 percent of the message.
- *Body language* communicates 55 percent of the message.

Yet, many of us do not utilize body language and tone to synchronize with our message and expect the other party to comprehend our message. When we want to communicate something to the other party, we may fail to align our body language (including facial expressions) and tone with what we are trying to convey. This can account for countless amounts of lost value.

Additionally, choosing a communication channel medium that is appropriate is important for the message. You may lose the opportunity to communicate with tone/body language when you use phone, emails, and texts. Therefore, if the message has a lot of room for miscommunication and involves an extremely impactful and nuanced message, then it may be wise to use a medium where there is greater control over the interpretation of the message.

Through the combination of our words/tone/body language and the channel, we end up encoding messages that the receiver needs to interpret. In effective communication, it's about taking ownership of the message that the receiver interpreted. This is opposed to people believing that encoding the message and sending it is simply enough. They also need to be accountable for how the recipient interpreted the message.

Sender → Encodes Message → Message → Decodes Message → Receiver

Remember, communication is about the message that the receiver decoded, not just the message you encoded.

Be a Team Player

It's important to get people to develop a team player mentality within the organization. It maintains a cohesive environment for them to reduce conflict and maintain a partnership mentality to help each other or move forward.

How do we accomplish that?

First of all, we need to establish clear expectations and guidelines on what it means to be a team player. Here are some considerations:

- **Be a team player that handles conflicts in a healthy manner** – Conflicts and disagreements can be healthy and productive because they allow us to come together to problem solve. However, excessive conflict can be damaging and result in a dysfunctional environment. Everyone must be clear on how to play their part in maintaining a feedback-rich and problem-solving environment, without making things personal and creating unhealthy conflict.

- **Have each other's backs** – Rather than having a self-oriented mindset, people should develop a mutually supportive mentality that allows for a collaborative environment. This doesn't mean ignoring your concerns, but rather understanding where your concerns fit in the overall scheme, so that good collaboration can be made.

- **Integrative life** – Many traditional cultures recommend maintaining work-life balances by having clear delineations and boundaries between the two. However, organizations with great cultures often promote an integrative life, which involves integrating work and life. This involves building relationships, friendships, and trusting relationships with colleagues. Often, this organically occurs as a culture develops and matures.

Minimize Unhealthy Communication

Unhealthy communication can often go unnoticed and ignored until it snowballs into a toxic work environment that is difficult to stabilize after the fact. It is easier to keep this at bay by managing gateway behaviors.

One of my favorite frameworks to monitor gateway behaviors to minimize unhealthy conflict is the "Four Horsemen of the Apocalypse" by Dr. John Gottman. This work was originally used for marriage counseling, but some companies have adopted it to minimize unhealthy conflict within teams. It highlights four toxic behaviors that can lead to a culture of unhealthy conflict if left unchecked. These are:

- **Criticism** – Making feedback personal.

- **Defensiveness** – Receiving feedback personally.

- **Contempt** – Sarcasm, ridiculing, name calling, eye-rolling (though it may seem humorous or harmless at first, it can add up to disrupt unity).

- **Stonewalling** – Avoiding contact and withdrawing altogether (pretty much ends the relationship).

I have found this frame to be very helpful because it identifies unhealthy behaviors at earlier phases before they become toxic. This is especially helpful in developing those who are not naturally in tune to emotional atmospheres, as it gives guidelines to preemptive behavior that can lead to unhealthy conflict.

12.2. Self-Management

On top of communication, people need to demonstrate self-management to be an effective member of self-directed teams and culture-focused organizations. Let's explore some elements.

Essential Self-Management Values

Accountability and Ownership

Everyone needs to be accountable and take ownership for their responsibilities and tasks. When people do not do this, it leads to excessive excuses and blame shifting. This leads to a vicious cycle of finger pointing, which doesn't resolve the issues and can be extremely exhausting to deal with. Therefore, we should hold people accountable and have them be accountable for themselves.

Even when we try to build a collaborative culture, some people will hide behind the collaboration to dilute their accountability. They may actually take advantage of these situations to dilute their accountability to mitigate their personal risk on potential failures. They may make excuses and blame everyone who was involved if something goes wrong. Don't let this happen!

People still need to be accountable for their responsibilities. If someone wants to use collaborative problem solving to approach their issues, it needs to be clear that it's still up to them to get the buy-in and collaboration to maximize results, rather than using it as a scapegoat opportunity. *Accountability still needs to be clear.*

Own it. Don't make excuses.

Be Actively Engaged

A higher degree of accountability involves proactively thinking and acting on behalf of the team or the organization. This requires *active engagement*. This is what gets people to take the extra mile even when no one is looking. This can involve looking for opportunities and issues, conceptualizing proactive solutions, collaborating, creating value, and being self-motivated to do the right things. Otherwise, it may lead to situations where people simply "count their hours," do the bare minimum, or practice destructive behavior when they can get away with it.

Play full out. Give a darn.

Have a Mindset for Continuous Improvement

On top of that, it takes a mentality of continuous improvement within people to take an organization to another level. Especially in today's society, existing status quos and processes can quickly become irrelevant. However, individuals may have a tendency to stick within their comfort zones and resist having to continuously improve themselves, as it can feel uncomfortable due to the changes required. This may limit their potential. In addition, developing people's true potential may involve a lot of feedback. People must be able to receive feedback constructively without taking it personally. Otherwise, they may end up resisting their own development.

Feedback is the breakfast of champions.
There's always a better way.

Taking Chances

Sometimes there are psychological inhibitors that prevent people from putting their best foot forward. For example, some people hold themselves back out of fear.

By empowering others to overcome their psychological blockers, it enables them to become better people and proactively problem solve. This can enable some of the highest leverage activities throughout the organization, especially strategy. Thus, it's not uncommon to see organizations encourage:

You don't make the shots you don't take. Dare to dream.

Overall, these are values that are meant to promote a growth mentality throughout the organization. In fact, many progressive companies tend to have these similar themes that enable more widespread empowerment and strategic thinking. Developing those attributes in others can unlock the potential for high leverage activities.

If we enable such themes, make sure there's sufficient people development efforts. Bear in mind that some progressive organizations have taken this too far without focusing on the fundamentals regarding foundational skillset development. If we do not couple this with actual skill development, it can have repercussions because it may open up vulnerability points and unnecessary risks by opening up the floodgate of unrefined ideas. That being said, it is still wiser to maintain such themes and couple them with sufficient people development efforts via coaching and training.

Connect with Yourself: Intrapersonal Awareness and Management

Your job can be a challenge! There is no doubt about it! There are goals to hit! You need to collaborate, but you hit brick walls! There are people who do things in a way that you simply cannot resonate with. *These all trigger emotions.*

Though many emotions can be beneficial to a situation, unhealthy emotions can lead to destructive behaviors and habits. This can significantly harm the business. This may not seem apparent in the short term, as it is difficult to measure the harm, but it has larger long-term repercussions. Therefore, it's important to be able to self-regulate by doing the following:

1. Take a moment to step back.
2. Identify how you feel. Then name it and claim it.
3. Convert that energy to a different emotion that is more productive.

That way, we can actually channel our harmful emotions into an emotion that is beneficial. This requires skills at emotional self-management and self-regulation. For example, if there was a situation that made you upset or angry, you can actually convert it to motivation, which is far more beneficial. Whatever made you upset is still likely an issue, but it puts you in a motivated position to address it in a productive manner.

This is actually harder than it sounds! When we get triggered, it takes a great amount of self-control to pause and then choose a more deliberate action for more productive results.

To get better at this, it can be helpful to get involved with *mindfulness* exercises. These can include meditation or exercises that bring you to a well-balanced state of mind. It involves keeping your mind clear and choosing a balanced lifestyle that keeps you recharged.

This keeps you in your *A game*. This prevents you from making rash decisions and starting discussions that can lead to instantaneous damage that is difficult to recover from. In addition, it helps you make great decisions and connections, which can create tremendous value. Therefore, maintaining mindfulness is a method of proactively creating value through self-regulation.

You may notice that getting buy-in for introducing emotional intelligence (EI) in your organization can be tough! I can empathize, because I personally had a unique relationship with the topic of emotional intelligence. I initially thought this topic was "fluffy" and "bubbly," and that those who practiced emotional intelligence believed you could "care" your way out of any problem, whether it made technical sense or not. However, I came to learn that this was a very superficial understanding of emotional intelligence. The deeper understanding actually leads to a tremendous increase in productivity through different aspects—greater self-management and greater results through improved coordination with people and teams.

There may be significant challenges in popularizing this concept, as there may be some who would oppose it due to poor understanding and beliefs that this is a "fluffy" topic that does not relate to them. Therefore, it is crucial for leaders of the organization to be bought into the concept and utilize the principles. Leaders who do not take the topic seriously send a message of unimportance throughout the organization, which leads to resistance from contributors. Additionally, it requires buy-in agents who are excellent at demonstrating those skills, achieving results, and resonating with people throughout the organization. Getting buy-in for EI throughout the organization may be a process that requires skillful promotion and perseverance of putting it into practice, reinforcing it, promoting it, and living it as an example.

Healthy Mindsets for Stress Management

It is without a doubt that work can be stressful. Therefore, it's no secret that some may have challenges dealing with stress in the workplace. People can get triggered for a multitude of reasons. In addition, stress management is a multifactorial issue, and we must recognize why someone has challenges with stress management so that they can be coached appropriately.

There tends to be a common overlying theme when someone gets excessively stressed. They typically adopt a *victim mentality*. They feel that the world is out to get them. They relinquish control to the world and develop a negative sentiment toward others. This can be an unhealthy trajectory because this mentality does not lead to any solution.

> *Don't be a victim.*
> *Acknowledge that you chose to be where you are.*

This requires taking ownership and acknowledging that they are choosing to make their decisions rather than being a victim of everything. If they can accept this, it empowers them with a sense of control. If they can get used to this and apply it in areas of their life, it creates a ripple effect that demonstrates ownership, better focus, peace of mind, and superior results. This can significantly decrease the stress over their lives and create a long-term stress-management solution. The sense of control can be empowering.

In addition, people tend to fantasize about other people's lives. They worry about things that are outside their control rather than focusing on what they have control over and how to improve their own lives. They may choose to obsess over the latest news and develop strong opinions over situations that have no relevance to them and are outside their control. This can perpetually drain their energy, as there is nothing they can do except stress about it.

Worry about things within your circle of influence,
not outside of it.

Rather, reallocating that energy to avenues that they have influence over can yield more fruit and regain more control of their lives. Subsequently, they can choose to build the amount of influence that they have, so they are in a better position to make a larger impact in the future. This grants them even more control over their lives on a long-term basis, which is far more effective than having a "victim" mentality.

Balancing personal lives reduces stress. Sometimes, people end up neglecting various aspects of their lives, which affects their well-being and increases their stress levels. People can have health, social, mental, or spiritual needs. If left in imbalance, people may develop a pattern of perpetual stress without realizing why. Sometimes people need to take control of balancing their personal lives to stabilize their stress level, so they don't damage their performance at work.

Proactive Time Management

People who have challenges managing time can find themselves over-burdened with work and trapped. They may blame their situation, but this is often a reflection of time management skill deficiencies. Let's look at various items that take up our time and how we could optimize our management of them.

- **Critical items** – These items are both urgent and important and must be dealt with immediately. Examples include taking care of a high-conflict situation in a team, managing an upset key client that is threatening to take their business elsewhere, and so on.

- **Proactive items** – There are a subset of items that are important but not as urgent. These are some of the most valuable items. The greatest take-home point is that we should prioritize on maximizing this category, as it is the strategic category that decreases future escalations from other categories. Bear in mind that you must intentionally reserve time for this, or you will never find time for it.

- **Inefficient tasks** – This category includes urgent tasks that are not as important or could have been prevented. We should proactively reduce the number of items in this category. Mismanagement in this category often leads to situations where people feel overloaded. This is often the result when boundaries or accountabilities are not clear. Also, it occurs when one hasn't learned to create efficiency by building systems, delegating, or saying *no* (when it's appropriate, of course), and so on.

- **Waste of time** – These items are neither urgent nor important, and you should immediately stop doing them. These items are a waste of time and we need to discipline ourselves to not partake in them. Examples include unproductive social media, television, games, and so on.

Utilizing this guide can greatly improve the productivity of our time, while decreasing the burden that we experience. You will never have more than twenty-four hours in a given day, so once you become very busy, the only way to increase productivity is to become more efficient.

For more information, look into the Eisenhower Time Matrix. This is a great model that uses a 2x2 matrix with dimensions of urgencies and importance for optimizing and managing one's time. It goes into greater detail regarding the different categories, relevant items, and appropriate action items.

12.3. Thinking

People should be capable of thinking for themselves and the organization. They have access to information and personally witness issues at the team level, which puts them in a good position for situational problem solving. This is especially the case when we utilize culture strategy, as it leverages people's ability to problem solve. This may be contrary to many traditional organizations where they want team members to not think and simply do what they're told.

If we don't develop people's ability to think, we may expose the organization to undue risks from:

- People making false claims
- Poor ideas and proposals
- Creation of disengaging situations due to unrefined ideas being shot down by management
- People being overcommitted on ideas that are not aligned with the functional needs of the organization, requiring management to put the ideas down with a hard *no* stance (this can lead to unpleasant moments)
- Fear of participating in collaboration (due to lack of confidence)

When it comes to thinking skills, it's important to differentiate between baseline-level and advanced-level thinking. This helps create realistic expectations when developing our team members because it reconciles the fact that there are varying levels of aptitude and experience regarding these thinking skills. It may not be realistic to expect advanced-level thinking skills from everyone. However, it is possible and necessary to establish a baseline level of thinking skills for most people.

- **Advanced thinking skills** – This is appropriate for specialists.
- **Baseline thinking skills** – This is appropriate for the majority.

If we try to develop everyone to have advanced-level thinking skills, it usually leads to a mutually frustrating environment for the managers and team members.

When developing these thinking skills within team members, you may notice varying degrees of attitudes on developing this. Some are excited to have the opportunity to develop themselves. Others have become so accustomed to being told what to do and say:

"Just tell me what to do!"

"That's not my job!"

This demonstrates a lack of ownership and desire to develop themselves and integrate with culture strategy. It may lead to an unsustainable situation, and either we would need to get their buy-in to build such skills, or they may not be a good fit.

Results-Oriented Thinking

Results-oriented thinking involves multiple factors. It requires being able to juggle multiple issues while simultaneously identifying priorities, risks, and other relevant issues.

Challenges with this form of thinking can quickly lead to situational misprioritization of tasks, which leads to problems that could have been avoided. Though we could expand upon this topic with advanced tactical considerations, let's explore a simplified baseline version that can be used for more widespread development.

- **Top three priorities** – What are the top three priorities of a given job? How do they know when to reposition tasks based on the priorities and urgencies of the current situation? What would they need to do?

Critical Thinking

Critical thinking involves the assessment of validity of information, reasoning, and conceptualizing solutions. This is important to prevent false claims from being spoken all the time by maintaining objectivity during collaborative discussions. This reins conversations in for more fruitful discussions.

Of course, we can go into great depths with advanced forms of critical assessments, including data gathering methodologies, statistics, quantifying assumptions, cross-referencing knowledge, and so on. However, we're not trying to turn everyone into data engineers and statisticians.

Rather, a baseline version of critical thinking can be utilized to maintain objectivity throughout the organization. Here are some key themes:

- **Evaluate information** – Evaluate objectivity, fact-checking, data, source, additional sources, and additional opinions.

- **Identify assumptions** – Identify biases, filter out hype and persuasion techniques, remove excessive emotions, and step back to look at the big picture.

- **Conclusions and decisions** – Solutions are based on objective information, current reality, goals, and alignment needs. This also involves overcoming sensitivities associated with discussing delicate topics.

Analytical Thinking

Some ideas need to be broken down into compartments, as issues can be multifaceted. Analytical thinking can be used to break ideas into smaller pieces to help get organized, identify hard-to-see issues, create processes to follow, and evaluate uncertainty.

Although we don't plan to make everyone into analysts and process engineers, we can certainly raise the bar on analytical thinking to get people on the same page during collaboration, discussions, and facilitated sessions.

A baseline version of analytical thinking can involve:

- **Patterns** – This involves breaking things down into patterns, cause-effect relationships, steps, flows, processes, affinities, and frames. Sometimes this type of thinking can be drawn out through participation in facilitated sessions using various frameworks.

- **Probabilities** – There are many unknowns involved in our work. However, we can make educated assessments of the impact and probabilities of these unknowns to help guide our decision-making process.

Thinking into the Future

A lot of value can be created, and many issues can be avoided, if we are proactive with our thinking. By envisioning a better future, we can proactively create it rather than remaining reactive and allowing things to happen by default.

Most people do not naturally think like this. This is an abstract thinking skillset that involves looking into possibilities that are not tangible.

In essence, we're trying to enable basic strategic thinking within people. Again, we're not expecting everyone to be advanced strategic planners. That would be quite involved and extensive, especially when dealing with advanced enterprise-level strategic plans. However, a baseline version of this can be made on a more universal level by promoting the following thought process:

1. Self-discovery of personal and organizational values.
2. Imagining the ideal work situation where there's alignment.
3. Working backward to identify the missing links.

Thinking into the future is challenging for some. It is very difficult to develop this skill for people who tend to think in the past and present. Managers who tend to naturally think about the future have additional struggles in developing others' future-thinking skills, as they often cannot understand why people have challenges with this. Sometimes, there are deeper psychological blockers preventing individuals from thinking this way. If you choose to train this skill, prepare to be patient, make it safe for them, and coach them by guiding them to refine their thoughts.

Hard Skills

Hard skills are still important, and every industry has their own set of capabilities and skills. It's the task- and process-based skillsets that are required to do a job. Obviously, people need to develop these skills to perform their role competently.

However, in general, I have seen an overemphasis on this. Most managers usually have an over-focus on hard skills when they supervise or train others. Incidentally, such emphasis usually doesn't adequately address many of the issues that arise within organizations, as many of those issues are due to collaboration breakdowns. In fact, many companies overcompensate for the lack of collaboration by over-focusing on everyone's technical or hard skills.

This may be effective in a business environment with predominantly routine tasks and very little change, as it's commonly seen in traditional companies. However, the current business landscape is changing at a more rapid rate and requires more adaptability, which involves greater collaboration. The companies that have already transitioned to developing baseline collaboration, management, and leadership skills tend to outcompete the others, especially when they do this in a way that considers various communication styles.

You can improve your communication and collaboration with Goal Pushers, Analyzers, Enthusiasts, and Stabilizers by remembering the Platinum Rule: Do unto others as they want done unto them. Focusing on emotional intelligence, you can develop your self-management skills and help others do the same. These are universal skills that managers need to hold themselves and their team members to. That leads us into our next discussion, which revolves around what managers leading a single team must learn and practice. Let's dig in.

CHAPTER 13

ESSENTIAL SKILLS FOR TEAM MANAGERS

When I began my transition to manage through an emphasis on people development rather than a task-focused approach, it felt really odd. I had a lot of doubts. I thought to myself, *This is going to be weird. The team won't be receptive of it.*

The truth is, if you haven't been managing like this before, it will be weird, and the team will push back. You can't undo long-term conditioning of a task-focused management dynamic overnight.

Let's say someone on your team escalates an issue to you. Rather than fixing the situation or directing them on what to do, you could engage in a coaching discussion.

"Hey boss, _____ just happened. What should I do?"

Rather than jumping in with a solution, you could take a step back and say:

"Hmm, what do you propose we should do?"

Likely they will respond with:

"What are you doing, boss? We got a real problem to fix."

It will feel odd for both of you, but you have to get over it. It'll be worth it if you truly adopt a mentality that is conducive for culture strategy and push through.

Now, if it's truly a risky situation that can potentially sink the business, you should definitely step in. However, in most cases, it's not, and it's an opportunity to develop and coach them. It's important to carry on.

To make this the new norm, there'll be many other issues that need to be simultaneously addressed, including:

- Developing your skills as a coach
- Getting their buy-in and engagement for this process
- Making the process safe (don't reprimand when work isn't done to your exact specifications, and don't reprimand when they bring up ideas)

It'll be challenging at first, but like any other skill, you'll get used to managing with a coaching and people development approach. If you stick with it, you'll notice your issues disappearing one by one, over time. On top of that, it builds infrastructure through people and sets the foundation for self-directed teams.

Initially, people may not see the value of developing themselves. They may even nod their heads and agree with you in front of you, but may passive-aggressively resist it. This results in going through the motions, but not actually materializing its value. This concept in culture strategy needs to be popularized to get buy-in and engagement within members of the organization.

Seeking a Deeper Understanding

While many folks might already be familiar with the concepts that will be discussed in this chapter, few actually understand their real significance and how to truly apply them. In fact, I have seen many people overuse the mechanical aspects of these concepts but underemphasize the true emotional connection with people. In that sense, it almost appears like they are using the frames to be manipulative. These frames are not meant to substitute true emotional or deeper-level connections between people. They are to be used as a guide to help uncover breakthroughs with people and to provide a guideline for healthy behaviors or connections.

13.1. Delegation and Coaching

Delegation is one of the most powerful tools that managers and supervisors can use for organizational success. However, there are challenges associated with learning how to do it effectively. With simple tasks, it's very easy to describe the situation. However, the more complex the task gets, the greater the likelihood for more confusion and misinterpretation. That's why it's important to establish clarity and set expectations in those situations.

Simplify to clarify.
Expectations create reality.

This involves breaking the complexities down to simpler components with clear expectations. Complicating the delegation with all the conditions, permutations, probabilities, and interrelatedness will give rise to confusion. This will usually freeze people's minds and lead to simple-minded behavior.

"Simple, clear instructions give rise to complex, intelligent behavior. Complex instructions give rise to stupid, simple-minded behavior."
—Unknown

We should also strive to manage through *agreements* of expectations. Through this, people can interpret the task as they see it and problem solve in their own manner to reach the goals. This increases ownership and mutual respect.

Delegation doesn't work in a single stroke. It's going to take a lot of repetition to truly achieve the behaviors that you want. So, plan to be patient, persistent, and consistent.

> *"Simplicity, consistency, and repetition—that's how you get through. It's a simple continuum that finally reaches a critical mass."*
>
> —Jack Welch

As you reinforce the agreements, use clear verbiage and direct communication.

> *Avoid using bet-hedging or weasel-wording, such as "try," "sorta," "guess," "kinda," and "but."*

Some people have a habit of doing this because they don't want to overcommit to potentially incorrect ideas. This may be appropriate when we are engaging in conversations that involve a lot of back and forth and verifying facts while we apply critical, analytical, and strategic thinking. However, this can cause confusion when delegating and setting expectations.

Performance Coaching Involves Adult Learning

You can't possibly expect your employee to get things right on the first go-around every single time. This takes performance coaching. This includes monitoring, connecting, collaborating, problem solving, establishing agreements, reinforcing, and following up.

It is nearly impossible to hire someone who simply just fits right into their job role. Even if there is a great fit, there are going to be many nuances that need to be positively or negatively reinforced to achieve optimal team synchronization. Therefore, it's important to take the effort to coach people for the sake of performance enhancement and alignment.

But remember, adjusting behavior is like learning a new skill. Always bear in mind that learning is hard. If we recognize this, then we can understand why it's going to need a lot of affirmations because what gets reinforced gets repeated. To do this, you'll have to create safe zones for people to learn to set them up to succeed.

I know what you're thinking. "God, this looks hard! Who has the time for this?" But in reality, you don't have time not to make time for this. At first glance, when you properly develop people, it may take a lot of time on the front end. But it saves you countless time and energy when the tasks are being completed for you on a continuous basis. This actually creates significantly more time for you as the manager.

THE ECONOMIC VALUE OF CO-CREATED SOLUTIONS

One of the benefits of coaching is co-creating solutions with the contributor, which has *substantial* value. To compare this phenomenon with an analogy, the value of co-created solutions can be likened to 35 percent extra credit in tests back in school. If there was a classroom full of students taking an exam, and a few people had a 35 percent extra credit for the exam, they wouldn't need to study as hard to outperform those who could ace it with 99 or 100 percent. Even if they got 70 percent, they would outperform others with a 105 percent. The value from co-created solutions works in a similar manner. Even if their idea is not the best in the world, as long as it's going toward the right general direction, the value from the resulting ownership and buy-in more than makes up for it.

However, it's important to recognize that achieving buy-in through this approach is actually a delicate process that can be disrupted by directives and even advice giving. These interfere with the conceptualization, development, and refinement of ideas.

Oftentimes, it's very difficult for a goal-oriented manager to resist the temptation of giving their advice or engaging in an autobiographical story. This is because goal-oriented managers were promoted because they were good at what they do, and they want to share their knowledge. It requires an exceptional amount of patience to actively listen without making hasty judgments and guide people's realizations. However, if we don't do this, we will fail at getting buy-in.

I was guilty of this myself, and I learned it much later, that the real value is in the buy-in. I could conceptualize a "better" solution than the collaborator, but my idea would actually still yield less long-term productivity. In the short term, my idea may outperform. However, because there was no buy-in, the collaborator wouldn't understand the ins and outs of the idea and would lack the ability to adapt situationally. They didn't own the idea and didn't know how to develop the idea further. Rather, if we co-created a solution, it would yield much more value through their buy-in.

Negative Reinforcement

Give feedback because your team members can't read your mind! Create an environment of trust where feedback is the "breakfast of champions," and people don't take it personally. Give feedback as soon as you can to the individual in question and not in front of others. This allows them to correlate exactly which behavior is being negatively reinforced.

This means that the manager must be skilled at evaluating good and bad behavior in terms of both productivity and team cohesion. The manager must also be good at articulating the impact of the associated behavior, while co-identifying potential causes that led to that behavior. This may involve the contributor's current gaps in communication, self-management, and thinking skills. The manager should also be aware of the contributor's personality style and aspiration when having these conversations. There should be a balance between providing advice and providing room to develop. If we give too much advice, we can come off as a micromanager, and people may develop a dependence on the manager for solutions, which will strip away their ability to develop themselves. Overall, the goal is to get people to be able to do their work independently.

When you strike up a conversation, using the following guide can help:

1. **State the behavior and impact** – In general, it is better to provide this negative feedback in private. Based on the situation, it may be wise to break the ice a little bit before beginning. Sometimes, you may uncover some things that are going on in the other person's life, which may reveal important information. I recommend stating the behavior directly, being specific, and stating the impact. Examples of impact can include: their behavior creates more burden on the manager, business productivity impact, damaged team relations/dynamic, and so on.

2. **Open up the discussion** – I recommend moving on to this step rather quickly, especially if it is a more severe situation, as there could be different kinds of emotions triggered in the recipient. Beating around the bush in Step 1 can cause a lot of angst. Here, the conversation can go multiple directions.

   Sidetrack you – This is actually quite common, and can come in many forms! They may make excuses, shift blame onto other people or situations, or bring up other things to distract you, hoping that you will focus on those things rather than the situation at hand. Recognize that the other person is trying to do this, and steer the conversation back. If excessive sidetracking conversation begins, it may be important to put that on the "parking lot," to acknowledge that it will be revisited another time, thereby recognizing the importance of it, but not letting the conversation steer itself in another direction.

   Agree with you – A team member with a great attitude will understand, agree with the situation, and want to improve. They may even thank you for being direct and caring about their development.

Agree with you in a patronizing way – This is in reality a sidetrack. They take a nonchalant attitude to get you off their tail without a true agreement of the situation. It may be necessary to dive deeper to reveal the real situation.

Disagree with you – Some may get offended, and some others may disagree with you. This can occur in different forms as well. For example, this may happen when bringing up an uncomfortable issue like personal hygiene, inappropriate appearances, or leaving a mess. It is important to remind them of the impact on the business/team/you (such as it creates a disruptive environment or forces the manager to have to micromanage them rather than doing more productive things). Sometimes, this can involve difficult conversations—for example, giving a promotion to someone else because of certain qualifications, and explaining it to the other applicant when he thinks he was better qualified.

Bring up good alternative perspectives – This is a true judgment call that a manager needs to make. Sometimes a valid perspective is brought up, and it reveals critical information to improve the situation. A truly trusting, open mentality and active listening are required to draw this out.

3. **Collaborate on solutions** – This involves asking them what they could do differently to achieve a better outcome. This involves guiding their thinking to reach their own solution. Sometimes, it requires helping them connect the dots. Or, it could help them see the risks of their proposed solutions. All in all, it's important for them to conceptualize and own the solution.

   The advantages of collaborating are better alignment, a higher chance of them following up, an ability for them to bring up detailed perspectives that only they could see, and allowing them to have their own custom solution (everyone solves problems differently). Additionally, if they have their own solution to it, they can manage curve balls and change their approach with their own adapted solution.

Collaborating on solutions requires a baseline set of skills and a mutually trusting relationship. This expectation may not be appropriate if they are totally new to the job, or when there is no trust, which may necessitate a more directive approach. However, the manager should strive to eventually move past the directive approach with all their team members and go for collaborative problem solving in the long term.

4. **Plan a follow-up** – A reasonable follow-up is recommended to demonstrate that you are holding them accountable for their results. Interestingly, I've found that performance improvement is very similar to building new habits. If there is no short-term improvement, perhaps a more direct approach is needed, with clarification of potential consequences or impact to them. Once a short-term improvement is achieved, it is important to continue to monitor for long-term sustained improvement. It's not atypical for someone to regress to their old habits, so it is important to positively reinforce improved behavior and negatively reinforce regressed behavior. Eventually, the goal is to get them to change their habits and have sustained improvement in results.

Providing these reinforcements may require training and practice! If you're not used to doing this, and you're struggling, it may be worthwhile to consider practicing and training for this. It wasn't until I got third-party opinions on my feedback techniques from role-playing that I realized how I was butchering it. Apparently, I had blind spots!

Positive Reinforcement

If you want a behavior repeated, it's good to positively reinforce it. Otherwise, people won't understand the positive impact of their actions.

This is often overlooked because some managers expect that doing a good job is part of the job. However, when using positive feedback as a manager's tool, it can:

- **Align expectations better** – Provides clarity to the contributor on what actions actually help the team.

- **Improve motivation and engagement** – Some people are motivated by appreciation more than anything else.

- **Condition people for the behaviors you want** – It's like "programming" people for productive behavior.

Just like negative feedback, it is important to state the exact behavior and its impact. Then, open up the discussion and show your gratitude:

1. **State the behavior and impact** – Be detailed so they know exactly which behavior was good because they won't know otherwise. Let it be from the heart. If it's too mechanical, it loses its meaning.

2. **Open up the discussion** – Hear them out. Most people appreciate it when a manager gives positive feedback. It can be a chance to connect.

3. **Show your gratitude** – As a rule of thumb, positive feedback can be either private (introverts prefer this) or public (some people love public praise).

Won't they get over-inflated egos and unrealistic expectations, and start asking for unrealistic raises? This is a genuine concern that I've seen some managers have. This is a result of:

- **Lack of a true partnership mentality between manager and team** – If the team members are looking for openings to squeeze the manager to get what they want, then a partnership mentality and mutual trust are not fully established.

- **Compensation actually does need to be equalized** – Sometimes, it reveals that the compensation structure needs to be reevaluated for equalization with the market—when it makes sense based on the health of the business or sustainable win-win prospects.

- **Meant in humor** – Sometimes, it's meant in humor. You just have to make sure it doesn't get out of hand.

Evaluate your own circumstances situationally so you can adapt accordingly.

Developmental Coaching: Producing Well-Balanced Contributors

Developmental coaching is a form of coaching that is meant to leverage who the coachees truly are, by developing their natural strengths and covering for their natural weaknesses. There is a greater emphasis on developing the universal skills, which usually involves communication, self-management, and thinking. This is designed to refine them into well-balanced contributors.

It's important to understand that developmental coaching needs are very different for every individual. Getting to know their personality profile and past experiences can help guide your coaching by helping you understand them better. Developmental coaching also provides an opportunity to confirm some functional aspects of their role during sessions:

- **Clarity, transparency, and alignment** – This is an opportunity to clarify team goals and individual goals, and review metrics during sessions.

- **Whether they are receiving adequate support** – We can learn whether the collaborator has adequate support for their job. This can include training, resources, and so on.

- **Get to know what's going on in their lives** – Sometimes, we can get to know major events that may impact their job and proactively address them. This requires a great deal of vulnerability and trust for the employee to open up and connect with the manager. Do not betray their trust. If that information is used against them, they may never open up again. Furthermore, it may tarnish the culture and send the message to keep to themselves within the organization.

Developmental coaching is a great way to connect with team members, get to know their story, and help them with certain aspects that they struggled with for a long time. Oftentimes, their imbalance in universal skillsets is something they carried with them their whole lives. Participation in this type of coaching will require the team member to be self-aware and vulnerable.

- **Individual self-awareness** – For this to work, developmental coaching utilizes self-introspection and discovery to acknowledge their own strengths and weaknesses so they can confront them. This is because it involves achieving growth through their own self-realizations and working toward bettering themselves. This requires a commitment to improve oneself and be vulnerable.

  For someone who is uncomfortable with self-introspection, it is not uncommon for them to resist this. That's why it's important to get buy-in for this. As a manager, it can help by living it and setting yourself as an example to demonstrate the value. Some may still resist until developmental coaching gets popularized throughout the organization. When they see their colleagues participating and improving, more people are likely to get on board.

- **Get to know their aspirations and priorities** – Most people have their own individual and personal goals. Get to know what they are! They may be deeply held dreams that they never dared to share with you. Then, discuss where the team is trying to go. Then evaluate whether there's a possible alignment to design a win-win scenario. Imagine the degree of motivation and engagement that can be captured when they're working toward their dreams.

  How about if they want something that's completely unrealistic after being asked about their personal goals? For example, if they want to work one day a week to simply relax while maintaining the same compensation, obviously, there's no alignment with the organization there. To answer that question, it's important to remember this isn't supposed to open up the floodgate for unreasonable demands. Instead, it's for exploring possible partnership opportunities with *win-win* situations. If unreasonable expectations develop, it's important to be realistic with them.

  Another challenge that opens up is when they overrate themselves by desiring higher positions, but their skills are underdeveloped. That can definitely occur, and in such situations, their expectations need to be grounded in reality. This way, they can evaluate whether it's worthwhile for them to walk the challenging path of developing such skills to get to the next level.

  How about if they want a higher position, and they demonstrate the aptitude, but there are no openings. In such cases, there is no functional alignment, and the business either needs to be in a position to create such an opening, or partner to fill this functional gap to co-create a situation where the role may be created.

- **Partner with them** – If you get to know their aspirations, and there's potential alignment with the team, then you can partner with them to create an individualized development plan. This can involve getting on the same page with the organization's goals, identifying areas of interest for the individual, identifying any current skill gaps, co-planning solutions, identifying where there are resource gaps, and so on. Oftentimes, it can spark topics of interest, proposals, and trajectories that will bring new capabilities to the team. Additionally, they tend to leverage their natural strengths to create growth trajectories that you never imagined.

Developmental coaching deepens the relationship between the manager and team member because the resulting skill development often improves the quality of their personal lives as well. Additionally, deeper relationships improve the sustainability of the organization because of greater retention, greater satisfaction, loyalty, and a pay-it-forward mentality to help others develop.

Coaching is one of the best retention perks for your best talent. Sometimes, people never had a coach or mentor their entire lives. By offering guidance for their lives, a deeper-level connection can be made. It can make an extremely profound impact on their lives. Because of that, it's actually more valuable to most people than other conventional benefits that other companies have to offer. This actually ends up being a powerful retention mechanism.

Truly Listen by Remaining Curious

Many management skills require a lot of active listening to truly dig deeper and identify the heart of situations.

> **Active and "naïve" listening** – Truly listen and don't get distracted. This involves remaining curious with an almost "naïve" mindset. Paraphrase in your own words to confirm with the other person that you understood them correctly.

This requires a lot of patience, self-management, and willingness to dig deeper. This is harder than it sounds. This is especially the case for:

- **Managers who form opinions quickly** – These managers tend to formulate opinions prematurely without truly listening. This tends to be the case for: Goal Pushers (want to give advice), Analyzers (want to analyze the logic), and Enthusiasts (want to share their own story)!

- **Dealing with differing personalities** – It is even more difficult to actively listen when dealing with differing personality types, as they tend to process and see the world differently. It requires a great amount of adaptation to listen and understand the world as they do.

These can prevent true listening and can interfere with information gathering, getting real buy-in, and codeveloping their own solutions. It can even interfere with building healthy and trusting relationships with others. That's why it's important to stay focused in the moment and connect with the individual.

When listening, be in the moment and connect.

The opportunity cost of not connecting with people is very high. There will be a lot of value that is lost due to ineffective coaching sessions, a failure to co-create solutions, and an inability to capture engagement. You'll accidentally lose their ownership and buy-in when you don't listen and default to directing them or giving advice. Remember, the benefit of directing or advising your own idea can have short-term improvements in productivity, but you lose the greater long-term benefits from true buy-in.

Know What Level They Are In

Unfortunately, delegation and coaching are not as clear-cut as how they have been discussed thus far. There are additional considerations to understand the best plan of attack because it actually depends on the employee's current skill level. Based on their level, a more directive approach may be appropriate, or a more coaching approach may be necessary. Let's look at how this applies based on Hersey and Blanchard's Situational Leadership Model—a frame that recommends different approaches based on employees' competency levels.

- **Level One: Unconsciously Incompetent** – At this level, everything is so new that the staff isn't aware of what they don't even know. This can be a confusing period for them. Therefore, a *directive* approach is needed because if you ask them on what they should do, they won't know what to say.

- **Level Two: Consciously Incompetent** – At this level, the staff is now consciously aware of what they don't know. It can be a stressful time for them, as they're going through the learning pains. Therefore, they will require a lot of *guidance*, where you discuss the situation together, but still tell them what to do.

- **Level Three: Consciously Competent** – Alas, they have developed competence by overcoming the challenges with developing new skills. Now, they have a competent understanding of the situation. To further develop and optimize their results, it requires *coaching* them, where they conceptualize solutions and propose them to you. There is a lot of buy-in as it's their own solution. At this point, you can help them by refining their solutions through your input for alignment with higher-level priorities, discussing necessary support and allocation of resources.

- **Level Four: Unconsciously Competent** – At this level, they're so competent at their role that it has become second nature to them. At this level, it becomes about *empowering* them during coaching sessions. Based on the trust level and the type of tasks, you can ask for update reports, align with them strategically, empower them to explore new directions, or even tell them to proceed as they see fit.

It's also important to recognize that the same person can be in different levels for different skills. That means you also need to be aware of what level they are in and for which skills. Even for highly experienced people, if it involves a new skill for them, then they will be back on Level One for that particular skill.

Dealing with Issues: Skill or Will?

We're still going to encounter problems and issues. To add to the complexity of coaching and delegation, we have to also consider whether the issue is due to a lack of skill or will. This actually impacts what the best approach is:

- **Incompetent and Willing** – If an individual has the will to perform, but does not have the skills, then it can represent a training opportunity. This likely involves a more directive approach or a *show and tell* training.

- **Competent and Willing** – If an individual is competent and willing, but hasn't been performing well, then they likely need to be empowered. This may involve creating a *safe zone* because they may have concerns that they might be "stepping on toes," or performing outside their duty to possibly face repercussions. This may also involve providing the necessary resources for them to move an effort forward.

- **Competent and Unwilling** – If an individual is competent but unwilling to perform, a deeper dive coaching session may be necessary to uncover the reason for resistance and see if it can be resolved.

- **Incompetent and Unwilling** – If an individual is not competent and not willing, then this may not be a good fit and an HR action may be necessary.

Performance Reviews

Traditionally, performance reviews are used to rate performance for the purpose of determining whether a staff will remain, needs improvement, stays as is, or deserves a raise or possible promotion. Performance reviews are often designed to standardize this process and are custom tailored toward a company's functional needs. During these reviews, it's recommended for employees to not only be aware of their own performance, but also the overall company or team performance as well:

- **Team and company goals** – How did the team or company do in relation to their goals and metrics? Are they aware?

- **Individual goals** – If applicable, what are the metrics that measure their individual performance? Do they know what they are? Did they reach them? Were there any other mutually agreed upon goals? Did they accomplish them?

This encourages employees to understand their functional performance and take an interest in the overall direction and financial health of the organization. This can minimize the adoption of an individualistic mentality, encourage holistic problem solving, and help ground unrealistic expectations for raises to reality.

Furthermore, managers have the opportunity for a qualitative assessment of the employee. It is also a chance to evaluate their alignment with the culture of the organization. Sample categories to assess can include teamwork, customer service (or stakeholder management), technical skills for the job, detail orientation, goal orientation, punctuality and reliability, leadership (if applicable), or others.

While this may provide a standardized way to evaluate performance, there is a missed opportunity if we only focus on that. Performance reviews are actually alignment opportunities with the team. This should not be a dreaded thing, nor should there be any surprises. If there are surprises during performance reviews, it's an indicator that there need to be more alignment efforts. Whether it be ninety days post-hire, quarterly, semi-annual, or annual reviews, use this as an opportunity to align with the team. Alignment related themes can include:

- **Self-reflection** – What are their thoughts on their overall performance? What are they most proud of? What was the most challenging? Is there anything about their role or how it's done that could be improved or changed?

- **Transparency on priorities** – Do they know what the priorities of the company are? Could their role in the company be made clearer?

- **Development plan** – What are their goals for their current role? Do they have the skills or resources to achieve those goals? How could the company and management have supported them better?

You may notice that a lot of these topics should be touched on during coaching sessions. That's why if there are surprises, it's usually a sign of misalignment, and may be a reminder to reevaluate how coaching or management is done.

13.2. Team Dynamic

Besides dealing with the relationships between managers and their team members, the manager is also responsible for the dynamic within the team. This an important responsibility, as it can greatly impact productivity and sustainability. This is a powerful and intangible aspect that must be managed to maximize the chances of developing self-directed teams and team-level problem solving. The manager has many tools and vehicles to influence the team dynamic, including:

- Organizational mission, vision, and values
- Rules of engagement and code of conduct
- Living it in everyday moments
- Coaching healthy team interactions
- Team meetings and sessions
- Supporting programs (onboarding, and so on)
- Refereeing the dynamic

This can set the tone for acceptable and unacceptable behavior. There are many tones that a manager must focus on:

- **Balanced environment** – Through a well-balanced focus on goals and people, we can establish a fair, focused, hard-working, synergistic, and collaborative environment.

- **Motivated environment** – Maximizes engagement within the team.

- **Feedback-rich environment** – Promotes a growth mentality, competent behavior, and a healthy environment for feedback.

- **Eliminating excessive conflict** – Maintaining healthy work environments that minimize unhealthy and destructive conflict.

- **Team development** – Promotes maturation into a self-directed team.

- **Morale and momentum** – Morale and momentum affect productivity.

- **Culture value alignment** – Promotes cohesion and collaboration by being a beacon for culture within the team.

Interestingly, whether the team dynamic is healthy can be used as a leading indicator of performance. Some organizations have begun using the emotional status of a team as an early leading indicator of performance because it tends to be the precursor to drops in performance in other measurable areas when unhealthy emotional dynamics of a team are not addressed. This allows for a proactive stance in managing a team's performance, as opposed to waiting for a quantifiable performance drop.

In such situations, relationships have already been harmed, and trust has been compromised, which becomes much more difficult to deal with after the fact. In such situations, turnover, backtracking plans, restructuring the organization, policy changes, and/or directive stances to improve performance may lead to further loss in trust, continuing the downward spiral of culture and performance, without ever getting to the root of the issue.

Balanced Environment

Everyone knows that businesses and teams need to meet goals to stay afloat. However, some businesses take it too far, and neglect the people aspect of it. This can be very destructive to the culture of the organization. Therefore, it's important for a good manager to champion the establishment of a healthy balance between goals and people.

Find the balance between goals and people.

Besides that, they must also demonstrate something that's not hard or soft skill related. It has to do with their intrinsic being as a person.

- **Character** – Does what they say they are going to do. Exhibits trustworthiness, respect, responsibility, and so on.

- **Ethics and values** – Has a heart for others. Exhibits honesty, values fairness, and so on.

Though this may appear self-evident, the importance of character, ethics, and values often gets overlooked. Many managers reach their position because they are goal-oriented or due to being an expert in their craft. Some may reach their goals while ignoring these intrinsic characteristics. They may be taking shortcuts, behave in extremely self-oriented manners, not have a heart for their customers or teams, and so on. These are deeper values that impact the manager's everyday decision.

If a manager lacks these characteristics, it may be exceptionally difficult to develop these attributes, as it may have to do with beliefs that may be deeply ingrained within them.

The moral and character framework of the manager is an integral part of keeping a team together. People do not want to follow or support someone who has questionable values, ethics, or concepts of fairness. People want to know that they can trust their manager to appropriately recognize and reward strong efforts and maintain a fair, balanced, and healthy work environment.

Provide recognition and rewards when due.

On the topic of fairness, I don't believe in treating people equally because people actually want different things—treating them equally leads to problems. Rather, people want to be treated fairly. Otherwise, a demotivating environment can inadvertently be created. Regarding this topic, it's important to note that:

- **The perception of fairness matters** – People tend to make a big deal about whether they think something is fair or not.

- **People are more sensitive to fairness (and change) than economic value** – To illustrate this point, if someone was given $100 for free, they would be grateful for it. However, if they saw someone else get $150, they would be unhappy that they were given only $100. As you can see, the perception of fairness is relative, and we need to be cognizant of that when we make decisions as a manager.

Establishing ground rules and agreements are great ways to keep things fair. However, there will be many moments when it may make sense to make exceptions on a case-by-case basis. Be warned, you must watch out for the dangers of making exceptions, such as:

- **Exceptions becoming the new norm** – This impacts the perception of fairness.

- **Exceptions cheapening your word and agreements.**

- **Damage coming not from the individual exceptions, but from the general perception of fairness being altered.**

Due to this, exceptions need to be evaluated on a case-by-case basis and should be made only in exceptional situations and granted very sparingly.

On top of that, there will be many instances when people try to push their luck and boundaries. In such situations, it becomes important to:

> **Demonstrate managerial courage and hold your ground** – There will be times when you need to stand firm and hold your ground. Otherwise, people may take advantage of you.

I'm not saying to do this in a heartless and soulless manner. This must be done while balancing your focus on people and goals. The manager must be aware of these considerations and make decisions on a case-by-case basis.

Motivated Environment

Motivation is tough! Almost all managers have encountered the conundrum where it feels like no one is motivated but themselves, and that they have to spend all their time herding the cats that try to get out of doing good work. It wasn't until I truly understood the following that a paradigm shift in my mind occurred:

You can't motivate another person,
but yet all people are motivated.

Remember that we are all different people with different personalities, motivated by different things, with different goals. There is a tendency for us to think that people are all the same and are motivated by the same things that would motivate us. However, that is the exact thought process that got people caught in the demotivated cat-herding situation.

Understand that motivation comes from within.

Understand what drives someone. This helps determine whether there is a possible *win-win* situation that simultaneously meets the team's needs and the individual's need. Of course, this needs to remain within realistic parameters to stay on point with the team's goals. Otherwise it would lead to a *lose-win* situation. Overall, looking for a *win-win* is far more effective. At the same time, it deepens the relationship between that person and the manager.

You can't motivate anyone, but you can only create
an environment for motivation to flourish.

We can also influence motivation by maintaining the environment that cultivates motivation. This is through addressing a combination of the following actions:

- **Maximize intrinsic motivators** – This is the primary motivating type that can capture long-term engagement and should be our main focus. Intrinsic motivators come from within a person and are driven by a deeper purpose. Here are some examples of intrinsic motivators: autonomy, recognition, sense of accomplishment, being part of a group. Some prefer challenges, some prefer routines, and some value a sense of fairness.

- **Apply extrinsic motivators as needed** – Extrinsic motivators include external factors such as praise, financial incentives, other rewards, or avoidance of negative outcomes. Though this can definitely achieve short-term boosts in productivity and be a good adjunctive focus, if we only use this type of motivator, the benefits are usually short-lived and create an unsustainable environment for continuous motivation.

- **Remove demotivators** – A manager should avoid demotivating their team members as it can be extremely damaging to the team dynamic. It is also important to remember that different things demotivate people in different ways. Here are some sample demotivators: personal attacks, managers taking all the credit and thus failing to recognize good work, not delivering on your word, actions not congruent with words, not listening, and not developing team members.

- **Don't forget pre-motivators** – Pre-motivators involve the initial ground rules and structure to keep a team together. It is important to remember that pre-motivators are essential as well and shouldn't be overlooked. Unfortunately, people are not perfect and may make decisions that are not in the best interest of the team. They may even take advantage of the team or the manager if given the opportunity. Thus, it is important to set some pre-motivators in place to keep that in check. Without this, unfortunately, team members may exploit openings, simply because they can.

  For instance, there may come a time when a manager has to make a hard stance to maintain an environment of professionalism. They may call out when team members engage in unhealthy conflict, show up late and unprepared, or do not buy in to the culture, or evaluate when a team member may not be the right fit for the team. Though we want to promote a culture of motivation, engagement, and collaboration, the manager does need to make it clear that taking advantage of trust that is given is not acceptable and that everyone is replaceable. This takes managerial courage, which some managers find difficult.

Feedback-Rich Environment

It's important to promote a feedback-rich environment to maximize the impact of positive reinforcement, feedback, coaching, and collaboration. Otherwise there may be a tendency for people to take things personally and have unnecessary defensiveness. When there is an environment where people take feedback defensively, it becomes exceptionally difficult to calibrate performance. Therefore, it's important to set the following themes:

- When giving feedback, don't make it personal.
- When receiving feedback, don't take it personally.

By reinforcing the value of feedback, we can create an environment that is more receptive to it. In fact, some organizations champion it as a path for personal growth. That way, rather than hiding from feedback, people look forward to it.

Feedback is the breakfast of champions.

This also applies to team members providing feedback to each other. This enables team-level problem solving and improves collaboration among team members. This significantly reduces the amount of escalations to the manager and increases organic problem solving.

Eliminate Excessive Conflicts

Although conflict can spur problem solving and collaboration, let's make sure it doesn't get out of hand. When it does escalate to that level, it actually becomes a high priority item to deal with. Some managers are stuck dealing with perpetual excessive conflict. They know how stressful a situation like this can be for themselves and their team. This can create an extremely toxic work environment that interferes with regular work and the development of the culture. There are several things that a manager can do to stabilize this situation.

- **Create agreements** – Get real with the team. Admit that you haven't been keeping up your end of the bargain by maintaining a healthy atmosphere, but you will be doing so moving forward. Establish rules of engagement and mutual agreements among the team to prevent it from getting out of hand again.

- **Don't get in the middle unless it gets out of hand** – Team members who are accustomed to Traditional Hierarchy may be used to bringing up escalating issues to ask you to, "Put this person in their place." Unfortunately, if you do that, you've just put yourself in the middle, and every issue that arises between them will be brought up to you. Rather, it's important for them to overcome their differences.

- **Coach them on collaboration** – Excessive conflict is usually the result of differences in opinions, differences in profile styles, and deficiencies in universal skillsets. This is an opportunity to coach them on those universal skills and teach them how to settle differences in opinions and communication styles.

- **Deal with unacceptable behavior** – If it really gets out of hand, you do have to intervene. If things are extremely heated, it may be important to allow a moment for all parties involved to cool down. Then, when that happens, get perspectives from those involved, and mediate peace if necessary.

- **Managerial hard stance** – If things are extremely sour and people have trouble making up on their own, there may be a moment where you have to put your foot down and take a hard stance. This may involve verbal or written warnings. Sometimes, people do need to learn the potential consequences of their behavior for them to get over it.

- **Get in front of the problem by providing clarity regularly** – Oftentimes, conflicts occur due to confusion and misinterpretations of priorities. Introducing regular alignment points is a great way to get in front of the problems to proactively address potential issues before they occur. This can prevent confusion and minimize escalations.

Team Development

A manager plays a critical role in developing their team through its various phases of development. Ultimately, the manager should guide the team to reach a self-directed team status. This is a key component and building block to achieve exponential growth using culture strategy. A manager should be familiar with the various phases and the key items that must be addressed to successfully guide the team to the next level.

Forming Phase

This is the "honeymoon" phase. This is where people have initially gathered together. People may be eager and excited to be in a new environment or with new people. They don't know each other very well, so they are very cordial and polite with each other. Everyone is trying to figure out what's going on.

In this phase, it's important for the manager to take a directive stance and provide a lot of clarity for the team. With clear expectations and rules of engagement, people will better understand what needs to be done to avoid reaching a confused state.

Storming Phase

During this phase, people begin testing each other's boundaries and bumping shoulders with each other. They're getting to know how they personally fit within the team, and understand the position, influence, and attitudes of others. This is important to occur for people because it means that they care about their individual performance, and they're trying to figure out how to accomplish their goals within the team dynamic.

Oftentimes, this phase will self-resolve and the team members will develop a natural equilibrium of power and influence with each other. In such situations, it's important to stay out of it and let it happen, or you will disrupt the flow and be in a position where you're stuck in the middle between people resolving perpetual issues. Organic resolution of this phase tends to happen when the culture of the organization is already established and there are good collaboration skills within the people.

Other times, this can be the most stressful phase of the team-development process. If it tends to get out of hand, you must step in and neutralize the excessive conflict. It may require a combination of coaching, situational reinforcement, and a hard stance for it to stop. This tends to happen more when there's a less established culture or lower baseline of collaboration skills.

Norming Phase

The Norming Phase occurs when people begin to understand the boundaries between each other and figure out what lines not to cross. This is often characterized by a peaceful state of unoptimized performance. High amounts of collaboration are not seen, as people view it as risking conflict, and they don't want to deal with it.

While the Storming Phase is potentially the most stressful phase, the Norming Phase is potentially the most dangerous phase. In reality, most teams actually get stuck in this phase and never reach the Performing

Phase. In fact, some teams get stuck here for so long that people have gotten accustomed and numb to dysfunction and think it's normal. It's not normal! In reality, they never progressed and got stuck.

The important action items are to coach, develop, and facilitate well. The manager needs to get buy-in from the team that differences in opinions are actually healthy and have the potential to create synergy. This will require coaching the universal skillsets, developing people, and facilitating synergistic collaboration.

Performing Phase

This is where we achieve the self-directed team status. The team is bringing up multiple perspectives, collaborating around them (rather than introducing excessive conflict), and coordinating to deliver great results. In this situation, the manager may actually feel like they're not needed anymore and begin wondering about the next challenge.

In such cases, it is possible to have the manager continue to deliver optimal results with a "stay-and-sustain" mentality. However, if we truly want to optimize such a manager, they should begin preparing their replacement so that the manager can work on developing the next team to further grow the business.

Though this may seem like it should move forward in a step-by-step manner, that's not how it always works. Actually, it's important to recognize that teams can move backward.

> **Major changes tend to start the process all over again** – It's important to understand this and try to foresee the various triggers that can start the process again to prepare the team and plan accordingly. Major changes can include team member change, major policy change, project change, leadership change, and so on.

For more details, refer to Tuckman's Four Stages of Team Development, which is a widely known and accepted model for understanding the various phases of team development. However, though it is widely known, few truly understand it and know how to apply it. The best way to utilize this frame is to predictably take your team to the Performing Phase, achieve a self-directed team, train your replacement, step out as a manager, and work on your next team.

Morale and Momentum

Throughout moments of hard work, it's important to remember that the morale and momentum of the team matter too. It can be so easy to get consumed with the goals and objectives of the team that we forget to take notice of fatigue that is kicking in, which can affect productivity as well.

Morale and momentum matter, too.

It's good to have an understanding of how frequently fatigue and morale dips occur, so that there can be a proactive rhythm to build team spirit. It can also help to have situational and spontaneous moments of small appreciative gestures. This can help maintain an environment that:

- Celebrates wins,
- Gives recognition, and
- When things go well, gives credit. When things go bad, takes the blame.

We can also consider using team-building events to improve morale and momentum. However, team-building events can sometimes be tricky, as people may have conflicting priorities (family and personal life), and there's a chance for it to backfire. With that in mind, here are some recommendations:

- **Bottom-up team events** – It actually works best when it's proposed from the bottom up.

- **Be a part of team-building events** – If team-building events are hosted, don't forget to participate. Also, don't get crazy inappropriate and do things that you'll regret (for example, get very drunk and compromise your credibility).

Another sustainable way to maintain morale and momentum is to encourage team members to have:

> **Work-life integration throughout the team** – Promote the building of trusting relationships and friendships within team members. This is opposed to the mentality of separating work and personal life.

Of course, none of this can be forced and it usually occurs organically as the culture of the team develops.

Culture Value Alignment

As a manager, you play a critical role in culture strategy by being the beacon for the team. You are either supporting the penetration of its values to your team, or you are blocking it. Culture strategy has the potential to tremendously benefit both your productivity and your team members' lives. So, get on board and be a culture champion! This means that you have to:

- Get buy-in to the collaborative culture from your team members,
- Live the collaborative culture, and
- Manage through developing others.

To truly maximize the impact of culture strategy, it helps to promote certain themes within the team dynamic. Here are some sample themes that are useful to implement within your team:

- **Empowerment** – Enabling people to reach heights they never thought possible.

- **Dare to dream** – It's okay to have goals. Let's see if we can achieve them together through win-win situations.

- **Take chances** – You don't make the shots you don't take.

To help propagate these themes, it means that we have to be comfortable being:

- **Transparent** – As long as it's not confidential, we want to be open and problem solve together.

- **Vulnerable** – This may feel like we're exposing potential weaknesses. We have to get over this and trust the team.

- **Advocating bottom-up management** – Get used to people proposing solutions, and drop the "It's my way or it's the highway" approach.

This also means that we have to look out for people who harm the culture because we need to:

- Protect the culture, and
- Referee the culture.

When people harm the culture, try to work it out with them and get their buy-in. However, if that doesn't work, it may become necessary to:

- **Defend the culture with a managerial hard stance** – If they don't buy in to the culture, it may not be a long-term fit. In that case, we may need to consider parting ways. Do this sparingly, when all else fails.

- **Muster up managerial courage** – For most people, managerial hard stances aren't easy decisions, nor do they feel good. However, there are times when people cross lines, and it becomes necessary to protect the culture. This may require mustering up the courage to do what is necessary.

We also have to live the culture when we are interfacing with the rest of the organization and varying cross-functions. That means that we have to:

- **Be open to sharing capabilities** – Be open to sharing ideas through cross-pollination and collaboration with the rest of the organization.

- **Do not hoard knowledge/staff/job** – Avoid protectionist behavior. This is harmful to the culture.

- **Promote a culture of internal mobility and change agility** – This means there's a possibility that the manager's team composition and responsibilities may change. For example, your team is asked to help out with knowledge transfer to a new team, your team member gets promoted to lead their own team, your team member gets assigned on rotation to learn new skills, and so on.

This may feel uncomfortable at first because it means we need to be open, vulnerable, and willing to adapt to change. But remember, when we all live these values together, we have the potential to truly make a difference and create an exponential organization.

13.3. Day-to-Day Tactics

As a manager, there are moments when we need to take a step back from work to plan and organize tasks for your team. There can be a seemingly never-ending stream of tasks that need to be organized and accomplished. Part of a manager's duties is to figure out what needs to get done. This falls in the realm of tactics.

To do this, we need to make time for tactics. Tasks don't plan and organize themselves. A manager needs to do this. This requires margin. If we're barely keeping our heads above the water, we won't have time for this.

For some managers, this can be extremely challenging because they find it boring and unstimulating. For others, they may be planning too much, and never get anything done. If you're the type of manager who abhors planning, ask yourself, "What kind of value can planning create for me? If I see the value, should I create time to do this?" If you're the type that overplans and gets paralyzed, ask yourself, "Can I anticipate everything? Don't certain things only reveal themselves as I do them?"

Monitoring and Updating Responsibilities

As a manager, you're accountable for the team results and your team members. That means you need to know what's going on. A major part of the manager's job is to monitor the team, so that you have your fingers on the pulse of what's going on. Ask yourself, "What helps to get a sense of where the team is at? If trouble was brewing, would I know about it? If not, are there better ways to monitor?" Let's look at a few ways we can incorporate monitoring practices as a manager.

Direct Observation

This is probably the most obvious form of monitoring as you can physically see and hear what's going on. However, it's important to understand the limitations to this. There are many things that will be occurring outside of your direct observation because you can only be at one place at a time. Therefore, it's important to diversify your arsenal of monitoring tools.

Processes and Data

The biggest benefits for processes and data are that they can provide objective data that can be made transparent to keep score. It's important to understand that we use this as a collaborative benchmarking tool for transparency, rather than making it seem like "Big Brother" is watching them. When we use data as objective benchmarking, it can help maintain alignment and even improve engagement.

This also increases our reach and visibility because it is possible to systemize data accumulation. We can use reports or dashboards to simplify the data for easier viewing. It's important to select vital metrics that are important business functions that are worth monitoring.

People

In culture strategy, there is a large emphasis on monitoring the situation through updates from key people that you have built a mutually trusting relationship with. This is valuable because it has the potential to gather critical pieces of information that would be difficult to gather otherwise.

A great vehicle for obtaining information through people is through coaching relationships. When you have your sessions, you can get extremely useful information that helps determine the team dynamic and skill level of your members. This is valuable information because it acts as an early indicator of larger issues. This gives us an early opportunity to proactively address issues before they start affecting our revenue, profits, market share, customer service, and so on.

Organizing Day-to-Day Tasks

As a manager, there is a substantially higher volume of tasks that need to be completed to keep a team together and reach objectives. This needs to be organized so that people know their roles and know what they need to do. On top of that, there are always going to be unexpected situations that occur throughout the day. Therefore, managers need to be able to shift priorities to adapt to the changing demands to stay on point. This requires a bigger picture understanding of the team's role and planning ahead.

Who's Doing What

A manager should ensure that tasks are coordinated among team members and completed toward the team objectives, without leaving functional gaps. This means they need a strong understanding of the staff roles, instructions, shifts, attendance, and so on. Bear in mind, managers are accountable for other people, not just themselves.

One common mistake made by managers is that they distribute work unevenly and unfairly. Oftentimes, they have "go-to" people and put all the work on them. That can potentially create issues because it can overwhelm those people, but it also interferes with the development and coaching of the other team members. Remember, when all team members are developed into well-balanced contributors, they take greater ownership, and the burden of work gets more evenly distributed and creates a healthier dynamic.

Adapt Situationally

Curve balls are thrown around all day. This causes priorities to shift on a regular basis. The manager needs to capture new information and reset the priorities for the team to safely reach their desired objectives. To do this, managers need to know how to shift priorities by cross-referencing with the bigger picture.

Some people struggle with this due to indecisiveness or challenges of seeing the bigger picture. They may need to overcome great obstacles to develop the necessary business acumen.

Plan Ahead

It's important to plan ahead and understand the bigger picture because it helps the manager understand how to shift priorities and adapt. This is done by understanding their team's role and how it integrates with the rest of the organization. The manager needs to know how their team interacts with other teams, departments, sponsors, and stakeholders. Additionally, there is a need to know what direction the organization is going and its future goals. That way, the manager can anticipate tactical considerations, such as potential risks, impacts, probabilities, resource needs, priorities, and so on. When we understand these considerations, we can proactively plan ahead to address them.

Knowledge of these considerations also helps refine the thought processes when adapting team priorities and collaborating with sponsors for resources. Remember, a team doesn't live in an isolated silo and isn't frozen in time. It needs to integrate with the rest of the organization and its future goals.

In Summary

Remember that initially, practicing these essential skills *will* feel weird and there will be pushback from the team. You're trying to undo long-term conditioning, which doesn't happen overnight. If you can get over the weirdness, it will be worth it to learn to delegate and coach with both negative and positive reinforcement. This will help you produce and retain well-balanced contributors, regardless of their current competence level. Thus, you can create a balanced, motivated, and feedback-rich environment that allows for team development. With these skills, you can then learn to manage multiple teams, as we'll discuss in the next chapter.

CHAPTER 14

ESSENTIAL SKILLS FOR LEADERS WHO MANAGE MULTIPLE TEAMS

I remember having a conversation with a gentleman who had a successful multimillion-dollar business in charge of multiple teams. He was a man who others would have thought had it all.

However, during that conversation, he opened up to me. He shared with me that he was exhausted, hated his business, and had sacrificed his family and personal life due to his professional aspirations. Filled with regret, he told me that he was willing to give up everything to get his family and life back.

When I dove deeper into the situation, the cause became quite clear. Unfortunately, he was in a situation that required leadership skills to oversee multiple teams, but he was still using management skills that were more appropriate for a single team. He never made the transition to building a culture of self-direction and adopting leadership skills. Trying to use management skills where leadership skills are required can be exhausting and unsustainable.

Looking back, it truly was an unfortunate situation. You don't need to sacrifice everything for business. In fact, there are many instances where people have both. We just need a different approach because it's a different situation.

Leadership skills utilize a different set of control levers – This allows you to run multiple teams more efficiently with less involvement of your time, energy, and stress.

Getting on the Same Page of What Leadership Means

One of the challenges in discussing leadership is that everyone seems to have a different definition of what it is. Some think it's synonymous with management, but it's very different from that. Some think it's all about inspiring. However, it's not as simple as that either. If that were the case, it would simply be cheerleading.

There are elements of being a visionary and generating results with influence. From the context of culture strategy, I believe the most functional definition for leadership is:

Building people infrastructure as described in culture strategy and leveraging value from self-directed teams to maximize impact and value.

To do this effectively, leaders need to get out of being in the middle of the day-to-day tasks of the team and be able to produce results by influencing from the outside. Being in the middle of the team is the manager's job. Leaders have to position themselves outside the daily grind to leverage results in an optimal manner.

You may be wondering, *Hmmm... if I'm not in the middle, how do I*

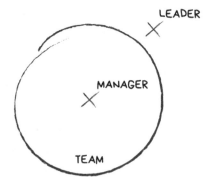

Managers positioned within the team, leaders positioned outside the team

leverage the team? That sounds like it would be hard. You're right. It is hard. You're not there to see what's going on, but you're still accountable for them. That's why it can feel very uncomfortable because it requires greater vulnerability than management. It also has a greater dependence on influence and buy-in skills.

This will require a different skillset from what leaders may be accustomed to. To achieve this, their primary control levers to generate value become:

- Developing other managers and leaders
- Strategy
- Mobilizing teams from the outside

This can be a challenging transition for charismatic leaders because it is difficult to replace yourself with a suitable manager. The team may miss you and resist the new manager.

It may take a lot of effort to coach and develop your management replacement to be accepted by people. To facilitate this transition, you may need to help transfer respect and credibility to them. Additionally, you can consider developing mass communication channels to simultaneously reach multiple teams for occasional alignment purposes without physically being there.

If a leader can figure out how to do this, they are in a position to influence and leverage multiple teams in a very sustainable and impactful way. This sets the stage for creating more value with less time, which can lead to a far greater impact.

14.1. Developing Other Managers and Leaders

The primary method of leveraging productivity as a leader involves developing other managers and leaders. This is the main vehicle for leaders to build people infrastructure to grow the organization. When applied correctly, it creates a deeper *partnering relationship* that promotes mutual trust with your managers. This interface also becomes a reliable method to monitor performance and align with them and their teams. This is also what enables leaders to have influence in multiples areas at once, without having to clone themselves.

True leaders develop other managers and leaders.

This is a critical component that greatly impacts the success of whether teams reach their objectives or complete their project. Without proper positioning of quality management and leadership, teams are more likely to fail or even internally implode. Many companies have a constant high demand for leaders and managers and little time for development. This often leads to people being promoted to their roles who don't actually have the necessary skills or aptitude. From that vantage point, it makes sense that projects fail due to poor leadership/management. That's why leaders should always be proactive in taking a greater role in developing the managers and leaders of tomorrow.

Choosing the Right Manager and Leader

Choosing the right candidate for a managerial/leadership position is very important, as these skills are more difficult to develop in others than team member-related skills.

This is a steep learning curve.

It may require multiple channels of learning, significant time, and financial investments to groom a leader. Understand that your candidate should have the tenacity to endure the challenges that would arise in their leadership journey, the courage to overcome deeper psychological blockers, and the openness to new ways of getting things done.

It involves overcoming many inner blockers.

This will require a great amount of drive, intrinsic motivation, vulnerability, and self-awareness. It will also require a flexible solution mentality. No one knows everything, and anyone who claims to can be problematic. It will require intuitiveness to identify gaps in their knowledge and skills and have the willingness to find appropriate solutions.

In addition, there are many difficult concepts to learn and skillsets that need to be developed, as these roles require managing a fine balance between people development and goals. Different candidates have varying degrees of aptitude regarding those skills, which makes it such that some have an easier time developing those skills. Therefore, it's wise to:

- Evaluate intrinsic motivation, intuitiveness, and whether they have a flexible and solution mentality.

- Evaluate aptitude to balance goals and people development.

Because these attributes are difficult to develop, you should be highly selective of whom you choose to groom. In fact, leadership/management skills are so challenging to teach that it is wise to reserve such efforts for developing HiPo's (high potentials).

On top of this, it's important that your managers are bought in to the culture strategy. Disagreement with culture strategy often leads to perpetual conflicts with your managers. They may agree with it at face value, but you need to evaluate whether it conflicts with their inner values. It will save a lot of hassle and headaches when trying to achieve alignment with the values of culture strategy.

- **Look past whether they only agree with the culture at face value** – At face value, people can easily nod their heads and pretend to agree but not really mean it.

- **Evaluate whether it conflicts with their core values** – For example, excessive dependence on hierarchal respect is seen as a form of conflicting value. Be aware, sometimes, they may lack the introspection to connect the dots and cross-reference values from culture strategy with their core beliefs. If we misdiagnose this, it can lead to a string of passive-aggressive behavior.

This leads into our next section: aligning the values of culture strategy with the manager.

Culture Strategy Value Alignment with Managers/Leaders

Managers have direct and regular interactions with team members. Through your managers, you gain access to people. Because of this, managers can enable culture strategy or block it. That's why it is important to align the values of culture strategy with the managers. This ensures a partnership mentality to enable this strategy to penetrate throughout the organization. There are several reasons why value alignment is essential in enabling organic and scalable growth of culture strategy:

- **The manager must be the beacon for culture for their team** – The experience of a contributor with the company is mostly dictated by the relationship with their manager more than anything else. So, if the manager is not bought in, then their entire team won't be bought in!

- **The manager must produce internally developed talent and people who may become future managers/leaders** – Managers are in a position to develop others. They are the gatekeeper, producer, and source for internal talent and potential future managers/leaders. If they are not bought in, then the supply of internally developed talent will be greatly hindered, which also deters growth prospects.

- **Managers must be open to share their knowledge, staff, and responsibility. Don't hoard!** – In an effort to protect their positions, some managers may have been hoarding their knowledge, their staff, or their job. As a result, some organizations find it very difficult to plan for successions, as the managers are holding their hoarded capabilities hostage. This is a very toxic behavior as it eliminates transparency, disrupts the potential to develop a culture of internal mobility, and hinders people from developing the ability to adapt to change.

If a manager is hoarding staff members, they are likely inhibiting the development of their team members. This will further hurt the overall work experience, affect overall engagement, and destroy several key strategic components of culture strategy.

There are several themes of culture strategy that must be represented at the manager level to maximize opportunities to develop and grow people. For example, managers must encourage:

- **Transparency** – This paves a path for greater engagement and collaborative problem solving.

- **Upward management** – Empowering and enabling team-level problem solving.

- **Internal mobility** – Enabling more stretch projects (which can increase the team capabilities) and likelihood of matching people with their desired role.

- **Team agility** – Encouraging adaptation, change, and improvement.

Managers have the potential to propagate or sabotage collaborative organizational cultures. There are some behaviors that may have been acceptable in traditional organizations, but they are actually very harmful to collaborative cultures.

Sometimes, this is a result of value-clashing occurring between Traditional Competitive and Synergistic Collaborative beliefs. People who overuse authority and create dysfunction may not be aware that they are doing it. They may believe that they are entitled to special privileges that make them invincible. If a team is having issues with an extremely hierarchal manager, then depending on the situation, it may be the manager who needs to be addressed.

If there is a philosophy mismatch,
it'll likely not work out long term.

Unfortunately, it doesn't work out with everyone. Value alignment can be challenging if there is a deeply held resistance by the manager. Many of the components of culture strategy require a partnered effort. If you can't get their buy-in, it may be a poor long-term fit. It will likely end up in a prolonged battle of disagreements and an eventual parting of ways.

Culture strategy is fair for managers, but some have trouble seeing it. Overall, managers need to be bought into this culture and see the opportunity in their own development as well. One of the reasons why they may resist is due to a protectionist mentality, which is caused by a fear of exposure and a fear of vulnerability. That's why a fair agreement should be made between managers and the organization to neutralize that concern and risk.

If a manager buys into a collaborative organization's
culture and invests in its infrastructure, then the
organization will invest in the manager's employability,
making them more valuable in the marketplace.

We can improve a manager's employability by investing in their skillsets. This can empower the manager to overcome their fears and openly contribute to the infrastructure of the organization. What helps them overcome this is assurance that their increased skillsets will improve their marketability, which can open up additional employment opportunities if their current situation doesn't work out.

That being said, we don't want to encourage our managers to leave. The goal is to have long-term retention. The strategy is to invest in them to improve their skillset, and thus their employability to give them peace of mind and buy-in to the culture. However, we want them to apply those skills in our organization! We encourage long-term retention with the following mentality:

> *"Train people well enough so they can leave, treat them well enough so they don't want to."*
>
> —Richard Branson

Leadership and Management Coaching

It's no secret that leadership/management development is hard! This can be a huge weight to bear because it's much more demanding than training simpler task-related skills. It involves self-awareness, overcoming countless obstacles, questioning the questions we ask, a willingness to restructure how we think, and much more. That's why there's no one trick to accomplish this.

There are certain people who have a strong aptitude for developing people and can help others absorb the relevant information much quicker, and even help them learn to apply it. It requires a great deal of foundational skills in emotional intelligence, communication, management, psychology of adult development, morale, momentum, and so on.

These leaders have the ability to build other leaders and self-directed teams at an amazingly rapid pace. They usually possess a *magnetic* quality that draws others toward them. When such individuals are identified, it may be wise to strategically allocate them to a position where they can develop large amounts of managers, leaders, and teams on behalf of the organization.

Whether leadership and management development comes naturally or not, these skills can be developed when you:

- **Diversify your efforts by hitting it from all angles** – I'm sure you've been in a situation where you've been telling a manager a concept a hundred times but couldn't get it through their heads. But after they hear it from someone else or take a training, they act as if they came up with a new brilliant "insight." However, in reality, it's what you were telling them for months or even years on end. Sometimes, they need to conceptualize a thought from a third perspective to materialize it. That's why it's good to have a diversified effort, otherwise it can greatly increase the frustration and slow down the rate of valuable realizations. This can be in the form of training or external coaching. Breaking these painful stalemates in a systemized manner can be extremely valuable for organizations.

- **Don't completely abdicate management/leadership** – It's not just sending them to training and letting go entirely! Training programs are partnered efforts. We can't entirely abdicate this responsibly altogether, or it won't work either. We need to touch base with coaching, discuss realizations, and discuss applications as well. At the very least, get to know their key take-home points from training.

Based on principles of adult learning and development by Michael Lombardo and Robert Eichinger, to maximize the impact of leadership development, we need a diversified approach with the following:

- **Training** – 10 percent of learning
- **Coaching** – 20 percent of learning
- **On-the-job application** – 70 percent of learning

The manager- or leader-in-training often needs guidance during their learning process. These concepts likely would not work out on the first go-around. Rather, it requires trying to apply these principles, making mistakes, getting back on their feet multiple times, adapting/

calibrating, trying again, actually succeeding, and having someone to celebrate with. Thus, the bulk of the learning actually comes from the trainee implementing it in their job, going through the hurdles and challenges of applying the skills, and properly assimilating the skills as they become habits.

Regarding Training, the 10 Percent of Learning

Training provides access to a holistic view of leadership topics. Examples of this include sending someone to a seminar, or providing individual study material like books and webinars. This gives the person the opportunity to have access to a broad range of topics and internalize the material in a way that makes sense to them. They also gain additional perspectives on the various topics through instructors and peers. Management topics/skills are relevant across all industries, and managers realize that they are not alone in the endeavor to develop these skills, which can be a comforting psychological factor via social support. Additionally, there's something about sitting in a room for longer periods of time learning about a particular topic with stories, discussions, and exercises that helps with knowledge retention and connecting the dots.

Regarding Coaching, the 20 Percent of Learning

Twenty percent of the learning is dependent on coaching. It's important to recognize that the learning curve to develop management and leadership skills is steeper than you would expect. Even if they receive training, it is likely that there may be a bombardment of information, and the trainee may struggle to make the connections. Therefore, it often requires a coach to point them in the right direction, and to help them understand the applications of various principles. It helps when a coach lets them know that this is a steep learning process and is going to be tough. When they fail, have conversations like, "Hey, I've been there. I tried that, and it hurt, it sucked. But hang in there, it's going to be fine because it's going to look different when you get better, and you will." A coach can sometimes help the individual identify personal or deeper level blockers for developing skillsets and work together to overcome them.

Regarding on-the-Job Application, the 70 Percent of Learning

Seventy percent of the learning will actually occur as they apply it on their job. Obviously, learning practical skills is not just simply talking about them. Even if they learn the topics from training or coaching, it won't internalize unless they apply it, have "cuts and bruises," and learn to overcome their challenges to find success. This gives them the opportunity to let the material soak in and marinate, see what works when they lead initiatives in their hands, see what doesn't work, and let these skills become habits. You can also help a manager accelerate their on-the-job learning through intentional accelerated efforts:

- **Stretch goals** – This can help mentees push their current limit by taking on a project that is slightly above their current capability, thereby breaking past their current limit.

- **Rotations** – This can be a great way to create a broader perspective in their management or leadership role.

- **Leadership pairing** – There are a lot of unwritten nuances to a leadership role that include deeper knowledge of existing processes and relationship dynamics that keep the business functions stable. Unfortunately, many managers/leaders who move into new roles often learn by trial and error, which often causes unnecessary friction and damage to the organization that can have a larger ripple effect on the overall culture. Therefore, leadership pairing can be a great way to capture such nuances to transfer existing knowledge and relationships beforehand. Good handovers can mitigate the likelihood of compromising current business functions.

Leadership development can be so challenging that it is usually wise to have a support group with coaching and leadership peers. This further allows for cross-pollination of ideas, and helps them overcome the internal conflicts that they encounter as they transition from contributor to manager, and then manager to leader. In fact, because the control levers for being a strong contributor, manager, and leader are all different, it can be an extremely confusing concept to grasp. Thus, these support systems aid in psychological reconciliation of these concepts.

Have a support group or community of knowledge sharing.

Engaging Their Inner Drive

Throughout leadership development, it is important to understand the inner drive of your mentee to optimize the impact of leadership coaching. Here's a brief summary of how people have different drives, and how it influences your approach in engaging them.

Goal Pushers

Typical leadership coaching: Give them big picture goals to strive for and support them with training and alignment. They like to shoot for overarching targets and tend to fill in the in-between details by themselves.

Understanding their drive: Make sure you talk about accomplishments, challenges, goals, and success. That's what motivates them.

Typical leadership challenge: They will likely need coaching on using influence rather than authority, connecting with people, and developing people.

Analyzers

Typical leadership coaching: Have them *architect* a bigger picture solution that's related to major business objectives. *Master planning* a schematic that maximizes effectiveness and efficiency motivates them.

Understanding their drive: Understanding things. Becoming an expert.

Typical leadership challenge: They will likely need coaching on connecting with people and seeing the big picture goal to get past "analysis paralysis."

Enthusiasts

Typical leadership coaching: Thrust them in situations that involve being in the middle of a lot of people. That's how they get empowered and are motivated by it. They tend to retrofit solutions within those situations rather than planning ahead. Then, coach them based on their realizations as they try things out.

Understanding their drive: Building communities and gathering people. Being in the center of attention. Looking good.

Typical leadership challenge: They will likely need coaching on the value of planning ahead, staying organized, and following up.

Stabilizers

Typical leadership coaching: Create "safe zones" and give them stretch goals. Hold their hand throughout the process.

Understanding their drive: They enjoy building deeper relationships and helping people.

Typical leadership challenge: They will likely need coaching on seeing the big picture goals and gaining confidence.

You May Need to Occasionally Discuss Overcoming Inner Blockers

This may feel uncomfortable, but there may be a need to coach them around overcoming inner blockers to help them progress and develop. These are inner factors that may actually be debilitating and handicapping them from thriving as a manager or leader. It would involve a deeper-level connection with the individual to identify the psychological blockers that are preventing them from succeeding. Help them to overcome them by guiding realizations or confronting those blockers. Common themes include fear (of failure, exposure, or the unknown), ego, unhealthy relationship with money/sales, blame shifting, past trauma, uncomfortable being hopeful, and so on. It identifies scarcity mentalities and aims to achieve a paradigm shift to realign their life to a more impactful purpose.

As you can imagine, these are not easy conversations to have, and one must be extremely comfortable being uncomfortable (most people feel uncomfortable going this deep) to help them overcome them. These blockers are preventing them from being able to give the gifts of their talents to the world. This encourages self-reflection and vulnerability. It requires a genuine interest in developing people by connecting with their inner selves, and being comfortable with discussing deep issues to enable intentional habit creation for maximum impact. It can facilitate much more impactful breakthroughs and paradigm shifts toward productive behavior than task-focused or skills-focused realizations. In fact, it can be one of the highest leverage activities that a leader can perform.

Trusting and Working with Your Manager

It's important to establish a trusting and healthy working relationship with your manager. The dynamic of managing a manager may be very different from the dynamic of managing contributors. First, it's important to recognize that:

Alignment is critical – Managers need to be more involved than simply participating in culture strategy as a contributor. They need to represent it and promote it within their team.

It's also important to recognize that it's a harder job because:

It's a broader responsibility – There is an enormous number of tasks that need to be managed. Managers must be able to figure out how to juggle this.

This may look overwhelming for them. But remember, they're not alone. They have a team. That means they can complete the tasks and responsibilities through various means:

They have the option of deciding how the tasks get done in the team – They need to figure out how to juggle the balance of completing tasks by either: doing it themselves, delegating, or building a system around it.

Throughout all of this, it's crucial to recognize:

You can't micromanage a manager – You can't force a manager to do it your way. Different managers will do things differently, and this may make you feel uncomfortable because you're not sure whether it's going to work out. Get over it. Actually, if you find yourself having to do this, you'll likely get exhausted from this, or you have the wrong manager.

You can guide them with bigger picture goals – Provide bigger picture landmarks and let them figure out how to achieve them. That's what their job is.

We want to encourage and establish a dynamic of:

Upward management – Let them evaluate what they need from you. Have them get used to working with the following mindset: give me X, so that I can do Y.

There will be times when you notice issues and want to get in the middle of the team. But it's important to:

Follow the chain of command – This means don't skip the chain.

Otherwise, you'll mess with the manager's dynamic with their team, which may eliminate their collaboration, self-direction, and problem solving. Your personal involvement can interfere with their dynamic. However, issues within their team can still arise, and it's important to deal with them by:

Working through the manager, not around them – If an issue arises, coach the manager on how to deal with it. Otherwise, you're messing with their "groove" and team dynamic.

If you get the right trusting and coaching dynamic with your manager, you'll gain a side benefit: improved visibility and monitoring of their team.

- **It's a great way to keep tabs on what's going on** – Ever since I did it this way, I know more about their teams without being there. This provides much more visibility than when you solely or excessively depend on metrics. This is because the coaching dynamic involves discussing current challenges, which provides visibility to issues that are deeper than metrics, such as team-related issues.

- **It identifies issues long before they become a serious problem** – By identifying these issues earlier on, it becomes easier to address them proactively, before they become real problems.

14.2. Strategy

Now that you have built the infrastructure to effectively oversee multiple self-directed teams through your managers, what next? You need to point them in the right direction! Otherwise they will go forward with their own uncoordinated directions and miss out on tremendous value that can be created from strategy. With well-thought-out strategic directions and coordinated efforts, we can amplify the levered results that are generated from our self-directed teams.

But strategy is another word that tends to create confusion. Everyone has a different definition and understanding of it. So, let's get on the same page with what it is with an overview. Furthermore, it will be described in more detail in Part V.

Set the Guiding Light for the Organization

Leaders can breathe life into a soulless environment by setting the tone of the organization. By doing so, they can bring in hope, vision, and inspiration. It's important to set the overall strategic direction and the guiding light that everyone should move toward. To do this, it all starts with:

> **Gaining a solid understanding of the current reality** – It's important to understand the current situation to strategize how to move forward. Defining this reality involves multiple perspectives including understanding the internal and external landscape, reading trends, anticipating upcoming challenges, conceptualizing possible solutions, cross-referencing tactics, applying business instincts, balancing larger scale priorities, and so on.

We don't live in a perfect world. Oftentimes, the situation can use improvement. If we can conceptualize a more favorable situation, then we can work toward that strategic direction. Ask yourself, how can we make things better? As we dive deeper into these thoughts, it's important to do the following:

- **While simultaneously being a realist, be a dreamer!** – This is the vision and the dream. It's important for the leader to understand that there are better ways than how things are done now. This doesn't mean being airy fairy, naïve, or green. This actually involves sizing up the scope of the situation by understanding how difficult the solution will be by cross-referencing it with reality.

- **Have both opportunity-driven and purpose-driven aspects to the overall strategy** – A strategic vision should capture market opportunities but also be purpose driven. If we only design opportunity-driven strategies, there's not much substance to engage everyone with. Ask yourself, what impact do we want to make as an organization? Where are the current opportunities?

- **Have a clear understanding of what this means** – It's important to understand how everything connects together. Strategic visions are very complex, and it's important to understand how different teams play their part. Otherwise, it's easy to get confused and wander in unpredictable directions.

None of this matters if you cannot help people see what you see. However, therein lies another form of challenge. Communicating these complex thoughts is a difficult task. When we conceptualize an overarching strategic direction, we have to get everyone on the same page. Here are some tips to accomplish this:

- **Define reality for people** – After conceptualizing a strong understanding of the current situation, one of the actions of a leader is to define this reality for people. A lot of people need help with seeing the reality of the situation. They hunger for that clarity. The leader can help people understand the current situation.

- **Understand the pain, challenges, and obstacles** – The stronger the pain of the current reality, the more you can build awareness. Make it tangible for the people. Help them see and feel this, then they can believe it. Help them realize that it doesn't have to be this way.

- **Help them connect the dots** – A strategic vision can be overwhelming for people. That's why it's important for the leader to help them connect the dots by breaking it down into bite-sized milestones and providing major landmarks. That makes it much easier to understand. Additionally, it creates "safe" boundaries to apply their own strategic thinking.

There are going to be major challenges along the way, so it's important to have the spirit to persevere and endure. People will look toward the leader for guidance, so it's important to have endurance. This involves being proactive and staying in front of the issues, rather than getting backfooted or reactive.

It's important to be very intentional when communicating the vision and its major milestones. Otherwise, there's a high likelihood of confusion or lack of buy-in. Here's a couple overly cautious examples when communicating the strategic direction to the organization.

- "We'll do XYZ and see what happens."
- "Let's go incremental."

This form of communication may be more precise because we don't know exactly what will happen, but you'll likely fail to get the buy-in and clarity that you need to pull a strategy forward. Such language is more appropriate for discussing in-depth nuances during strategy formulation.

To Work toward the Vision, Develop Strategy Skills in Others

Now that we've established the current reality and shared the vision, we need to make it come to life by getting everyone moving in the same direction! To accomplish this, we have to get past the notion that strategy is for the "big wigs" or that it's an exclusive skillset. That is a prescriptive approach that ultimately leads to confusion and lack of buy-in. We have to make strategy more accessible. That means we have to encourage team-level strategies.

> **Promote team-level strategies** – This involves the co-creation of strategies and collaborative involvement of relevant parties. This creates advantages by maximizing alignment, collaboration, engagement, and buy-in. In addition, there is improved execution and adaptability exhibited by the teams.

However, we can't jump right into this if people haven't been sufficiently developed. This requires the teams and managers to meet the leader in the middle. But that won't happen unless we develop them. This approach requires development of the strategy skills of people. On first glance, this can seem like a daunting task. But let's break it down.

- **Universal collaboration skills** – Many efforts in culture strategy were a prelude to enabling strategic capabilities within teams. The improved engagement, collaboration, and management skills are essential building blocks to further develop strategic skills within teams. That's because team-level strategies encompass a great deal of this. Therefore, evaluate whether there is sufficient people infrastructure to build strategy skills within teams.

- **Strategic thinking skills** – Developing strategic thinking within people can be a challenging process. Though there are people who have natural inclinations for this skillset, most people struggle with it because strategic thinking involves working with the unknown, the future, and the abstract. This is not comfortable for the majority of the population because most people tend to think in the present and have tangible thoughts. Fortunately, we don't need advanced strategic thinking out of everyone, but we do need at least the basics.

- **Essential strategy hard skills** – This involves going through the strategic planning process to develop team-level strategies. Oftentimes, a facilitative approach can work well in guiding relevant strategy topics, even if everyone isn't an expert in strategic planning. This has a major advantage in bringing together relevant parties to develop the team-level strategies. This can include tacticians, cross-functional support, sponsors, executioners, and so on. Carefully assess which perspectives are really needed and bring the necessary parties together.

Leaders need to make situational assessments of the strategic capabilities of the teams when they decide how much to involve them and when it's "safe" to let go. This should be done with a "crawl, walk, run" mentality, and shouldn't abdicate team-level strategies too quickly, nor should leaders avoid getting teams involved and developing them. In fact, in earlier stages, leaders will likely need to get involved in developing and coaching strategic skills in others.

Understanding why people resist participating in strategy. Getting people involved in strategy is easier said than done. There's usually a lot of resistance with this from people. I found that the root cause of resistance is typically tied to deeper psychological blockers associated with upbringing, painful experiences, being told no throughout their entire lives, or never achieving anything they hoped for (making hope into a painful topic). They're also concerned that they will get their thoughts shot down, accidently overcommit their position, and step on their boss's toes to get labeled as the "black sheep," or expose other vulnerabilities. Help them overcome these factors by:

- **Diving deeper** – Explore why they avoid thinking about the future.

- **Creating "safe zones"** – Make it safe because this can be a scary topic for most people.

- **Overcoming psychological blockers** – This may require helping people confront their inner inhibiting factors.

- **Establishing mutual trust** – A mutually trusting environment is essential for this to work, due to exposing vulnerabilities from both sides.

Leaders should create an environment that enables and energizes others to dream and develop their own personal aspirations along with team strategies. Then, work with them to achieve their own goals by overlapping areas of alignment between personal and organizational goals. This creates the greatest engagement with the strategy of the organization because their own aspirations are vested into the company's goals.

Maintaining the Ecosystem for Strategy to Thrive

One of the things that took me a long time to realize is that strategy in the modern era is different. In the past, it was all about creating a prescriptive higher-level strategy, and disseminating it for people to do. That doesn't work as effectively in today's society, as it is extremely rigid and unadaptable. Such outdated strategic approaches are beginning to cause many organizations to have a downward spiral because they lose relevance in the market for customers and talent.

To adapt, we need to establish a paradigm shift of strategy to an alignment focus. This involves combining a refined enterprise-level strategy and integrating it with team-level strategies. When we do this, we gain the potential to harness value from well-positioned strategies as well as improved adaptability and engagement. To promote this, we should:

- **Maintain an ecosystem of strategy at all levels** – This means we need to be open to encourage team-level strategies. Even if they're not ready yet or their skill levels aren't refined, there should be an adequate effort to develop them.

    This also requires making cross-functional decisions at a higher level to promote the ecosystem of team-level strategies. This involves the advocation of a partnership mentality to create margin, transparency, strategic alignment, strategic skill development, and bottom-up management when appropriate. Multiple departments play a role in this.

- **Align team-level strategies with the enterprise-level strategy** – Team-level strategies need to integrate with the higher-level strategy to ensure that everyone's going in the same direction. Though we want the individual teams to have their own strategy, it cannot be designed as an isolated silo. It still needs to integrate with the rest of the organization.

    As various strategies are formulated, there will be competing priorities due to differing goals and perspectives. This needs to be balanced and prioritized because resources need to be allocated for different strategies. This is because there are limited resources in the organization. Therefore, it's essential to get alignment on the holistic viewpoint to get everyone on the same page, maximize collaboration, and minimize political disputes.

There can be a tremendous amount of value in developing strategic capabilities in others, as it enables sustainable long-term problem solving within teams and managers. It significantly reduces the dependencies on the leader for direction of the organization, as they are contributing to the direction as well. In addition, by aiding in co-creation of the future, issues with buy-in and alignment are greatly reduced.

14.3. Mobilizing People from an Outside Position

If you take a moment and think about it, successfully creating self-directed teams and stepping out by deploying managers creates a new challenge and paradox. Since the self-directed team is already doing things themselves, you may notice that if you direct them, it interferes with their flow!

So, how do you capture levered value or push for a strategic direction then? You're right in recognizing that you would have to mobilize them in a different way, so you don't mess with their groove. This requires a paradigm shift in how you approach the teams. You need to mobilize with *insights*, *influence*, and *buy-in* as opposed to directives.

When we guide their insights and get their buy-in, the self-directed teams will problem solve to fill in missing gaps and implement accordingly. These approaches provide direction without being prescriptive. The resulting difference is that they own their own solution.

Because this is insight-based, it's important to understand the overlapping principles behind this philosophy of mobilization and adult learning. With that in mind, you'll have to overcome the following challenges:

- Knowledge transfer is difficult.
- Traditional approaches do not maximize knowledge absorption.
- Attention is a limited resource.
- People absorb information differently.

That means we need to have our meetings and announcements designed to maximize resonance.

> *"What you hear, you forget. What you see, you remember.*
> *What you do, you understand."*
>
> —T. Harv Eker

Riding this wave will require a different mindset and skillset. Here are a couple approaches that companies have adopted within their regular practice.

- **Facilitative meetings** – This is opposed to having prescriptive meetings. This utilizes collaborative problem solving to optimize a plan of attack and co-creating solutions, which maximizes buy-in.

- **Mobilizing presentations** – This is opposed to prescriptive announcements and directives. This utilizes presentations that focus on connecting, stories, visual representations, and so on. This is designed to maximize knowledge absorption, resonance, and buy-in.

Some companies have implemented unique practices within regular meetings, including modification of traditional forms of meetings and announcements to adopt alternative practices that maximize resonance. Let's explore a couple adaptations.

- **Visual meetings** – This form of facilitative meetings uses visuals rather than written notes because more people understand and follow along better with images than with words.

- **Narrative memos** – This form of meeting uses short storytelling memos to describe a situation rather than using PowerPoint presentations. It appeals to the human instinct of learning and transferring knowledge through stories rather than slides and bullet points.

Obviously, you should do what makes sense for your organization. Just bear in mind that traditional approaches may have some limitations when mobilizing self-directed teams, and it may be worth considering a different approach if you're not getting the resonance and engagement.

Facilitative Meetings

The main purpose of facilitative meetings is to promote untarnished problem solving during meetings. This is to harness the pure essence of ideas and skills of the people whom you've come to trust and depend on. This can be difficult when you are their boss because you have a stake in their results and hold their job at bay. This requires earning the trust as if you are their "nonsupervisory" facilitator even though you still are their supervisor, which is a very delicate balance.

The greatest advantage of "nonsupervisory" facilitation is that it preserves the autonomy of self-directed teams and maximizes their engagement during this co-planning process. This gives ample opportunities for people to participate and refine their thought processes. Because they co-created the plan, they will know it inside and out, which improves their buy-in (obviously, since it's their own ideas), and can adapt the plan to changing scenarios. This further improves the success rate of their efforts.

This is accomplished through structured discussions to guide focused problem solving and to minimize derailing situations. This maintains the environment for collaborators to problem solve and develop solutions, while maintaining the essence of the self-directed teams. I find this to be an extremely delicate process, just like coaching. In fact, I find it an even more delicate and refined skill than coaching.

One of the goals of facilitation is to avoid monopolizing the discussion to capture the essence of people's ideas, which can be very difficult. Imagine that you are leading a facilitation to gather ideas to solve a situation, but a lot of silly ideas come out. It can be hard to avoid saying things like, "Hey, that wasn't the best idea that you came up with" and slamming them down, which signals everyone to shut up and agree with you. Another killer of problem solving is saying the words, "Prove it," which is often said when the validity of a statement is questionable.

Remember, facilitation is very different from simply having meetings to discuss and getting everyone to agree. In the latter, it is very typical for a few dominant extroverts to dominate the conversation while others remain quiet. When one of them brings something up, they get shot down and end up agreeing with the dominant person at the end. This results in a plan with minimal perspectives, lack of engagement, lack of alignment, and continued challenges with adaptability when changes are thrown at the team. In fact, bosses are usually guilty of doing this the most.

> **The boss and facilitator paradox.** It's difficult to establish a "safe zone" when the boss is facilitating because they have control over whether the contributor keeps their job in the company.

Bosses end up doing this because they believe the ideas brought up are inferior and they don't want the meeting to derail with incompetent ideas, so they overtake opposing ideas. However, this is due to a perpetual underdevelopment of the contributors because the contributors haven't had a chance to refine their thinking skills, or they lack sufficient overall knowledge of the situation. It may also signal gaps in the facilitator's skills.

Bosses also overtake facilitation sessions due to a lack of foresight in the value of alignment. Oftentimes they do not see when the value of alignment exceeds that of the idea. Personally, I've found that the long-term economic value of alignment is often superior to that of the quality of the idea (as long as the idea is going in the right general direction), due to greater adaptability, ownership, and opportunities for continuous development of the contributors, especially as they learn from their mistakes.

Facilitation Tips

Any honest facilitator has had sessions go south and derail, especially when they are newer to facilitation. Oftentimes, this is a result of opening up everything for discussion. To prevent this, the facilitator must know exactly what is open for discussion and what is not. If we are too loose with this, it could easily lead to loss of control of the situation. It is recommended to put the exact topic for discussion into the agenda and maintain those boundaries.

A skilled facilitator must be prepared to handle various situations. They can be faced with challenging scenarios that can interfere with facilitation, including people who do not speak, people who always speak first, and people who won't stop talking and get off topic. Here are some additional considerations that they have to keep in mind:

- **Connecting with the collaborators** – This is important for getting engagement, getting real ideas out, balancing the perspective, and engaging the quieter ones.

- **Setting the tone** – It's important to set the tone right by making it safe to participate, following processes, and following any rules of engagement.

- **Staying on track** – At times, there may be a need to deal with problem people, manage derails or rabbit holes, put certain discussions on the "parking lot" to revisit later, and so on.

A facilitator's role is not to contaminate the process with their ideas but facilitate the group's ideas. Actually, a great facilitator does not participate in the ideation, and the best ones maintain a "nonsupervisory" feel during the facilitation. Therefore, it is not uncommon for a facilitator to delegate the following:

- **Scribe** – Preparing and sending out agendas, notes, recordings, minutes.

- **Champion** – Identifying calls to action, measurables, deadlines, follow-ups.

- **Sergeant** – Time keeping, meeting logistics, making sure it starts on time.

This allows the facilitator to purely focus on the facilitation and not get distracted. This also reduces the "supervisory" feel, which can improve the probability that true facilitation is achieved. Sometimes, if it makes practical sense, even the facilitation can be delegated to a third party, especially for more complicated situations.

Overall, organizations with facilitative meetings have more effective solutions, engagement, and execution. It creates a competitive edge over organizations that are using prescriptive meetings. This will manifest in the form of continuous adaptation, innovation, and sustainable self-direction.

Mobilization through Presentations

There are times when a leader must reach goals by influencing a larger number of people at once. In such cases, facilitative meetings may not be the technique of choice, and presentations become more effective. However, this isn't about having a professional PowerPoint slide deck and demonstrating expertise on highly complicated topics. The goal should be to optimally deliver a message that will get the audience to mobilize and produce results. If this is the goal, then it becomes increasingly evident that connecting with the audience is essential in achieving results. The message needs to resonate with the audience, connect with them, optimize engagement, get buy-in, and provide clarity.

It is very important for the presenter to be clear with the goal of the presentation. Usually, "to share information" is not a compelling enough reason to successfully engage an audience. Have a purpose or a goal that you're trying to accomplish, and then sell it. This can involve getting buy-in to a strategy, mobilizing people, selling the value of a product, getting approval for the project, or whatever else you are faced with. When that becomes clear to the presenter, the psychology of the persuasion becomes paramount and is built into the structure of the presentation.

Simplification of the message and optimal engagement techniques such as storytelling help to connect with the audience. It's not about the slide deck, looking smart, or getting excessively granular. These can actually be deterrents to engaging an audience for the goal of the presentation.

Many leaders actively develop and refine their public speaking and storytelling skills. This is because these skills become more relevant as their scope of responsibilities increases because their role has a greater reliance on mobilizing people and getting buy-in. By increasing engagement levels during their presentations, they can make a larger impact. Various techniques can be employed to maximize engagement, such as:

- Utilizing exercises such as icebreakers, demonstrations, and facilitation breakouts.

- Utilizing presentation soft skills to their advantage such as posture, tone, body language, and elimination of "ummms." These can be important skills that can be learned and practiced.

Advanced Leadership Techniques

The role and possibilities of leadership can be limitless. Beyond these facilitation and mobilization tools, there are other techniques that leaders can use to leverage more value from people and teams. Here are a few additional advanced techniques that leaders can apply to create even more value:

Form Strategic Alliances

Form strategic alliances to tackle common issues bigger than your team(s) can handle alone. There can be a large problem that is impacting your business that is bigger than the scope of what your team(s) can handle. In such cases, it wouldn't be surprising to see that it's a common problem for others as well. By creating strategic alliances, which can be within the organization or even outside it, you can tackle a common challenge that no one can address by themselves. This way, you can group the resources, expertise, capabilities, and networks of multiple formidable allies to vanquish a common challenge, so that everyone can benefit.

Build a Community

This can be used to create exceptional value for the organization. That's because people don't just want a job in life. They want to be a part of something bigger than themselves. Community building can help with that by providing purpose and camaraderie. This increases the sense of purpose, improves engagement, deepens relationships with companionship, becomes a support group for similar challenges, and promotes work-life integration. This inherently helps with cross-pollination of knowledge, networks, and capabilities. When you bring people together as a community, you frequently encounter another added benefit of creating new innovative trajectories in business. You never know what synergistic value will come about when you mix a community of people together.

Become a Thought Leader

Leaders can become a thought leader to promote ideas that can synergistically benefit the business. Establishing authority over a topic builds credibility, which can help in outreach to customers, educating customers, outreach for recruitment, and standardizing internal education. It can even lead to additional capabilities, processes, business lines, or other opportunities.

This added credibility could help your organization by reducing barriers when acquiring new customers or talent. Not only that, it will help you get better quality ones. This is because you will get the ones who intentionally sought you out based on your expertise and credibility. This will help you differentiate yourself from your competitors. It even builds retention and loyalty from your customers or talent. This can be done through various vehicles including presentations, coaching, consulting, online vehicles, articles, books, and so on.

In Summary

In this chapter, we've discussed essential skills for leaders who manage multiple teams. These leadership skills utilize a different set of control levers that allow you to run multiple teams more efficiently and with less time, energy, and stress involvement.

True leaders develop other managers and leaders. You now know the importance of choosing managers who align with the culture strategy, and who you can then coach to engage their inner drive, regardless of their personality type. Trust is critical, as is strategy, in setting a guiding light for the organization. You can communicate that through facilitative meetings that promote problem solving, and advanced leadership techniques that create even more value. How, though, do we really connect culture with strategy? How do we create an environment that allows strategy to thrive at all levels? That's what we'll discuss in Part V.

PART V

CONNECTING CULTURE WITH STRATEGY

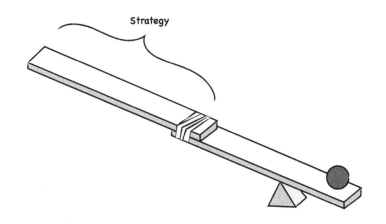

Strategy

GETTING TEAMS ON BOARD WITH STRATEGIC THINKING

Imagine this scenario: You have conceptualized a high-level strategy and want to implement it across the organization. You've gathered information regarding the current reality, utilized strategic frameworks, and conceptualized a strategic vision. Now, you want to get it implemented, and you want to discuss the tactical considerations with your team to have it executed.

You host a meeting to introduce the strategic direction and try to facilitate it. However, your managers and teams are not engaged. In fact, whenever they bring up ideas, they are bad ideas, and you have to shoot them down. This causes the room to get quiet, and it becomes awkward. Eventually, a brave soul finally speaks up, and you don't think it's a bad idea this time. So, you compliment that idea and everyone agrees. It gets decided that everyone will follow that idea.

However, as time progresses, the results are not satisfactory. You set up additional meetings, but they are just as unproductive as the first meeting. Your job is not feeling satisfactory, and the team members are not happy. You feel like you are herding cats. You begin asking yourself:

"Why can't I get everyone moving in the same direction?"

"What's going wrong?"

"Why can't we strategize and get on the same page?"

Now this time, imagine a different scenario. An overarching strategic direction was set and everyone is bought in. Most teams create their own strategic plans for review and approval. Only a few of the teams need closer handholding for planning. Different teams and departments are collaboratively working together to implement their plans, rather than having internal disputes. Feedback and approval are given based upon financial and strategic alignment considerations. Throughout implementation, you give guidance and support only where needed.

So, what's the difference? Why did the latter situation go so much smoother? Answering that involves going deeper into how strategy works.

15.1. Understanding the Strategy Chasm

Believe it or not, this is a common dilemma that exists between strategic senior leaders and operational managers. It actually leads to a great deal of frustration between such individuals. It happens more often than many leaders realize, and they are not alone in encountering such situations. Unfortunately, many strategic leaders have succumbed to believing that this is just the way it is. They think it's inevitable. That is not the case. It's only true if we don't reevaluate how we do things. It's one of those things that needs to be approached from a different angle.

To explain this phenomenon, we have to understand the paradox of the *strategy chasm*. If we understand this better, we have an improved chance of bridging this chasm. Long story short, it all boils down to differences in how people think and process the world. Strategists often think from a futuristic, abstract, and bigger picture perspective, whereas operational managers often think in present and tangible steps.

This may sound trivial at first, but personally I think it can be the most challenging tension point to reconcile.

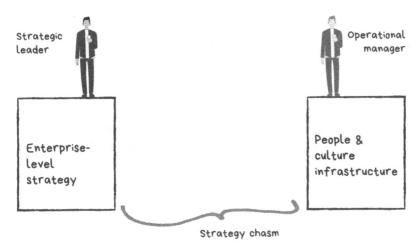

Visualization of the strategy chasm

When we acknowledge this, we can shift our focus to understanding the components to bridge this gap. Let's take a look at a diagram of this. You'll notice how the initial building blocks are culture infrastructure and enterprise-level strategy. We need to start with this to have a fighting chance.

- It all begins with *culture infrastructure* – This is why we spent the greater part of the book discussing how to build culture infrastructure. Strategy is actually the leverage of culture infrastructure.

- Well-positioned *enterprise-level strategy* – We need to have a well-designed and well-positioned enterprise-level strategy to set the tone and overall direction of the organization. It becomes the guiding light for people to work toward. Though we touched on this briefly in some aspects of the book, we will spend more time on it in the final chapter.

Understanding Why Team-Level Strategies Are Dependent on a Conducive Culture

Enabling team-level strategies requires a well-developed culture. This is because strategies require an extremely broad spectrum of perspectives for problem solving. However, it could result in more instances of disagreements and conflicts. This will require a higher standard of collaboration among people to reconcile this. Furthermore, there needs to be buy-in and engagement for an environment that promotes strategy at all levels. Many organizations attempt to force this strategic capability prematurely. They struggle and fail to harness this value, while not realizing what the real issue is.

Additionally, this requires managers and leaders to be skilled at managing people's ideas and proposals. Unfortunately, leaders are often the ones who kill this environment without realizing it. They often have the habit of steamrolling others or habitually giving advice without developing others' ideas. Rather than doing this, it's important to:

- Be a coach to develop others' thinking skills
- Ask and listen to their thoughts
- Guide the development of their ideas through questions, rather than directing or giving advice
- If their ideas have gaps, help them see it, and let them revise their own ideas

Once we have the initial building blocks in place, we need to bridge the strategy chasm with intentional efforts. This requires involvement from both sides with a partnership mentality by meeting in the middle. This doesn't work if only one side is expected to cross the entire chasm by themselves.

From the team's perspective (managers and team members), we need to be committed in improving strategic skills. This involves:

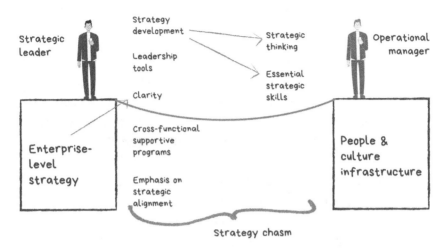

Visualization of the components to bridge the strategy chasm

- Getting involved with *strategic thinking* – This involves developing the mindset to think in the future, possibilities, and uncertainty. Oftentimes, this involves facing psychological blockers that are inhibiting them from doing so. We will be spending the remainder of this chapter discussing this.

- Building and applying *essential strategy skills* – There are many essential hard skills involved in strategy to initiate it, plan it, and execute it. These skills can be applied during facilitative sessions and throughout everyday moments during implementation. We discuss these considerations further in the next chapter.

From the leadership's perspective, we need to focus on the following:

- *Develop strategy skills* within teams – This involves the development of both strategic thinking and essential skills. It requires giving the teams a chance to get involved in strategy as well as providing situational development and guidance. It also involves setting the right tone by maintaining a conducive environment that guides discussions while maintaining the "safety" of involvement.

- *Apply leadership skills* to engage and mobilize teams – Strategy requires the same leadership principles that have already been described throughout the book. Even in strategy, we need to maintain the mindset of using everyday moments for coaching and development. We have to apply leadership tools to facilitate and mobilize self-directed teams from an "outside" position. That means we can't steamroll everyone and overtake discussions.

- *Create clarity* on the enterprise-level strategy – Just because we created an enterprise-level strategy, it doesn't mean that others understand it. Enterprise-level strategies embody complex thoughts that need to be simplified for easier consumption. We also need to create clarity on how it applies to different people and teams. We will discuss this in the final chapter.

- *Adjust cross-functions* to support an ecosystem of team-level strategies – Cross-functional processes and support programs can impact the initiation and sustainability of team-level strategies. It is worth reevaluating whether they are either supporting or inhibiting the ecosystem for team-level strategies. This is further described in Chapter 17.

- Emphasize a partnership mentality to maximize the interface between enterprise-level strategy and team-level strategies for *strategic alignment* – When we enable team-level strategies, we have to ensure that we also achieve alignment with the enterprise-level strategy. This will require mutual trust and a partnership mentality when we initiate, plan, and execute strategies. This is because there will be vulnerable moments that require mutual trust to overcome as we make decisions throughout the strategic process on how we provide resources, knowledge capabilities, and transparency to information. We will discuss this further in Chapter 17.

Bridging This Chasm Unlocks Levered Value

Just by transforming the organization into a healthier and conducive culture, we've already unlocked tremendous value by creating self-directed teams and increasing engagement, buy-in, sense of purpose, situational problem solving, and adaptation. However, we can unlock further value by integrating strategy throughout the organization, which increases the leverage of the people infrastructure that we've built. This is because we are creating additional value through:

- **Riding market trends** – No one can deny that exceptional value can be captured by riding market trends. Integrating strategy allows us to extrapolate this as an organization more effectively.

- **Creating synergy between teams** – Whether it's through cross-pollination from similar functions, improved collaboration between cross-functions, or even better integration of processes, synergistic value can be captured by strategically positioning teams. This is one form of value that many traditional organizations struggle to harness due to the collaboration breakdown that occurs between their teams.

- **Maximizing value and reducing risk** – Through successfully implemented team-level strategies, we can generate more value by providing solutions with more market relevance, proactive thinking, situational problem solving, and greater engagement from the teams. We also exhibit a reduced number of issues and problems that tend to arise, thereby reducing risk.

- **Creating innovative solutions** – New and unexpected value can be created through innovative problem solving. This occurs by enabling people, which provides more eyes, minds, and hands to create solutions that would otherwise not have been conceptualized.

When you combine these benefits together, it can be extremely impactful. Imagine having an organization that looks ahead and can move in the same overall direction, while maintaining the ability to situationally adapt at various levels and still maintain alignment. This can establish self-directed growth and long-term viability for the organization by becoming a powerful infrastructure to sustain scalability and growth. We can even establish significant growth trajectories that you did not expect were possible. Ask yourself, "What's that worth to me?"

15.2. Enabling Strategic Thinking at Every Level

The definition and connotations of strategy are used loosely. Different people and organizations seem to have their own definition, which can cause confusion. This actually introduces needless blockers and debates.

Let's get on the same page for the sake of reading this book. At the end of the day, it's not about what these things are called. If you want to call it something else in your work, feel free to do so. Rather than focusing on the nomenclature of different approaches, it's important that the necessary actions are being done.

- **Strategy** – This broader term describes all topics of strategy. This involves the skills in strategy (thinking and essential skills), different phases (initiation, planning, execution), different levels (team-level and enterprise level), and approaches (linear versus alignment-focused).

- **Enterprise-level strategy** – This is the higher-level strategy usually defined by senior leaders. This is the overarching strategic direction of the organization.

- **Team-level strategy** – These smaller scope strategies are used at team levels to proactively plan their own goals. This should be aligned with the enterprise-level strategy.

- **Strategic thinking** – These skills are involved with thinking ahead. This should occur throughout every level and every activity. This is also known as proactive thinking or innovative thinking.

Strategic Thinking Involves Thinking about the Future

In its very essence, strategic thinking involves thinking about a desired future state and working toward it. It includes identifying issues before they occur and proactively addressing them. This involves imagining what's possible, conceptualizing the outcome before actually doing it, and working toward the endgame.

It's about thinking about the end first.

This tends to be a more theoretical and abstract skill than it is a concrete skill. This is because it lacks a tangible component, as it involves the future.

Though there are those who naturally spend their time and energy thinking about the future, most people tend to focus on the present and past. A lot of people have challenges thinking about the future and conceptualizing what they want. Most do not have the habit of thinking that far ahead, and only do it when asked or trained to do so. This is an important skill to develop when you want to be on the same page in strategy.

Strategic Thinking Involves Everything We Do

One of the misconceptions that people have about strategic thinking is that it only occurs in an isolated planning phase in the beginning. Either that, or they think it only involves senior executives who formulate overarching enterprise-level strategies. However, that can't be further from the truth because it can involve everyone and encompass everything that we do.

It's not just for the "big wigs" or the executives.

When we develop a widespread mentality to envision goals, plan for them, and strive for them, we can unlock additional capabilities. This mindset can be applied to anything. Therefore, it makes sense to get the teams involved with strategic thinking. This can manifest in multiple forms, which can create benefits for the organization by:

- **Applying it in day-to-day tasks and execution** – This can help identify reoccurring issues that can be addressed and have new solutions adapted to the plan to navigate around such obstacles. Furthermore, this improves ownership, situational adaptation, partnership mentality with a bottom-up management approach, and better precision for allocating resources.

- **Applying it by co-creating strategic plans to increase perspectives, alignment, and engagement** – Co-creating strategic plans can improve alignment and merge multiple perspectives to create better solutions. This includes perspectives from the sponsorship-level, cross-functional, execution-related, and team-level considerations. Furthermore, we also increase the engagement level and situational adaptability of the teams when we co-create plans.

- **Applying it in unexpected avenues!** – When we choose to intentionally develop strategic skills within others, it can create new trajectories in value that can yield significant dividends by improving results in unexpected ways and encouraging the discovery of unexplored possibilities.

Widespread Strategic Thinking Involves Trusting and Letting Go

We just described the benefits of decentralizing strategic decisions to your teams. This means that we need to let go more, be vulnerable, and lean in to trust your managers and teams. Now, some organizations have genuine concerns that by involving more individuals in strategic thinking, it can increase the risk exposure of the organization due to a lack of consensus, inviting chaos, and generating suboptimal plans.

It is true that it doesn't make sense to decentralize everything by getting everyone involved for everything under the sun. First, that doesn't make logistical sense. Second, it does open up vulnerability points. However, most organizations tend to overcentralize strategic decisions, thereby creating side effects of misalignment, lack of perspectives, and lack of engagement. To get past this and move forward, we need to be aware that:

There is a paradox between centralizing
and decentralizing decisions.

There needs to be a distinction between acceptable and unacceptable risk. A good practice is to centralize extremely critical and delicate strategic issues. If feasible, we should aim to decentralize anything else when it is possible. If the teams haven't developed sufficient strategic skills yet, we should work to eventually get them there. Below are some guidelines that can help you decide what to centralize and decentralize. In general, it is better to centralize if there is:

- **Involvement of highly impactful decisions or risks** – Examples of such risks can include:
  - *Impact risk* – Key large-scale strategic decisions that can be the difference between setting the direction of the organization for success or failure.
  - *Financial risk* – Critical resource allocation decisions that involve considerable financial investments or those that can impact the preservation of liquidity for sustainability.

- *Time duration risk* – Critical long-term strategies that involve an extremely long run time to materialize (for example, several years or even decades).
- *Market risk* – Critical market positioning decisions that can make or break the company.

- **A conflict of interest or sensitive/confidential information** – Decisions that involve confidential information should still be centralized.

- **An underdevelopment of strategy skills within your managers/ teams** – If this is the case, don't decentralize too much too soon, but rather focus on incrementally increasing involvement, promoting strategic thinking in our everyday moments, and developing them through coaching/facilitation.

This can create a guideline to help insulate that risk, while still maintaining an environment to promote and develop team-level strategies. Even still, strategic skill levels within managers/teams can continuously be developed to eventually get more of their involvement in critical decisions.

Setting Up Strategic Thinking for Success

To enable these capabilities, we need to create an environment that embraces strategic thinking at all levels. This doesn't occur accidently, nor does it occur by forcing people to do it. First, we need to reassess the maturity of the culture.

If the culture is not adequately developed,
then refocus on developing the culture.

After that, you have to make an intentional effort to make room for strategy. Strategy does not occur naturally and organically. It involves resources and margin, whether it be through pulling time and energy from people out of their current work demands or building separate teams for it. Other times, margin can be created by identifying inefficiencies and improving them.

> Create *margin* – Strategic thinking can't occur when we're barely keeping our heads above water. We need to create margin for it and proactively block out time for strategy.

Then, we also have to ensure that the organization is set up to encourage widespread strategic thinking. We can do this through a combination of means:

- Encourage using "white space" for strategic thinking – Key individuals should block out time to think strategically. This is a chance to do research, understand trends, and conceptualize solutions so they can consider implementing them or bring them to the discussion table.

- Have a healthy schedule of facilitation-focused meetings where strategy can be discussed – Having the appropriate format and frequency of facilitation-focused meetings is a great way for companies to get on the same page and coordinate. This is a great place to foster and guide strategic thinking within others.

- Reinforce and refine others' strategic thinking in your everyday moments – There will be countless situational moments where there are opportunities to coach and develop strategic thinking within people. Live it and breathe it in your everyday moments. Encourage other managers and leaders to do the same, so we can reach more people.

15.3. Different Types of Strategic Thinking

Throughout the day-to-day grind of work, it's easy for people to lose touch with what's happening from a bird's-eye perspective, and how it applies to their everyday lives. It's because these are intangible factors that have a vague connection to them and their daily work. They get stuck with their routines and begin accepting it for what it is. However, to enable strategic thinking, we have to get past their current reality, and have people conceptualize a desired future state.

This involves going from a mentality of "what is" to "what if."

To enable this type of thinking, we need them to have an overall outlook to understand the current situation and anticipate trends. Once they have an understanding of that, they can conceptualize solutions. Then, they can actually work to make them come alive.

Stepping Back and Understanding the Landscape

Let's dive deeper into what we can do to understand the current situation. This involves an overview of what's happening around people beyond what they can perceive with their normal five senses from their involvement with the current team. First, we understand:

- **External considerations:** *macroeconomics* – External factors that involve macroeconomics include considerations that are beyond your or even your organization's control. This includes economic, social, technological, environmental, and political factors, and so on. We can stay in touch with these factors with research and analysis. Understand the relevant trends to identify *opportunities* to ride the wave or identify *threats* to make plans to mitigate the risk.

- **External considerations:** *microeconomics* – Microeconomic factors are considerations within your industry. This involves the overall market environment for customers, competitors, vendors, talent, and so on. We can gather such information from various customer interfaces, surveys, and market research. Understanding microeconomic factors and their trends can also identify *opportunities* to capitalize on and which *threats* to mitigate.

- **Internal considerations** – Internal factors are considerations within the organization. This can involve capabilities, processes, culture, mental capital, and so on. We can gather information through direct observations, open communication channels, data, and surveys. This helps identify *strengths* to capitalize on and *weaknesses* that should be covered.

Baseline Strategic Thinking Skill #1: Future-First Strategic Thinking

If you choose to embark upon developing strategic thinking capabilities within someone who does not naturally think in such a way, I advise coaching the future-first strategic-thinking technique because it's less technique sensitive and easier to develop in others. This form of strategic thinking involves:

> *Thinking about the future first, then moving*
> *backward and filling in the gaps.*

This involves developing two major visions: a personal vision and a team vision. Then, the focus shifts toward identifying the overlapping alignment between the two.

> *Find alignment between personal goals and team goals.*

Future-first strategic thinking has an added benefit of engaging the individual's inner core, their desires, their strengths, what they want in life, and their drive. Everyone has a gift or something unique to offer, and sometimes it's not easy to see. Other times it's not easy to bring it out. The individual should search their inner being to visualize where they want to go in life. Defining the following can help with this:

- Personal mission and vision statements
- Personal strengths and weaknesses

This requires a strong understanding of yourself, what you enjoy, what you are good at, what you don't like, and what you are bad at. Your values come into play along with your priorities. I've encountered many individuals who truly struggle searching deep in their soul to understand what they want. Sometimes there are deeper psychological blockers that are subconsciously inhibiting them from drawing it out, and they may need some help in doing so.

After they recognize their personal vision, they can begin imagining an amazing goal for the team. It should be designed to truly optimize support of the organization and serve our customers in the best manner. It should also be something they would be proud of being a part of. This has the added benefit of conceptualizing strategic solutions that are only visible from their vantage point. Here are some tips that may help with this:

- Imagine an "ideal" state for the team or envision a *moonshot* goal.
- Create a team mission and vision statement.
- Reference the enterprise-level strategy to ensure alignment.

Then, the potential alignment between the personal and team goals can be conceptualized. With this, people become highly engaged because their own personal aspirations are tied to the success of the team and organization. Then, we can work toward achieving that dream together.

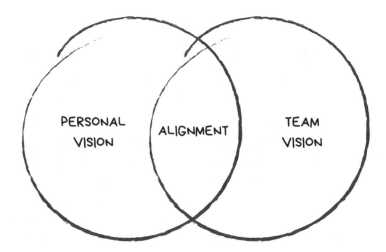

Visualization of alignment between personal and team visions

Some managers may be concerned that focusing on their contributors' long-term vision can lead them to push for a direction that's not beneficial for the organization. That is indeed possible, which is why it is good to focus on the overlap between personal goals and team goals, where there is alignment. This helps negate the risk, while at the same time maximizing engagement. Let's face it: without engaging what people want, they don't really care. So, we still need to engage their personal dreams.

All in all, this approach engages their deeper values and drives them to envision a future that they desire. The advantage to this approach of strategic thinking is that it is less technique/operator sensitive, faster, easier to train, and easier to get participation from collaborators who may not be accustomed to strategic thinking. Therefore, this is easier to scale in a widespread manner across the organization. The disadvantage of this approach to strategy is that the resulting strategies don't evaluate the feasibility of what is technically possible with precision. There is another type of strategic thinking that is more appropriate for such scenarios.

Specialized Strategic Thinking Skill: Precision-Based Strategic Thinking

There is another form of strategic thinking that has a greater amount of precision and involves an "architected" approach. This type of thinking is often used for overarching enterprise-level strategies and advanced technology product-based strategies, due to their dependence on high degrees of precision. This is because of their highly impactful nature or larger technical risk (if the idea is not technically possible, it will fail). In such situations, slight imprecision can have potentially devastating impacts. In this approach, we are building the strategy up from countless possibilities and technical considerations to determine the best possible vision. This approach yields greater precision, while simultaneously pushing the boundaries of its moving pieces to conceptualize a desired state.

Precision-based strategic thinking involves gathering the moving pieces behind several disciplines, then putting them together in a harmonious "ideal" balance to evaluate the limits of what would be possible. This is much more operator and technique sensitive as it requires skills in:

- Understanding how multiple disciplines interconnect
- Understanding the most current innovations of multiple disciplines
- Having a strong understanding of the business needs
- Interconnecting multiple disciplines to harness synergies as it relates to the business needs
- Adapting the disciplines when the needs of the business change

You start this by beginning with an overarching issue or pain point. From there, you need to identify hypothetical solutions and relevant disciplines that provide capabilities that can build into the solutions. Then, you need to identify the different philosophical approaches that can deliver on those capabilities, along with potential processes/

methodologies that deliver the tactical components of the desired approach. Then you begin a process of elimination to remove the irrelevant ones by assessing the pros/cons and interdependencies. The resulting outcome becomes the "master planned" vision.

1. **Identify the *overarching issue*** – Identify and truly understand the pain point or problem.
2. **Visualize a *hypothetical solution*** – Conceptualize potential hypothetical and meaningful solutions to the overarching issue.
3. **Identify relevant *disciplines*** – Identify all relevant disciplines that can provide capabilities that build into the hypothetical solution.
4. **Identify different *approaches*** – Identify different philosophical approaches within the disciplines that can deliver the desired capabilities.
5. **Identify various *processes* and *methodologies*** – Identify various processes/methodologies that are in line with the philosophical approaches.
6. **Evaluate the *advantages* and *disadvantages*** – This involves an analysis of the pros/cons of all the processes, approaches, and disciplines. Eliminate the ones that don't have clear benefits with a process of elimination.
7. **Understand the *competing factors*** – When you have this many moving pieces, when one of the factors gets overemphasized, it adversely impacts the others. Take a step back and understand how they compete with each other.
8. **Find a *balanced solution* that pushes the limits** – Select the most appropriate balance of processes, philosophies, and capabilities that may best optimize the solution for the overarching issue. This becomes the master plan and vision that pushes capabilities to the limit.
9. ***Test and adapt accordingly*** – Even with a well-thought-out and balanced solution, there is a need for continuous adaptation and shifting of gears, as further information reveals itself while plans get materialized and implemented.

*Inside the mind of a precision-based strategic thinker: spider diagram
of thought processes for precision-based strategic thinking*

As you read those steps, I typically get one of two responses. Either, "What the heck is this?" or "That's what I do!" If you're the former, don't worry because this is likely not expected of you unless you're heavily involved with strategic planning. If you're the latter, it may be important to recognize that the majority of people will not be able to keep up with this. This is important to recognize when you try to get on the same page with them.

As one can imagine, this approach requires a voracious uptake of information and appetite for knowledge. Not everyone has the aptitude or interest to dissect issues in this manner. In fact, most people get as far as learning a single process or approach in their entire career. This is important to recognize because one of the common problems that causes the strategy chasm is that there is an expectation from senior leaders that everyone will think in this way. Obviously, this is unrealistic.

It is important to note that there are those who naturally do this. For those who do this, strategic thinking does not only occur in organized meetings. In fact, every waking moment is a data gathering and compartmentalization exercise. That means that every hallway chat, side discussion, technical update, current event, update to macroeconomic conditions, internal/external policy, and so on are all relevant information. Then, they process all this information to create a well-thought-out solution.

The challenge of precision-based strategic thinking is that it's harder to get people bought in. Precision-based strategic thinking is highly appropriate for precision-sensitive strategies that should be centralized. However, leaders who use this form of strategic thinking usually live on the strategic side of the strategy chasm. This means that their biggest challenge isn't conceptualizing advanced strategies, it's getting others to see them and buy into them.

If you have this challenge, then try to meet them in their world rather than expecting precision-based strategic thinking from them. Encourage baseline forms of strategic thinking and focus on alignment in the middle. It will likely bear more fruit and reduce frustration.

Baseline Strategic Thinking Skill #2: Strategic Thinking in Facilitated Sessions

Facilitated strategy sessions can be a valuable tool to promote strategic thinking in others in an organized manner. These sessions use frameworks to guide members in strategic thought processes that they would otherwise have difficulty conceptualizing. These insights can be extremely valuable, as team members can apply them to all aspects of their work and be engaged in the strategic process.

Strategy frameworks can guide thinking,
realizations, and insights.

It's no secret that certain aspects of strategy can be advanced. Facilitated strategy makes it possible to get more people involved, as the frameworks help bridge strategy skill gaps.

Frameworks bridge strategy skill gaps, by making
discussions more accessible to people.

This can be utilized for many different circumstances including situational analysis, gathering information, diagnosing, digging deeper, achieving alignment, guiding thinking, exploring possibilities, co-creating solutions, and so on. This achieves benefits in many ways. It:

- Gathers an increased number of perspectives
- Improves teamwork and gets them on the same page
- Maximizes involvement, buy-in, and engagement through a co-creation process
- Maximizes alignment throughout the organization
- Offers a structured format to collaborate around a specific issue
- Offers a structured format to minimize derailing situations

This requires skillful maneuvering of facilitation techniques to introduce the relevant angles and thought processes for the team. Without a skilled strategy facilitator, it can be challenging to guide discussions with pinpoint precision and appropriate guidance as necessary. In fact, many strategy facilitators have their own library of frameworks and tools for different scenarios. We cover an overview of the strategic process in the following chapter.

Collaborators must also bring their "A game" and demonstrate universal collaboration standards. Naturally, this occurs when a conducive culture has taken root and baseline collaboration has been properly developed within people. Otherwise, such efforts are likely to be met with resistance.

By continuously developing the strategic capabilities of our people, we further strengthen the infrastructure of the organization. However, it can be tough to identify the people who have thinking skill gaps, and what those skill gaps are. You may not have access to everyone on an everyday basis, and some people hide their skill deficiencies. Through the strategy facilitation process, it is possible to uncover where the strategic thinking gaps are.

By uncovering specificities in thinking skill gaps, it can create opportunities for development. For example, strategic thinking facilitation often works in tandem with analytical, critical, and tactical thinking, and so on. By better identifying the specificities of where people have room for improvement, you can aim to develop their abilities with greater precision and success.

15.4. Managing Strategic Collaboration

To truly promote team-level strategies, it involves much more than simply trying to develop strategic thinking skills in others. It also requires fostering an environment where team-level strategies can flourish. This means setting the right tone where strategic thinking and discussions can thrive.

Setting the Tone for Strategy: Enable and Remove Blockers

To successfully build a rich environment of team-level strategies, it's important to understand the typical reasons why people don't think strategically, or why these discussions fail. It may come as a surprise to many that the most common reason for this is due to psychological blockers. These can include ego, fear, insecurities, need for control, lack of curiosity, and so on. Therefore, we need to set the right tone to unblock this. Below are ten strategic tones for success:

Strategy Rule #1: No Single Person Sees the Entire Process

It's important for everyone to understand that no single person has full visibility of the entire process. This is a valuable tone to set as it promotes teamwork and cohesion. This mindset helps promote an atmosphere of mutual respect and openness to others' ideas.

This also helps tone down the presence of bosses and domineering extroverts. Oftentimes, they can have an excessive presence that eliminates the atmosphere for ideation and collaboration. This mindset makes it easier for them to acknowledge that they may have blind spots and need to hear out additional perspectives.

This mindset also promotes greater participation for more reserved collaborators. It increases accountability for them to come up with ideas, rather than spacing out and agreeing with others. It gives them the courage to speak up as they recognize that their silence and passivity actually harm the process as they may see components that aren't visible to others.

Strategy Rule #2: Strategy Is Messy, Unknown, and Risky

Strategy is messy! It's not clean-cut. There's uncertainty because we're talking about the future. There's risk, and nothing can be known for certain because no one has a crystal ball that tells the future.

This can drive perfectionists crazy. They may find themselves unable to commit to anything due to uncertainty. Also, when things don't go according to plan, they may get very frustrated. They would need to get over this tendency to participate in strategic thinking and discussions.

Strategy Rule #3: Dare to Dream

Strategy requires thinking about the future. Some people's brain literally shuts down when they try to think about the unknown, hope, risk, and future. This may be indicative of significant psychological blockers inhibiting their mind to think in this way. Oftentimes, this may be associated with trauma or broken hope.

Therefore, it's common to see organizations that utilize culture strategy to have core values that emphasize thinking about the future. Such common values include: "dare to hope," "don't be afraid to try," and so on. Through such messaging, we can make it safe to dream and hope again. This can reactivate future-based thinking on a widespread level.

Strategy Rule #4: Failure Is One Step Closer to Success

Strategy means that we have to take chances and accept the possibility that things may not work out. We have to be okay with weighing our options and rolling the dice. It simply means that we may need to shift gears if things don't go according to plan.

Throughout this process, we will gain a stronger understanding of the situation, which will position us for a better *next play*. Of course, we should anticipate such risks beforehand and consider a *vanguard* play to test the waters before deploying full-blown investments, if applicable.

This is very difficult for some to accept because they have been indoctrinated with the idea that "you must finish what you start" and "failure is not acceptable." Though we do want to follow through with our commitments, we also have to reevaluate whether we're "betting more chips on a dying effort" or getting "analysis paralysis" from trying to prevent any form of failure at all costs.

Strategy Rule #5: Curiosity Is a Muscle to Develop

Strategy requires a continuous curiosity to want to understand things. This requires a child-like curiosity to better understand situations.

When you see young children, they constantly ask their parents "why?" Remember that child-like curiosity? Where did that go? As a society, we may have been conditioned to stop being so curious by our parents, teachers, and bosses because such curiosity was inconvenient to them. We were always being told "no," "curiosity killed the cat," and to behave. Somewhere along the way, the curiosity died out.

It's time to bring that back. It'll be difficult at first, but if you keep at it, it will come back. It's like a muscle and needs to be continuously exercised to get used to it again. Work it out!

Strategy Rule #6: Strategy Is a Bird's-Eye View

One of the key elements of strategic discussions is to have a bird's-eye overview of the situation. Some people have a habit of jumping straight into action without strategizing (usually out of action orientation). They're so used to doing things this way, and they have trouble taking a step back to look at the full picture. In fact, they may find strategic discussions to be boring and irrelevant.

The moment we jump into action mode, the strategic discussion has ended, and it becomes about tactics and execution. Then, we will fail to bring all of the ideas to the table, evaluate them, consider options, and plan accordingly. It takes discipline to stay in a bird's-eye perspective. If someone jumps into action, it has to be stopped. Then, take a step back, and reconvene the big picture discussion.

Strategy Rule #7: Be Willing to Talk about Sensitive Issues

Strategy involves the discussion of potentially sensitive issues. This can involve political issues, environmental issues, social issues, and so on. Unfortunately, if the sensitivity of the issues prevails throughout the discussion, we won't be able to collaborate on the best possible strategies.

We have to accept that it is what it is, talk about the considerations objectively, and weigh things in from a neutral perspective, so we can steer the discussion properly. It doesn't mean to be insensitive to such issues, but we must acknowledge that we have to get past them to talk strategy.

Strategy Rule #8: Co-Creating a Plan Takes Patience

Co-creating strategic plans is going to require patience. A lot of people are accustomed to *action, action, action*, and are not accustomed to collaboration. In fact, such people will think that this involves excessive discussions.

It's true that it creates more work on the front end. But it creates even more value by preventing a lot of problems on the back end throughout execution. Significant value is generated by maximizing alignment and engagement throughout the co-creation process. This in turn minimizes the escalating issues and fires that need to be put out later on because it empowers the team to adapt their solutions along the way.

So, be patient! Of course, it doesn't mean to waste each other's time either. We should definitely be efficient with our discussions and respectful of everyone's time.

Strategy Rule #9: Play Full Out in This Safe Environment

Most people perceive involvement with strategy to be a risky move. They are often concerned that they may say something "silly" and get shot down. Other times, they may accidently overcommit and be labeled as "aggressive" or as the "black sheep" of the organization.

Therefore, it's important to make this a safe environment. Avoid punishing people for participating. If anything, use derailing moments as coaching, developmental, training, or facilitation opportunities.

This is so that contributors feel comfortable to play full out. Some find it easy to let go and get involved, while others have deeply etched fears in doing so. So, be cognizant of this, and be courteous as mutual trust gets built.

Strategy Rule #10: Unite on Terminology

Terminology creates a lot more problems than you may realize. Organizations call different steps and components of strategic processes differently. Industries, professions, backgrounds, methodologies, and strategy approaches call the same components by different names. This can lead to needless debates that don't move the conversation forward.

Therefore, unite on terminology. We can't let it get in our way. It's not about what it's called. It just matters that it gets done.

Strategic Leaders versus Operational Managers/Teams: The Most Painful Tension Point

I find that the most difficult, painful, and complicating tension point exists between strategic leaders and operational managers/teams. I personally had many challenging instances where I was communicating in a completely different wavelength with implementers. This led to many problems, disagreements, and mutual disappointment. I was surprised to realize that the majority of the population does not naturally think in this way.

This was harder than reconciling the tension point with the Goal Pushers, Analysts, Enthusiasts, and Stabilizers.

Strategic thinking is an abstract skill that involves considering future possibilities. Implementers typically live in the present moment and focus on tangible tasks. The chasm between the two is so large that it takes a great amount of commitment from both ends to meet in the middle. Though this may be difficult, if you can bridge this, it can be very rewarding. It sets the stage for greater leverage within the organization.

Utilizing Situational Moments: Set People Up for Success, Not Failure

Throughout the course of our work, there will be countless circumstances where situational moments can be used to develop and reinforce strategic thinking. We can do this by *relating everything back to strategy*.

As people discuss actions and plans, it's easy to get engrossed in their current situation and forget the big picture. Therefore, it's important to relate it back to the overall strategy. *Does this help us get closer to our vision?* If the answer is no, it may be worth reconsidering. This takes some discipline.

Like any other skill, strategic thinking has a learning curve. Trying to teach advanced strategy to a strategy beginner will likely end in mutual frustration. That's like asking someone who just learned to drive a car to go on the highway. They might get themselves killed! Remember to approach this with a "crawl, walk, run" mentality.

Don't ask someone who just figured out how to use the turn signal to do a highway drive.

If you set the right tone to enable strategic thinking at team levels, prepare for an influx of ideas and proposals. At first, a lot of them may be unrefined ideas due to misdirection and myopia. Prepare to receive those ideas as coaching moments to help contributors assess the risk, refine their thoughts, see the big picture, and prioritize. We can also couple this with training. Otherwise, we may inadvertently shoot ideas down and kill the safety of proposals, and it may become difficult to encourage team-level strategy again.

Be prepared to catch, coach, develop, and
facilitate an influx of ideas and proposals.

This is going to require a lot of patience, and you'll likely be pushed to your limit as you deal with the random trajectory of ideas. Touch up on your emotional intelligence skills because it will likely be frustrating. You're still going to have moments of weakness and steamroll people accidently. It's okay. Learn from it and get better. Developing strategy in others is a skill like anything else. Lean into the baseline strategic thinking skills and strategy rules outlined in this chapter, and you will set yourself and others up for success.

This may be the most painful tension point to reconcile.
Prepare to be extremely patient.

Now we're ready to discuss essential strategy hard skills.

CHAPTER 16

ESSENTIAL STRATEGIC SKILLS FOR STRATEGY AND INNOVATION

Strategy is a lot like the game of chess. We need to think several steps ahead, see the bird's-eye view, anticipate the future, predict our opponent, and maneuver to beat them. This is similar to the concept of strategic thinking, as it involves the mindset to see the bigger picture, think ahead, and anticipate the impact of our decisions.

On top of that, in chess, we also need a fundamental understanding of how the game works, the various moves, and the different plans of attack at our disposal. Obviously, we can't play the game competently without knowing how the rook and the knight move, or what the common set of plays is.

This mirrors the topic of essential strategy hard skills, as it involves understanding the steps and considerations necessary in the strategic process. In the previous chapter, we only discussed the mindset of thinking proactively and strategically. We haven't yet described the essential steps in the strategic process.

That's what we are going to cover in this chapter. We will look at the steps involved in initiating, planning, and executing strategies. We will cover various steps and frameworks that can be useful to guide our thinking with structured approaches. This will be with a facilitated team-level strategy focus. We will also discuss how to merge strategy with tactical and execution considerations to better coordinate our efforts.

As you read this chapter, on first glance, it may appear overly optimistic to get all the teams involved in this because there is a lot involved. Yes, it's true there's a lot involved. That's why we recommend a facilitated approach, so everyone doesn't need to know the steps inside and out. Only the facilitator needs to know them well so they can provide guidance. Others need to play their role by participating, collaborating, understanding the discussions, making valuable realizations, applying them, and taking ownership in their respective roles.

Additionally, the degree of team involvement is dependent on the proficiency level of the teams. As a rule of thumb, the more competent they are, the earlier they can get involved in the process. We may need to focus on their strategic skill development and increase involvement with teams incrementally if they are not ready yet. This involves centralizing the earlier parts of the strategic process and decentralizing the later parts until they are ready. That being said, we should make an active effort to develop their strategic capabilities to get greater involvement in the long run.

Use the Frames as a Standard, Not an Exact Methodology

It's important to recognize that this should be used as a standard rather than an exact methodology. Every company has their own unique situation and priorities. Some steps may not be relevant in your situation, and other times there are additional steps that are relevant. Let's look at various ways you can apply this standard within your organization:

- **As a guideline for discussions** – For some organizations, they are not at a point where it makes sense to develop a structured process yet. They can use this chapter as a reference to guide their strategy discussions forward.

- **Model for developing a formalized process** – For some larger organizations, they may be in a position where they need to develop a formal structured process for strategy. They can use this as a model.

- **Guide for training** – Even without a formalized process, walking through these steps with people is a great way to build their strategic mind and skillset.

- **Take pieces and adapt them to your existing methodology** – Some organizations already have existing strategy processes. Another perspective is always useful in identifying gaps in their existing structure and adapting it.

- **To gain a holistic outlook on strategy when you have a fragmented approach** – Some organizations have very different work processes or methodologies to organize their strategies, and they may have challenges reaching their goals due to having a fragmented approach. In such cases, they can use this chapter to gain a holistic perspective on strategy to identify areas to improve their current processes.

Overview of the Strategic Process

Overall, there are three key phases in the life cycle of a strategy. Bear in mind that this chapter is more of an overview than a comprehensive description of the strategic process. We're not trying to make everyone into expert strategy facilitators with this chapter. That topic alone could represent an entire book on its own. Let's explore the key phases:

- **Strategy Initiation** – Getting it off the ground. This involves gathering information, trends, getting on the same page, and conceptualizing an overall solution to the issues.
  - *Pre-Strategy Initiation* – "Let's get to know our situation!"
  - *Strategy Initiation* – "Let's create a solution!"

1. Pre-Strategy Initiation

Let's get to know
our situation

2. Strategy Initiation

Guiding Light

Let's create a solution

**3. Strategic Planning:
1st Phase**

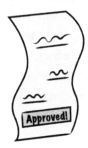

Let's start planning

**4. Strategic Planning:
2nd Phase**

Let's get organized

**5. Strategy Execution:
1st Phase**

Let's get it done

**6. Strategy Execution:
2nd Phase**

It's not done until it's done

- **Strategic Planning** – This is where we start introducing tactical components to the strategy. What are the considerations? How do we plan to make this a reality?
  - *Strategic Planning First Phase* – "Let's start planning!"
  - *Strategic Planning Second Phase* – "Let's get organized!"

- **Strategy Execution** – Getting it done. Though there are coordination-related processes involved in it, most of this topic actually involves buy-in, coaching, morale, momentum, and so on.
  - *Strategy Execution First Phase* – "Let's get it done!"
  - *Strategy Execution Second Phase* – "It's not done until it's done!"

It's not surprising to see similar steps being called under different names in different companies and methodologies. To make things even more confusing, sometimes the same terminology may be describing one component in one approach, while it means a different component in another one! This leads to a lot of confusion and disagreement, when in actuality they're talking about the same things, but using different terminology.

Don't get bogged down on terminology. It's important to note that it isn't about what it's called, as long as we can get on the same page, and as long as it gets done. The fundamentals are the most important things, so let's discuss them.

16.1. Strategy Initiation

Strategy Initiation involves getting the strategy off the ground by getting to know our situation and creating a solution, while using this as an opportunity to maximize alignment, clarity, engagement, and ownership. Unfortunately, this is often an overlooked, ignored, or underemphasized stage.

Oftentimes for many organizations, the entire Strategy Initiation stage gets centralized and completed by the senior leadership team. This is likely because such decisions are often highly impactful and delicate, and they want to mitigate the chance of having chaotic disagreements. Other times, the value of this stage is underestimated and it is skipped.

That traditional style of strategy is becoming more and more obsolete, as this leads to a great deal of misalignment. That leaves only the senior leadership looking toward the long-term vision and figuring out how to be strategic on behalf of the organization. Now, we need to get more people involved to become more innovative and adaptable to stay relevant with the market.

The degree of team involvement for Strategy Initiation should be evaluated situationally. This can depend on the proficiencies of teams. The more capable they are with strategy, the earlier we can bring them along in this process. Overall, there tends to be greater demonstration of competencies within teams in closer proximities to transformative leaders because they tend to develop strategic capabilities around them. That's why we should aim to be such leaders.

Additionally, it can be more challenging to get quality involvement from teams within larger organizations due to difficulties in maintaining a standardized quality in capabilities. Other times, we may face challenges when we try to involve chronically underdeveloped managers/ teams due to larger existing proficiency gaps.

That being said, even if we're not ready to get managers/teams involved due to current proficiency gaps, we should still aim to develop them with further people development efforts and provide opportunities for them to get involved. There are massive benefits in having multiple teams throughout the organization looking and strategizing for the long-term vision.

"Let's Get to Know our Situation!" Pre-Strategy Initiation

I. Pre-Strategy Initiation

Let's get to know
our situation

The main theme for this step is gathering and analyzing information. This is usually done before we get together for facilitative collaboration, as it can be time consuming and involve data processing. This involves gathering the information that we need to enhance our decision-making process. Capturing good data is important because flawed information will lead to ineffective strategic plans and results. Here are some ways we can evaluate the quality of the information:

- Fact checking
- Evaluating relevance of data
- Evaluating reliability of our sources
- Having multiple perspectives

Once we have data, we can analyze it to assess for trends and patterns. This is to help us visualize future scenarios, so we can plan around them.

Another source for data can surface when organizations become more transparent with data. This is especially the case for larger organizations, which usually have an overabundance of data that is not being utilized or shared. Being transparent with data can create opportunities for teams to process the information and conceptualize strategies.

External Data

It's important for people to know what's going on around them. A business doesn't function as a lone island because external factors can impact it. This is not something for only the senior leaders to know, but also for managers/teams to look at. This allows us to identify our *risks* and *opportunities*. Let's explore different types of information that we can gather:

- **External factors:** *macroeconomics* – These are much broader external factors, and most companies usually have very little influence over them. Our focus should be to understand them to capitalize on trends or plan around them.

  - This includes economic, political, legal, social, technology, and environmental factors.

- **External factors:** *microeconomics* – These are more market- and industry-specific external factors. With coordinated efforts, companies can influence their position in this. This deals with customers, competitors, vendors, and so on.

  - *Customers* – It's important to remember that at the end of the day, companies cannot exist without their customers. That's why it's essential to have a good feel of the pulse for what their customers want.
    We can utilize good market research, customer assessments, net promoter scores, focus groups, and so on.

Also, teams that regularly interface with customers may have good insights.

By anticipating what they want, it allows you to be one step ahead of the curve. The company that understands its customers the best will stick around the longest.

- *Competitors* – Competitors can play a major factor in the market condition. They can influence market share, offer competing products, and even shift the market landscape. Therefore, it's important to understand them as well.

  When we evaluate the overall condition of the market or industry, it's also important to understand "intangible competitors," including the threat of product substitutes and barriers for new entrants to the market. They're not current and real competitors from the traditional viewpoint, but they can also impact the market landscape.

  A common mistake is to over-focus on our competitors. If we over-focus on our competitors, we're actually playing a reactionary game. Although it's important to monitor our competitors and see what cards they may be holding, if we overemphasize this, we're always playing catch-up. Rather, by truly focusing on what our customers want and playing our hand accordingly, we can stay ahead of the curve.

- *Vendors* – Vendors play a role in being able to provide quality products or services to our business, or help us to develop competent processes.

- *Talent* – Our availability of talent can impact our capacity to build great businesses.

Internal Data

We also have to take a good look inside our organization. By understanding ourselves as an organization or team, we will be able to make better and sound decisions. This helps us gain better introspection on our *strengths* and *weaknesses*.

- **Internal factors:** *intangible factors* – There are many intangible factors that make up a business. This can be harder for some to see because there are no physical objects associated with them. Regardless, they are critical components to a thriving business and should be evaluated.

  - *Quality of the culture* – This is an absolutely essential component to achieve organic, sustainable, innovative, and exponential growth for the organization. In fact, most of this book focused on this factor and how to maximize it within our people and culture infrastructure, as it can greatly impact the strength of the organization's foundation.

    The truth and reality of the situation is that if we have an unhealthy organizational culture, even if we engage our resources with strategies, we won't get the outcome that we want. It must be conducive for self-direction, collaboration, upward management, team-level strategy, and so on. It also includes the quality of baseline skills, trust, depth of relationships, engagement, adaptiveness, degree of alignment, and more. Unfortunately, this is often overlooked in many organizations, and it's why they struggle to achieve their goals.

  - *Knowledge/process capabilities* – This involves the collective mental capital or know-how of getting things done. This can include organized or structured processes, or even unstructured forms of "tribal knowledge." Such capabilities can include the knowledge of sales, marketing, operations, finance, HR, strategy, product development, technology, and so on.

- **Internal factors:** *tangible factors* – Tangible factors are a lot easier to measure and evaluate because they are concrete, and information is readily available in financial statements or other sources of data. We often do not need to go out of our way extensively to measure this. These can include financial, plant, materials, technology, and other factors.

"Let's Create a Solution!" Strategy Initiation

2. Strategy Initiation

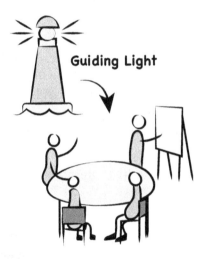

Let's create a solution

It's time to visualize the big picture and future. In this phase, we begin gathering together for the collaborative strategic process. This involves applying the information that we gathered from the previous step, cross-referencing the enterprise-level strategy, and conceptualizing strategies and goals.

Analyze Data and Trends Together

It's time to take the information that we accumulated and begin processing and discussing trends as a team. This helps people connect the dots and sheds light on which direction the team or organization needs to go.

Depending on the situation, there may be a need to perform number crunching to ascertain trends in data (financial, market, gap analysis, and so on). If we have specialized people or teams available for trend analysis, it should be done by them before gathering for strategic collaboration. This is because it involves more specialized skills and more time to process the information.

We're not trying to make everyone into master statisticians, financiers, market research experts, and so on. But we can prepare the information, have the teams look at it together, make realizations together, and problem solve together.

Putting it together. We take the internal and external information that was gathered from the previous phase to collaboratively evaluate its validity, get consensus on the key issues, and identify potential strategic directions. This can be done through a SWOT Analysis, which assesses strengths, weaknesses, opportunities, and threats.

- *Strengths* – These are positive internal characteristics that we can capitalize on.

- *Weaknesses* – These are negative internal characteristics where we can leverage our strengths to cover up vulnerabilities.

- *Opportunities* – These are positive external trends that we can invest in by leveraging our strengths.

- *Threats* – These are negative external trends that we need to identify and then prepare mitigation plans.

Are we delivering on expectations? As a business, we have to relate our efforts with our customers or stakeholders, otherwise we will eventually lose our relevance.

If we have customer assessment information available, we can take this information to identify what's important to them, and determine how we are performing in those areas. In a nutshell, we need to be performing stronger in higher priority items (as they see them) than in lower priority items. This helps identify whether we are on the right track of balancing our strategic priorities. Oftentimes, there's an imbalance that will be uncovered that can help us determine:

- *Areas to invest more* – When something is important to the customer, but we are not performing well there, it means that we are underperforming. We need to allocate more resources to improve our performance there.

- *Overkill areas* – When something is not important to the customer, but we are performing very well, it means we are overkilling it and wasting resources. We should reallocate those resources to areas where we need to improve.

You cannot be a ten out of ten in everything. That would entail unlimited resources, and there's no such thing. Rather, we have to be strategic about where we focus our efforts so that we can maximize our relevance.

For teams that directly interface with customers, it's very easy for them to see how their work impacts the customers. However, there are other teams that don't interface with them, but rather influence them indirectly. We can sometimes evaluate those indirect impacts with this method.

Even if we can't, teams that don't interface with customers still have a very clear "customer," which is their boss. They are a clear stakeholder who will have opinions on what the priorities are and how they are performing. This can be used for teams that have a behind-the-scenes role.

Formulate a Strategy That Solves the Gaps

Now that we've assessed trends and identified gaps, pain points, and possible solutions, it's time to conceptualize a strategy as a team. It needs to be designed to solve problems and create a sustainable competitive advantage. A strategy is not limited to the highest level of the organization. It can also be created at the team level. This is important to do because the enterprise-level strategy usually has little resonance with teams and it's difficult for people to connect the dots and relate to it.

However, it's important to note that the team-level strategy still needs to be going in the same direction as the enterprise-level strategy. Ask yourself, *What are the major things that need to be accomplished to support that strategy?* Then ask yourself, *What else do we need to accomplish that only we can see?*

As you do that, get a healthy dose of reality by referring to the discussions from the previous step. It can also be a good source for potential directions that were unearthed from the collaborative analysis. But don't be dragged down by cynicism and realism. Use strategic-thinking skills to envision a future! *Be bold! Think outside the box and reach for the skies! If your strategy doesn't make you at least a little nervous, it's not ambitious enough.*

Depending on the situation, this may be more effective to fabricate with a fewer number of people who represent the team and are familiar with strategy. Otherwise, we may engage in excessive and standstill debates regarding this. If you anticipate this, design this with a smaller group, and then bring more people in for subsequent discussions.

Additionally, if it hasn't been done already, it can be beneficial to create a team-level mission, vision, and values:

- **Team-level mission** – Who are you, what do you represent?
- **Team-level vision** – What impact do you dream of making?
- **Team-level values** – What values keep you together and delivering impact?

Do note that it takes a competent strategy proficiency to formulate a functional MVV that doesn't end up collecting dust or end up as a fancy poster on the wall. So make the judgment call accordingly.

Some ask, "How are enterprise-level strategies different from team-level strategies?" Enterprise-level strategies have more considerations, and should be centralized due to their larger impact and complexities. In addition, one of the most difficult parts about enterprise-level strategies is communicating them in a way that makes sense to everybody. Therefore, a big component of senior leaders' responsibilities is breaking down the enterprise-level vision into bite-sized milestones and getting people on the same page. We discuss the conceptualization of enterprise-level strategies and creating clarity around them further in Chapter 18.

All for One and One for All: United We Stand and Divided We Fall

I know this sounds cliché and corny, but it's the truth. It's important to recognize that strategies are interrelated. The enterprise-level strategy depends on a healthy balance of multiple team-level strategies to successfully move forward together. Therefore, it's important for teams to understand the importance of this balance.

If one strategy takes a hit, we all take a hit.

We accomplish this by looking at the overall picture together, which involves looking at the enterprise-level strategy and contrasting it with the multiple team-level strategies. By understanding how different teams play their role in the overall picture, we can get a consensus on the strategic priorities. This will provide clarity for allocating resources to different team-level strategies based on the agreed-upon priorities. It's essential to get on the same page on this from the beginning.

> **Balancing strategies** – Take a step back, look beyond the confines of the team, and identify the critical strategic components that

make up the organization. Going through this helps people understand the interdependence of strategies for the success of the organization.

It's amazing to see how many companies don't do this. It may appear superfluous to get teams to see the overall big picture together, but it improves alignment and prevents a lot of hassle at the tail end of strategic initiatives.

Be proactive with getting the organization on the same page with strategic priorities, or face the consequences later on. There's a tendency for teams to become myopic and forget that strategies are interdependent with one another. When we lose sight of this, we can easily adopt a mentality of only looking after our own team, rather than making decisions that are best for the organization. To all teams, their work will always look like the highest priority to them. It's human nature to think like this.

This results in teams working as isolated silos, which creates internal bickering for the limited resources that are available to the organization. It introduces unnecessary bureaucracy and the organization will have trouble getting back on the same page.

Setting Strategic Goals

By now, teams should have an understanding of the current reality, possible trends, enterprise-level strategy, co-created team-level strategy, and the overall balance of strategies.

Now it's time to take the overarching team-level strategy and break it down into smaller bite-size pieces. If we are provided with the enterprise-level strategic goals, we can superimpose them with the team-level strategy to create corresponding team-level goals to help us stay aligned.

Setting team-level strategic goals creates
landmarks and milestones.

You'll notice that sometimes certain strategic goals have no choice but to be subjective in nature. In such cases, it's wise to use them to increase the clarity of the strategy to help more people understand it. When doing so, it's important to keep them at a bird's-eye vantage point so we don't encroach on the tactical components of the strategy. Remember, strategic goals are different from objectives (discussed in the next phase), which are more tactical in nature.

When possible, though, it is a good practice to set measurable success criteria for the strategic goals, especially in operations-heavy businesses with plenty of historical and comparable data. This will provide clarity on the definition of success. If we manage to consolidate measurable strategic goals from all of the key teams, we can extrapolate that information and fabricate a:

> Balanced scorecard – A strategic performance management metrics that takes a balanced perspective of the overall strategy. This approach results in a co-created version of a Balanced Scorecard, which is largely different from a traditional version that was conceptualized from a centralized top-down position. Therefore, this has the same benefits of engagement, buy-in, and ownership that are exhibited from culture strategy.

We will be taking those strategic goals into the next phase of the process: Strategic Planning. So, make clear ones. The clearer they are, the easier it is to plan for them.

16.2. Strategic Planning

At this point, the strategy can still be very vague for most people. Now, it's time to break down the strategy and materialize it into more tangible and tactical items. This stage involves converting our vision into an organized schedule, plan, action items, and deliverables.

It is wise to use the Strategic Planning phase to gather perspectives from execution, cross-functions, and sponsors during planning sessions. This will maximize alignment and take into account holistic and implementation considerations of the strategy. It's especially valuable to involve executioners, as they are the ones who will push the strategy forward and will need to understand the holistic considerations. A common mistake is to leave them out because they often struggle to synchronize with conversations during strategy sessions. If such gaps exist, rather than isolating them from the process, co-creating strategic plans can be used as potential developmental opportunities to improve their proficiencies in strategy. There is value in co-creating strategic plans together, as it improves ownership and adaptability.

It is quite common for various strategies to encounter speed bumps, changes, or roadblocks along the way. That is because there are a great deal of uncertainties and risks associated with strategy. When such situations occur, a less adaptable team or organization would be less capable of maneuvering around such situations, largely due to poor communication and coordination. When the right hand doesn't know what the left hand wants, and isn't communicating with the head, chaos will ensue. Many of those problems can actually be overcome by having a strong understanding of the priorities and risk, thereby making situational decisions or coordinated efforts based on said priorities.

Traditionally, many companies crafted a strategic plan from a higher-level standpoint and delegated the execution to later have it fail at the execution phase. Then, they would wonder why this occurred. Isolating this process inherently creates a weaker understanding and decreased ownership of the effort. There is something psychological about co-creating a solution, where people have more inner drive to see the plan come to fruition.

Historically this may have worked in the past when there was less emphasis on adaptability to stay competitive. Today's marketplace is more competitive than ever with a greater need to adapt to the changing landscape and execute better. Currently, there is a great deal of emphasis that involves executioners and holistic collaboration during strategic planning sessions as a method to create alignment. Furthermore, if teams demonstrate competence in strategic planning, they can own the planning process and make proposals to you.

"Let's Start Planning!" Strategic Planning First Phase

3. Strategic Planning:
1st Phase

Let's start planning

The first part of Strategic Planning is to convert the strategic vision and goals into something more tangible, so that we can further break it down into granular action items in the following phase. As an overview, we will cover:

- Tactical priorities
- Understanding the stakeholders
- Making the strategy "official"
- Defining objective deliverables

Varying strategy methodologies have different emphasis on these steps. Some frameworks skip this and go straight into action items, whereas others focus more on the earlier steps. In addition, there are many overlapping concepts with project-related approaches, like Project Management, Agile, and Objectives and Key Results (OKR), to name a few. These approaches usually have a heavier emphasis on tactics and execution.

You may already have existing methodologies that overlap with many of these steps. Regardless, it may be valuable to review these steps to capture existing gaps in your current processes or to gain additional perspectives. Other times, you may not have a formal process yet. In such cases, it's good to go through the thought processes on an informal basis to get on the same page. Otherwise, it may be time to create structured processes within your organization. Evaluate your organization on a case-by-case basis to identify what makes sense to you.

Tactical Priorities

It is important for a team to understand what their tactical priorities are, which should be based on their strategic goals. Is it revenue, a particular metric, deadline, budget, or something else? This will help determine which parameters of our goals are rigid, and which are flexible. This helps the team adapt during the occurrence of unforeseen circumstances.

Understanding tactical priorities guides our
thinking when unforeseen situations occur.

It is impossible for every part of our plan to roll out without hiccups, as we are dealing with uncertainty and have a finite amount of resources. Therefore, it is important to be on the same page with these priorities, so we know where to shift our attention and resources if we encounter such obstacles. Here are some sample methods that we could use to frame these priorities:

- **Cost versus time versus scope** – This is often used in project management, which is appropriate for temporary initiatives.

When unforeseen circumstances occur, we can adapt either the budget, deadline, or scope of the project to still meet the main goal. The team just needs to know which parameters are the most flexible.

- **Top three priorities** – This is often used in operations-based situations, which involve repetitive work. It's difficult for teams to remember countless priorities. Therefore, by focusing on the top three, it's easier for them to prioritize throughout their day-to-day functions.

Understand the Stakeholders

A team should not be working as an individual silo without understanding the different stakeholders and how they impact the team. That would lead to coordination-related problems that could have been anticipated and avoided. Therefore, it is important for a team to understand who the various stakeholders are, along with their influence and their attitudes. This will help them better understand the buy-in landscape, organize tasks, and keep people aligned, and will later assist in determining the best communication plan.

- **Influence** – Who are the stakeholders, and how do they influence the success of the strategy? This can involve decision-making authority, sponsorship, technical perspectives, cross-functional representation, and so on.

- **Attitude** – What is their attitude in regard to the strategy? Are they in support of it? Are they against it?

Making the Strategy "Official"

If we have a structured system to organize strategies, it's time to get the ball rolling on making this "official." Up until now, we had many great higher-level discussions; however, the strategy likely hasn't been approved with clear agreements and resource engagement. This is not a *one-off step*. It will require further refinement as more tactical considerations are ironed out in subsequent steps. This is often done in the form of business cases, which serve multiple purposes.

- **Organize the process** – Business cases can be a useful step to formalize proposals, approvals, and documentation to get different parties on the same page. Typical components often include: team name, rules of engagement, current problem, proposed solutions, benefits, cost, deliverables, milestones, constraints, assumptions, risks, external dependencies.

- **Formalize the strategy** – Business cases provides a route to get an official stamp of approval to move the strategy forward. This allows people to get on the same page and support it. Usually, this isn't a one-step process. Finalizing the approval and integrating resources will likely occur as the plan is further materialized because we don't have all the information yet.

- **Create clarity on agreements** – This is an opportunity to gain clarity on the agreements between teams and stakeholders. Important elements can include success criteria, deliverables, budget, deadlines, reporting standards, and so on.

Some organizations (especially smaller ones) don't have formal structures. In those situations, strategies often move forward through verbal agreements or resulting documentation from facilitative discussions alone. As they scale, it may become more challenging to keep track of the numerous strategies, and they may want to consider creating a formalized process to organize strategies, whether it's through an annual, quarterly, or standalone strategic initiative basis.

Define Objective Deliverables

Now that we've had a chance to organize many of our preliminary thoughts from this stage, it is time to commit to setting objectives with clear deliverables. Objectives are written with the intent to be concrete and tangible. The purpose of this is to create detailed requirements that have little potential for misinterpretation, which will minimize future misunderstandings. This will greatly reduce confusion in the subsequent planning and execution phases. This is in preparation of further breaking them down to action items and tactics.

- **SMART objectives** – This is a guideline that helps us write objectives to improve clarity with clear expectations for what success looks like.

  Specific – Be specific. If we are too big picture with this, then we are being too vague.

  Measurable – Use measurables. If you can't measure it, it's hard to define success.

  Attainable – Ask yourself, "Is it realistic?" If it's not, it can kill engagement.

  Relevant – Ask yourself, "Does it relate to the strategic goal?"

  Time-bound – Have a set deadline. Without a deadline, it's too open-ended.

When designing objectives, it is useful to refer to the strategic goals to ensure alignment with them. To clarify the difference between goals and objectives, goals are more higher-level to make strategies more bite-sized. However, they will still be too abstract and vague for most people to digest. Objectives take those ideas and make them tangible enough for people to prepare for detailed task-planning and execution.

"Let's Get Organized!" Strategic Planning Second Phase

4. Strategic Planning:
2nd Phase

Let's get organized

The purpose of this phase of Strategic Planning is to convert our objectives into actionable items in preparation for execution. We also take into account additional tactical considerations to anticipate the required resources that we need and potential risks that the team may face during implementation. We will cover:

- Breaking down the tasks
- Keeping stakeholders on the same page
- Knowing our budget
- Considering what can go wrong

When this is well-prepared, a clear picture/path is laid out for the execution phase. A good strategic plan lays the groundwork for successful execution, which predominantly focuses on buy-in, engagement, coaching, coordination, and momentum. With an unclear plan, it makes it extremely difficult to have a smooth execution, as it becomes exponentially difficult to achieve buy-in for something that people don't know what they're buying into.

Breaking Down Tasks

During this step, the team takes the objectives and breaks them down into actionable items. This is where items become much more granular and detailed-oriented. Tasks should be designed to reach the eventual objectives. Subsequently, they can be used to assign roles and deadlines.

It's important to recognize that there are many ways to organize tasks based on your situation. Task breakdown can be based upon common industry practices, methodology, or approach. It is wise to understand your team's custom needs. Evaluate possible "best practices" and whether they are applicable to your situation. Bear in mind that at the end of the day, it's what keeps us organized and market competitive, and what works. The simplest form of managing tasks is:

- **Who, what, and when** – This is literally just a list of who needs to do what by when. This may be appropriate for simpler task management needs.

Other times, there may be a need to have specialized task breakdown methodologies. Here are some examples:

- **Gannt chart** – This task management process is used in project management to focus on task sequence and interdependencies. This may be appropriate for task-heavy initiatives.

- **Agile methodology** – This is an adaptive form of project management that relies on continuous adaptation through iteration-based breakdowns. It has gained popularity in software development and marketing.

- **And more.**

Some task management processes also have the potential for integrating task breakdowns with time and resource expenditures. This can be helpful if reporting and data are a high priority throughout the execution process.

Keeping Stakeholders on the Same Page

Communication is a key component to strategic initiatives. If there is a communication breakdown with key stakeholders, it can lead to extremely challenging problems throughout execution. Many issues stem from a lack of coordination and collaboration.

Now that we've had a chance to identify relevant stakeholders and organize a task breakdown in previous steps, we can conceptualize a stakeholder communication plan to coordinate this endeavor.

- **Communications plan part 1** – Understand the key tasks and roles of the stakeholders. Are they responsible (for example, sponsor, approver), accountable (for example, team lead, manager), consultative (for example, subject matter expert, cross-functional support), or people to keep informed (for example, contributor or strategy targets)?

- **Communications plan part 2** – What is the appropriate frequency, medium, and format of communicating with the stakeholders?

Remember, the role of stakeholders can also vary based on their influence and attitude. For example, if there is insufficient support and significant resistance from key stakeholders, it can put a great strain on execution and adversely impact the initiative. Adapting an effective communications plan will maximize support and minimize the damage from potential resistance.

What's the Budget?

All strategic initiatives need resources to move them forward. Anytime we have an active strategic effort, we are engaging resources into it, whether we are aware of it or not. This can be in the form of a budget with dollar amounts, or even the allocation of manpower or talent.

Budgeting projects the resources required to move the strategy forward. This gets various parties to understand the anticipated resources, make informed decisions, and allocate resources accordingly. This can be done in two ways:

- **Using historicals or comparables** – Budgeting can be done with estimates and ranges using historical and comparable information from other similar strategic initiatives as reference points. It's simpler, quicker, and easier to train. The downside is that it can be less accurate, as it doesn't get as detailed.

- **Adding up components** – Budgeting can also be done by adding up the individual components to anticipate the overall sum. It's much more granular and can be more accurate. However, it is more technique sensitive and time-consuming, and a harder skill to develop.

We also need to consider whether the items in the budget are new expenses or reallocation of already existing expenses. We can do this by evaluating whether the components are green cash or blue cash.

- **Green cash** – Actual cash that needs to be spent with invoices and payments.
- **Blue cash** – Cash that the company is already spending, or it's being reallocated for the initiative (for example, allocating team members).

Who Sets the Budget? The decision on how budgeting gets determined is important because it has a profound impact on the financial health of the organization and outcome of initiatives. Therefore, it can be a sensitive decision, as it can have a large ripple effect. Let's look at some of the considerations:

- **Preservational top-down budgeting** – When managers or teams have not developed sufficient strategy competencies or mutual trust is not present, budgeting often gets centralized to provide guardrails and preserve the financial health of the organization. However, this is at the cost of diminished adaptability, increased rigidity, and loss of ownership.

- **Adaptable bottom-up budgeting** – Strategies have uncertainties, and budgets can be challenging to forecast accurately. If similar initiatives have been done before, it may be possible to be more accurate as we have access to past information. Otherwise, there is a high possibility that our forecasts may be inaccurate, and we may need to account for variability. This may require a more adaptable form of budgeting that can occur through bottom-up proposals from teams or managers. To accomplish this, teams and managers need to demonstrate competencies in budget management and reliably reaching objectives. They also need an open and mutually trusting relationship with the sponsor. This enables them to be more fluid with resource allocation to better achieve results due to improved adaptability during execution and ownership. Managers will try to stay within the confines of the budget to deliver results, and additional resources will only be requested when they are really needed.

What Can Go Wrong?

Every initiative has risk inherent within it. Whenever we deal with anything regarding the future, there are uncertainties. Whenever there are uncertainties, unforeseen situations can occur that can impact the initiative. Therefore, it is wise to anticipate such possibilities based on the probability and impact of the risk.

- **Probability** – What is the likelihood that the risk will occur?

- **Impact** – How large of an impact will the risk have on the organization?

Obviously, higher probabilities and higher impacts are deemed higher risks. Once everyone gets on the same page regarding the probability and impact, it becomes possible to design risk mitigating plans for such uncertainties.

> **Risk mitigation plan** – In the event that those risks occur, what is the game plan?

Interestingly, some individuals have challenges conceptualizing risk. Some people's minds draw a blank when ideas of future uncertainties and risks are involved. Other people have an altered perception of risk, causing them to underestimate or overestimate the probability and impact. Either form of thinking can harm the initiative by affecting the preparation and risk mitigation plan. Therefore, it is important to get on the same page on risk and prepare accordingly.

16.3. Strategy Execution

Initially, like many others, I had mistaken how Strategy Execution worked. When I was receiving training and coaching on this topic, I thought I was going to learn about various tactical methodologies to get an initiative moving forward and break it down in a granular and organized manner to complete tasks in a quality and timely manner. Although this was part of it, I was very surprised that 80 percent of the training was on emotional management, and only 20 percent of it was on the tactical part.

It was eye-opening to make the realization that successful execution is actually more contingent on managing the emotions of people, more so than the thinking or planning component! I asked myself, "Why am I learning about emotions? I didn't decide to receive training and coaching for this!" That was an interesting realization and paradigm shift because that execution depended on buy-in more so than the quality of the laid-out plan. Ever since gaining this insight, I approached execution differently and experienced greater success.

With traditional mindsets, Strategy Execution is perceived as a two-component process: *Know → Do*. If that was the case, then all we'd have to do is create a plan and tell people what to do. From there, people should be able to figure things out to do their jobs well.

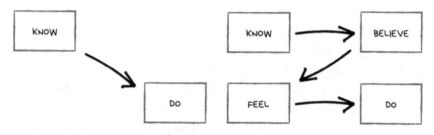

Difference between traditional and modern approaches to strategy execution

However, that is becoming an increasingly outdated model that tends to get outcompeted by organizations that focus on alignment and buy-in. The topic of buy-in really hinges on the emotional management of the situation. The following demonstrates the current reality better, which utilizes proper culture and people infrastructure: *Know → Believe → Feel → Do*.

The importance of this frame highlights the fact that knowing what to do is not enough for most people to do the job properly. People need to get beyond the knowing and actually believe in it. This usually requires communicating it in a way that adapts to their communication style and highlights "What's in it for me? (WIIFM)." Furthermore, the communication must engage their emotions so they feel something regarding the strategy (such as inspired, excited, proud, or happy). Then, people are engaged to do the tasks in a way that is truly conducive to the strategy. If not, there will be an environment where people do just enough work to not get themselves in trouble by management, or passive-aggressively do something else that is counterproductive if they think that they can get away with it. This leads to disengaged mindsets and loss of ownership. Subsequently, we'll lose the adaptability and innovation of the team.

"Let's Get It Done!" Strategy Execution First Phase

5. Strategy Execution:
1st Phase

Let's get it done

Buy-In and Momentum

The buy-in, morale, and momentum of Strategy Execution is critical to maintain high performance and productivity. People do not act as robots. They behave in patterns congruent with the morale and momentum of the situation. When this is high, our productivity shoots up. When this is low, our productivity drops. Therefore, it's important to recognize:

There's a large economic value of morale and momentum.

If we can recognize this, then it makes sense to invest in it and maintain it. It's as if people have a fuel tank to carry morale, and they can't run on empty. New fuel needs to be pumped in.

This can become more complicated when strategies involve multiple stakeholders from multiple teams who have differing motives and even conflicts of interest. It can even involve people outside the organization. To navigate that realm, we need to rely upon our ability to get buy-in.

Buy-in involves getting results with influence.

This involves many skills similar to those discussed in change management and leadership. Get to know your audience, their influence, and their attitude. Understand why they think the way they do, and how to get their buy-in. Craft a message that speaks to their core and resonates with them in order to gain their support. Engage people with a WIIFM approach.

For strategic initiatives with a longer timeline, it may be wise to have a *fast forward project* or *line-of-sight project*. A smaller short-term project can demonstrate the feasibility of the strategy to generate an initial jumpstart to the momentum. Remember to keep the momentum fueled throughout the strategy. Some managers have a natural blind spot to this and don't realize that people are running on empty.

Don't forget, it's important to celebrate wins when you can!

Back to the Fundamentals: Managing and Leading

There are a lot of moving pieces involved when you execute strategies. We've discussed a lot of tactical components during Strategic Planning. Now, it's time to get organized and coordinate the tasks to reach the end goal. Throughout Strategy Execution, it's important to exercise good management and leadership skills when you delegate, coach, manage team dynamics, use tactics, facilitate, mobilize, and think ahead.

There will be countless opportunities to develop people throughout execution with coaching moments. The executioner must be bought in to the idea of using such moments to invest in their people. This is harder than it sounds because executioners are faced with the pressures of reaching the strategic goals. This involves going back to the fundamentals and demonstrating skills in:

- Coaching and feedback, and
- Balancing goals and people development.

This can become more complicated when strategies have to bring in collaborators from multiple sources to work together. This is because it may involve situations where executioners have to work with people who don't directly report to them, interacting with different departments, managing upward to senior leaders, engaging external stakeholders (for example, customers, vendors, regulatory), and so on. To overcome this, it will be important to:

- Develop partnership mentalities with stakeholders, and
- Apply political skills.

This is another reason why culture strategy should be at an enterprise level. These political factors can definitely add challenges and complexities to execution. They can actually become significant obstacles for successful strategy implementation. That's why it's important to reevaluate our culture to determine whether we truly have a conducive culture at an enterprise level. If we get everyone on the same page with culture strategy, a lot of the political challenges can be greatly mitigated. This improves the success rate of strategic endeavors.

Adapting with Change Requests

Uncertainties will always be present because no initiative is without risk. Therefore, as risks become reality, changes are often requested or required. These change requests can occur due to several reasons, such as: when unforeseen circumstances occur, planned risks become reality, new information is revealed, or senior leadership changes the requirements.

As change requests occur due to unforeseen circumstances, it is important to lean back on the tactical priorities as a guide for decision-making, because the allocation of resources, timeline, or objectives may need to be adjusted. Having a clear understanding of the priorities is important to adapt in a way that is consistent with the strategic direction, especially when we hit speed bumps. When planned risks become reality, fall back on your risk mitigation plans.

Lean back on priorities and risk mitigation plans.

If the change request is made from senior leadership, it is important for them to recognize that it may uproot some of the previous work that has already been done, which can impact the initiative. It is important for the executioner to have a strong understanding of the implications of the initiative and communicate them clearly. Then, the senior leader can decide if the change is worth the impact to the initiative. This usually requires a mutually trusting relationship and a conducive culture to be in effect.

Maintain a partner mentality with senior leadership.

If we maintain a partnership mentality throughout this process, then we can successfully navigate around changes and risks. This improves our adaptability throughout the execution process, which significantly improves our success rate. It also maintains an environment of having a proactive and solution mindset. That atmosphere can solve many problems before they occur.

Keep a proactive and solution mindset.

Gathering Data and Reporting

Status reports are a necessary part of the execution of a strategy. They provide transparency throughout the process and ensure that we're on track. This involves:

- Gathering data
- Assessing the health of the situation
- Reporting updates

It's important to get on the same page and be intentional with a clear methodology on how this will be done. Some task breakdown frameworks have integrated tracking components associated with their processes. Some can simultaneously cross-reference them based on time and resources. However, even if we don't have such sophisticated mechanisms, it's important to gather information and evaluate whether we're on track based on:

- **Tasks** – Have we accomplished what we needed to get done? Are there major blockers? Can we get around them?
- **Time** – Are we on track for the deadline? Are we early? Are we late?
- **Resources** – Have we spent according to the budget? Are we under the budget? Are we above the budget?

Once we've evaluated the situation, updates need to be made to senior leaders. The format is extremely variable based on the organization's custom needs. Overall, most senior leaders prefer a simpler format, such as an *executive summary* or *three-sentence update*. Others want integrated financial reporting or other formats with customized preferences. Here are some sample reporting frameworks:

- **Executive summary** – Formal and simple summary.
- **Three-sentence updates** – An even simpler summary with a three-sentence limit.
- **Dashboard reports** – Automated and simplified data reporting into a dashboard.
- **Integration with financial data** – Financial officers may prefer integrated financial data in reports to track current progress based on expenses.
- **Green, yellow, or red light** – Simple visual representation that demonstrates whether we are on track.
- **And more.**

It's important to get on the same page with everyone on how to interpret whether we are on track. Even if you don't use the green/yellow/red light format as an official process, it is wise to apply a similar mentality when communicating update reports. "Green light" indicates that everything is good, "yellow light" indicates that there is a potential issue but the team is trying to handle it, and "red light" indicates that there is trouble and the team needs help. However, people can use this the wrong way:

- **Overreacting "red light"** – Some executioners communicate "red light" when it really is a "yellow light," which can create a boy-crying-wolf effect. It may succeed in getting the attention to improve the situation, but people will take notice that the urgency that was communicated was excessive, and this will erode trust for future efforts.

- **Everything is "green"** – Other people may communicate that everything is fine, even if it is a "yellow light" situation. Then, when it eventually becomes a "red light" situation, it gets brought up. This can erode trust as well, as it gives little time to prepare or conceptualize supporting solutions. Then, it creates a situation where it is perceived that the executioner's ability to assess the situation is compromised. This can force senior leaders to overcompensate with micromanagement and over-supervision. This is due to concerns that an underlying "yellow light" may be present when leaders are being told that everything is fine.

"It's Not Over until It's Over!" Strategy Execution Second Phase

6. Strategy Execution: 2nd Phase

It's not done until it's done

The second phase of Strategy Execution involves the closing phase of the strategy. This is an important step because it can greatly impact whether the organization obtains the intended benefits of the strategy. Unfortunately, this is often overlooked.

This is also known as the "forgotten step."

This is because people get disinterested during this step, let their guard down, or have no incentive to do this well because it's not correlated to their performance ratings.

Haven't you seen initiatives get implemented successfully, but the transition or closure is a mess? It leads to vague handovers, which cause a great deal of confusion. This is especially the case for strategies that involve process creation or improvements. Oftentimes, there are subsequent teams that need to maintain the process, but there was a messy transition. What's the point of doing the strategy if no one applies what was created? This introduces a new set of problems on the maintenance side and creates a lot of fires that need to be put out afterward.

Therefore, let's recognize that this is a critical step in the strategy process, and have a clean finish.

Smooth Closing or Transitioning

A strategic initiative can close due to multiple reasons. Let's explore some possible scenarios:

- Successful completion of the strategy
- Integration with another initiative
- Termination due to irrelevancy
- Termination due to resources having dried up

At the close of an initiative, it's important to transition smoothly. This minimizes the post-strategy "fires" that commonly occur otherwise: This can include:

- Proper reports to relevant stakeholders
- Return of resources
- Integration with any relevant department
- Any follow-up maintenance
- Updates to organizational processes and documentation
- Knowledge handover or training

By having a clean follow-through at the end, we can maximize the impact of our strategy.

Learning from Experience through Retrospectives

Many lessons will be learned throughout the lifespan of a strategic initiative, including valuable knowledge capabilities and practical know-how. That's why it is important to capitalize on them, reflect on them, problem solve for improvement, share the realizations, and even provide feedback to the leaders.

This maximizes cross-pollination of ideas.

This promotes cross-pollination of ideas and realizations throughout the organization, especially if we set up a platform where teams share their learnings with each other. This way, the value of the people infrastructure continues to strengthen as an organization performs more strategic initiatives. These are sample questions we can address during retrospectives:

- **Start** – What should we start doing?
- **Stop** – What should we stop doing?
- **Continue** – What should we continue doing?
- **Kudos** – Paying compliments to work well done.

We can also perform retrospectives throughout the lifespan of the strategy. This can be based on iterations, or set time frames such as biweekly, monthly, or quarterly frequencies. Ultimately, it's based on what makes sense for the organization.

These are the essential hard skills required to approach strategy like a game of chess—seeing the bigger picture, thinking ahead, and anticipating the impact of our decisions. There is a lot involved, but with a facilitated approach, everyone can take ownership of their respective roles. Together, you can work through the six stages of getting to know your situation, creating a solution, planning, getting organized, getting it done, and closing the strategy. Next, we'll discuss being strategic with this strategy, so you can create and maintain an ecosystem that maximizes alignment.

CHAPTER 17

BEING STRATEGIC WITH STRATEGY

I'm sure you know what it feels like. You have a strategic direction that you'd like to lead everyone toward. You'd like people to be proactively thinking at their respective levels. However, it doesn't seem like everyone is on the same page. What would it mean to you if you had an organization that was thinking strategically together? One of the goals of culture strategy is to accomplish this. However, this is easier said than done. There's so much that has to be built into this before we can accomplish it.

That's why we spent the majority of the book discussing how to develop the appropriate culture and people infrastructure. Without this, the teams wouldn't be able to handle the collaboration, facilitation, and leadership standards that are involved in strategy. Subsequently, we spent the last couple of chapters describing how to promote proactive thinking and develop strategic capabilities within your managers/teams.

A lot of what we've discussed in this book culminates to this chapter. Now that we have the necessary moving pieces in position, we can focus on building an ecosystem of strategy. In essence, this is being strategic with strategy. This becomes possible with a conducive culture because it functions as the internal strategy that propagates all other strategies.

Now, we can get proactive thinking and innovation to occur at respective team levels.

However, strategy involves a dynamic and interactive process among multiple parties. It's so easy to make the mistake of overcentralizing strategies or letting go too soon when decentralizing strategies. It's easy to overlook the cross-functional support required to promote team-level strategies. It's easy to lose patience and give up on developing the strategic capabilities of our people.

It's about finding that right balance. To top it off, this is a moving target as the position of this balance is dynamically changing as team-level strategic capabilities are built and mutual trust is further developed. This requires taking an additional step back and looking at all your other strategic efforts. By taking a step back and being a "conductor" for multiple strategies, it allows us to maximize alignment to produce a greater impact. In a musical performance, without such a conductor, we'll fail to capture the true potential of the musicians' group efforts, no matter how good they are. Likewise, strategies in an organization need a conductor to maximize the alignment between them.

17.1. Paradigm Shift: A New Approach to Strategy

The old model of strategy involves a very top-down approach, trickling down to granular action items and checklists. However, this model is becoming increasingly obsolete because it yields less effective results by executioners due to reduced engagement and ownership. Consequently, it has a diminished potential to adapt to the changing environment and thus is less competitive.

That is why there is a trend for companies to increase their focus on strategy alignment more so than strategic planning and execution. In general, many organizations already have very well-thought-out strategic plans. However, history has shown that this isn't enough to differentiate themselves and dominate others in the marketplace. If that's the case, you might naturally wonder how some organizations outcompete others, when many of them have great plans.

They may think that the differentiating factor is in the execution, because the organization that executes the plan the best will outcompete the others. Well, that does seem to create short-term differentiation. However, even that doesn't hold up long-term results.

In fact, the organization that continues to sustain long-term dominance demonstrates the strongest strategic alignment. This fosters adaptability because this alignment keeps the organization in tune with the various changes that are occurring.

Such organizations demonstrate the strongest understanding of their customers and ability to adapt to the market. Then, they can realign themselves internally to continuously adapt with the changing situations, and they will outcompete their competitors. This is especially the case in today's marketplace, as it is changing at a more rapid rate than it ever has.

> *It's not about having the smartest plan.*
> *It's not about having the strongest execution.*
> *Though they are important, it's about having the greatest*
> *alignment and adaptability.*

Strategy alignment requires constant adaptation through continuous collaboration and demonstration of leadership. This is more so than in organizations that have a greater emphasis on planning or execution. Therefore, it has a greater dependency on the maturation state of the people infrastructure and culture. By improving this infrastructure within the organization, people are more suited to achieve greater alignment through improved collaboration and leadership.

Different Ways Strategic Alignment Creates Value

Strategic alignment has the potential to merge the best of worlds. In fact, we gain the potential to create synergistic value between strategic planning and execution through an alignment focus and widespread strategic thinking. Here are some ways this can manifest:

- Clearer alignment with the enterprise-level strategy is present throughout departments and teams.

- Team-level strategic plans can be created, which improves relevance and adaptation because teams possess ground-level knowledge.

- There is a partnership mentality and continuous adaptation throughout execution.

- Projects have higher success rates, achievements are celebrated, and people cross-pollinate their learnings.

- There is greater morale, ownership, momentum, engagement, people development, coaching, and facilitation.

- Multiple perspectives are captured within strategic efforts to maximize ways to deliver value to customers and move forward toward long-term visions.

- This approach to strategy creates opportunities to develop strategic capabilities within people.

Common Areas of Strategy Misalignment

It's important to understand the various components that need to be aligned when we are creating and maintaining an ecosystem of strategy. There are actually multiple interfaces of alignment that need to be optimized. If we are not cognizant of the many interfaces involved, it is easy to overlook them and leave a large gap, thereby compromising the effectiveness of the ecosystem. Here are common strategy misalignment issues that typically arise:

- **Between strategic plans and execution** – This occurs when we isolate strategic planning and execution. This results in decreased engagement, ownership, and adaptability throughout the implementation processes. We can improve this by developing team-level strategic capabilities and increasing teams' involvement in strategic planning.

- **Between the organization and external customers or stakeholders** – When the teams are not engaged in strategic thinking and the planning process, they can get disconnected from needs of the external customers or stakeholders. This can also be the result of an inadequately positioned enterprise-level strategy due to a poor understanding of the consumer expectations.

- **Between centralized enterprise-level strategies and peripheral team-level strategies** – This happens when we do not adequately interface the enterprise-level strategy with team-level strategies. This can be due to lack of clear communication, mismanaging strategy facilitation, and decentralizing too many strategies to underdeveloped teams by letting go too soon.

- **Between centralized cross-functions and peripheral team-level strategies** – It is important that cross-functional support be designed to maximize the development and implementation of team-level strategies. If such processes create excessive rigidity, lack of transparency, lack of partnership mentality, and inadequate access to necessary resources, then they can constrain the propagation of team-level strategies.

- **Between different team-level strategies** – Misalignment between different peripheral strategies can occur when there is a lack of clarity on the enterprise-level strategies and poor strategy approval/screening processes. Overall, this leads to an imbalance of strategies that is riddled with internal conflicts and non-synergistic efforts.

17.2. Transitioning from Linear to Life Cycle Management of Strategy

In the previous chapter, we discussed a *linear management* of strategies that sequentially goes from initiation to planning to execution. Though this is useful when managing a strategy as an isolated unit, it doesn't address the misalignment that can occur from a holistic standpoint. This needs a broader approach that involves managing the overall strategy ecosystem to address these gaps.

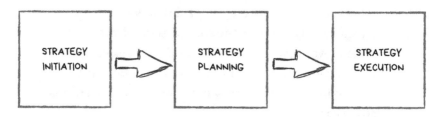

Visualization of linear management of strategy

To maximize our strategy ecosystem and alignment, we need to transition the way we manage strategies. This requires a mindset shift toward the *life cycle management* of team-level strategies, rather than the individual strategies themselves. This allows us to create exceptional results through greater leverage of self-direction and team-level strategies by intentionally promoting an environment of innovation, strategy, engagement, and ownership.

In order to accomplish this, we need to focus on enabling various components of this ecosystem to effectively support this value maximizer, so we can be strategic with strategy. Rather than focusing on the strategy itself, we're focusing on how to create an environment where team-led strategies thrive. This is what eventually enables us to achieve organic, scalable, and innovative strategies.

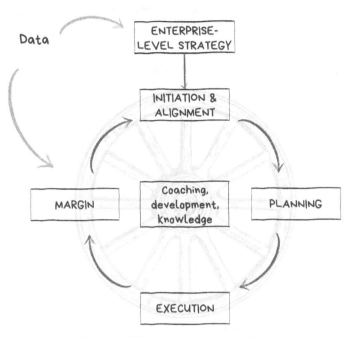

Visualization of life-cycle management of strategy

Naturally, a prudent mind will be initially skeptical to this approach. There are still many unanswered questions. They would be right. To enable this, we would need to address the following concerns:

- How do you ensure that team-level strategies are aligned with the enterprise-level strategy?
- How do you maximize the involvement of self-directed teams and develop their competencies in strategy?
- Where do they get time for this?

These are fair concerns because if they are left unaddressed, they can cause problems and disorder throughout the organization. We would need to counteract these issues using a holistic approach that builds up the ecosystem of strategies. Let's look at the components in the diagram to illustrate this better.

In the diagram above, the outside rim of the wheel represents the team's involvement. The linear progression of the strategy can be seen within the cycle: initiation, planning, and execution. With this approach, we have the ultimate goal of decentralizing more of the strategic process to the team and supporting them. Notice that their cycle goes from:

1. **Team margin** – Teams need bandwidth and resources to get involved with strategies. Creating this margin will require a partnership effort among teams and senior leaders.

2. **Strategy initiation and alignment** – Strategies can be initiated by the team, senior leadership, or together. Wherever they originated from, they need to be aligned with the enterprise-level strategy. This ensures that we're all moving in the same direction.

3. **Strategic planning** – This involves team-level strategic planning. Teams (or at the very least, their key people) should create or co-create the strategic plan, as they have a better understanding of the execution-related concerns and obstacles. This also gives them an opportunity to develop and refine their planning skills, which improves the quality of their execution due to increased ownership.

4. **Strategy execution** – This involves team-level strategy execution. If teams were involved in planning, they would break out of the traditional prescription-based execution mentality. This increases engagement and ownership, and improves situational adaptation.

Develop Teams' Strategic Capabilities

This type of ecosystem is highly dependent on the strategic capabilities of teams. It's important to develop their capabilities since the team's current skill levels are the basis for striking the right balance between centralizing and decentralizing strategic decisions.

This type of transformative ecosystem is not going to be built overnight. This may involve a gradual and challenging transition to develop the strategic capabilities of the teams. On top of that, teams and managers within the same organization can exhibit differing proficiencies in strategy. As the strategic capabilities of teams develop and mature, we can decentralize more of the strategic process to them.

Sometimes, this can be an extremely uncomfortable and vulnerable experience for leaders if they're not used to doing this. Leaders know all too well how quickly these situations can derail when they let go too soon and there is a lack of strategy skills. At the same time, they know the frustration of overcentralizing strategies, leading to teams that are disengaged and not on the same page. Even when a balance has been established, it still takes a leap of faith to push the boundaries to reach the next incremental level.

However, it's important to get over this because the strategic capabilities of the teams are the largest determining variable for success of this ecosystem. That's why we need to have the mindset of continuous growth and development for our people, even in the realm of strategy. Let's explore differing levels that teams commonly exhibit:

Level One Team

These teams are simply a workforce. They still need to be told how to execute tasks and they may have challenges adapting. The entire strategic process will likely have to be centralized until they exhibit further maturation and development. To accomplish objectives, we need to organize the tasks that need to be completed on a repetitious basis so that they can be allocated to various staff members. It may even involve micromanagement of staff, roles, instructions, shifts, hours, and so on. Obviously, this is not a sustainable situation, and should only be done on an interim basis until we develop our teams.

Level Two Team

These teams can handle and are responsible for execution-related coordination. Most of the strategic planning process will have to be centralized and handed over to them at the execution phase. Most of the repetitious tasks should be done independently by the teams, and they should have the ability to adapt to shifting priorities, as priorities can change on a regular basis. Therefore, the manager/team needs to capture new information and reset the priorities to adapt and predictably reach their desired objectives. This requires the team to have a keen business acumen and a mind that can understand the major priorities of an initiative. This involves understanding the big picture, risks, probabilities, impacts, resources, and even politics.

Level Three Team

These teams are responsible for a more holistic involvement in co-planning the tactical aspects of a strategy under structured parameters. This involves breaking down and organizing new tasks from established organizational processes. They demonstrate a proficiency in budgeting, resource planning, risk management, stakeholder identification, communication planning, and other tactical considerations. They can adopt a bird's-eye, tactical view more than the previous levels. Strategy initiation and higher-level strategic planning are centralized, and then handed over for the detailed tactics and execution.

Level Four Team

These teams are responsible for designing tactics with more open-ended parameters. This is usually done with less structured restrictions after tangible and measurable objectives are determined by senior leaders. The team must be able to understand the objectives and take it from there. It likely involves procurement of capabilities, "best practice" process selection, integrating processes, and customized planning. They can take a higher-level planning perspective to competently manage the associated priorities, objectives, stakeholders, budget, risk, and so on (with less guidance, even under open-ended situations). The enterprise-level strategy and initiation of team-level strategies are centralized, but most of the planning is handed over.

Level Five Team

These teams get involved as early as the initiation of the strategic efforts. This involves having a strong understanding of external/internal trends and knowing how to capitalize on them to reach a desired state. This requires having a strong understanding of the current reality, but being an idealist at the same time. Such teams have the potential to take the enterprise-level strategy, formulate and integrate a team-level strategy with it, and design strategic goals to shoot for, and they possess the tactical planning capabilities to push it through. The enterprise-level strategy is centralized, whereas most of the strategic process is decentralized, whilst ensuring alignment with the overall strategic direction and sponsorship.

Level Six Team

These teams have the potential to create brand new strategic directions that are innovative. They are proposed from a bottom-up direction to capitalize on opportunities missed by the enterprise-level strategic push. This is much more than being creative. It involves all the capabilities in the previous levels, an innovative mindset, and the ownership to be accountable for it. Verifying alignment among strategic efforts and sponsorship is centralized, but most aspects are decentralized.

17.3. How to Promote an Ecosystem of Strategy as a Leader

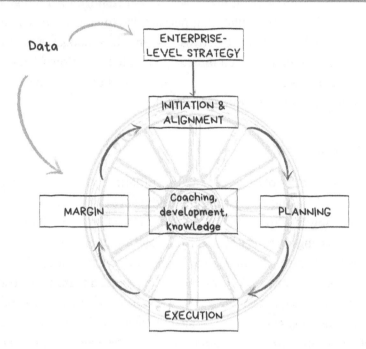

Promoting team-level strategies cannot occur in a vacuum. It doesn't happen naturally, and the ecosystem needs to be supported by the senior leadership.

Let's take a look at the other components of the ecosystem, beyond the "wheel" that represents team-level strategies. That's how we can visualize how leaders can optimize this process. You'll notice that there are pieces that are dependent on senior leader involvement, which include: enterprise-level strategy, data, coaching/development, margin, and initiation/alignment. To optimize these interfaces, senior leaders can do the following:

- Tip #1 – Maximize coaching, development, and engagement with strategy.

- Tip #2 – Align the enterprise-level strategy with team-level strategies.
- Tip #3 – Provide cross-functional support and sponsorship of this ecosystem.

Tip #1: Maximize Coaching, Development, and Engagement with Strategy

Initially, leaders will still need to get involved with the strategic planning and execution processes as they are opportunities to coach and develop people. Remember, strategy is hard. You can't suddenly let go and expect everything to come together. In fact, running through these processes is a great way to gauge the skill levels of your teams and people. As team-level strategic capabilities improve, leaders can step back and focus on the overall direction and management of the ecosystem. Let's visualize how leaders can optimize this process:

COACHING AND DEVELOPMENT IN STRATEGY

If people are not adequately developed to competently manage strategy, they will not be able to keep up. Senior leadership should evaluate and ensure that there are sufficient people development efforts throughout the organization. Teams should be given more access to developmental opportunities, whether through training, coaching, developmental programs, access to knowledge capital, and so on.

ENGAGEMENT IN STRATEGY

Team-led strategy relies on the engagement and buy-in of teams. It's important for leaders to understand their role in this. This is because there are many touch points where leaders can enable or kill the engagement throughout the life cycle of a strategy. Unfortunately, many of them have blind spots in this, which results in compromised outcomes and misalignment. Therefore, it's important to optimize their involvement in the strategy continuum. Let's look at how leaders could be maximizing engagement with people throughout the touch points of the process, or even inadvertently disengaging people.

- **Engaging people in strategic planning** – Leaders can empower, facilitate, or co-create plans with teams to increase their ownership and develop their strategic thinking and planning skills. This increases their ownership throughout the process.

- **Disengaging people in strategic planning** – When leaders over-centralize planning, it creates a chasm between the people and that results in misalignment. It can be caused by poor facilitation as well. Many larger traditional organizations that have an over-reliance on centralized strategic planning fit in this category. They may have a great strategic plan, but are unable to align and execute it well.

    On the opposite side, another way we could be getting disengagement in strategic planning is if we let go and abdicate it too soon, or don't do it at all. This leaves everyone wandering around aimlessly.

- **Engaging people in strategy execution** – Leaders can build momentum and morale throughout the strategic process. Additionally, leaders can use situational moments as opportunities to provide feedback, coach, and develop their people. This improves accountability, motivation, and engagement.

    At the conclusion of initiatives, successes should be celebrated to maintain spirit and morale. If the strategy isn't working out, leaders should prepare to shift gears, with an emphasis on communicating, connecting, and getting the people's buy-in for change.

- **Disengaging people in strategy execution** – This can happen when leaders are extremely prescriptive and fail to get buy-in, ownership, and engagement throughout the process. Additionally, this can occur when they don't use everyday moments to coach and develop others. They may also be forgetting to caretake the morale and momentum, which can greatly affect success.

Even if the strategy is successful, there may be a lack of celebrations, which can put a damper on morale and momentum. Furthermore, if the strategy is not getting the desired results, they typically shift gears without getting buy-in. Sometimes, this results in major changes, such as structural reorganizations, layoffs, process changes, and so on, which further damages relationships and the people's trust.

There is a tendency for teams in closer proximity to leaders, who can keep teams engaged in the strategic process, to exhibit stronger capabilities in strategy. This gives us some insight on how we may be able to develop these capabilities within teams. We can ask ourselves the following:

- Are we investing in or developing our own leadership skills to involve others while simultaneously reaching goals?
- Is there any way to strategically position our existing leaders who are skilled at this to increase their reach within the organization?
- Are we investing in developing leadership skills in others to do the same?

If we're continuously struggling in developing strategic capabilities within the organization, it may be worth reassessing our leadership skills in involving others in strategy while reaching goals. This can be deceivingly harder than it sounds.

Tip #2: Align the Enterprise-Level Strategy with Team-Level Strategies

When we enable team-level strategies, we have to be cognizant that there is an enterprise-level strategy going in a top-down direction that has to interface with team-level strategies going in a bottom-up direction. There are also multiple strategies that are competing for the same limited resources available within the organization. That means there are interfacing junctions between various strategic efforts that have to be managed. To reconcile this, leaders should do the following:

- Be cognizant of the current team-level capabilities when centralizing/decentralizing strategy – It's important to be aware of the strategic capabilities of your teams. Even within the same organization, different teams will exhibit varying degrees of strategic competencies. Being aware of these considerations will help guide how much of the strategic process should be centralized or decentralized. At the same time, it's also important to take occasional leaps of faith to increase involvement in the strategic process when you think that the team may be ready. This creates a continuous trajectory of growth and development.

- Formulate a clear enterprise-level strategy – When enterprise-level strategies are formulated, they should be clear and simple to resonate with people. This allows teams to reference them to maintain alignment when setting the overall direction of team-level strategies. Many organizations have enterprise-level strategies, but they are often poorly designed for resonance. We will discuss how to create a well-positioned enterprise-level strategy in the final chapter.

- Communicate the enterprise-level strategy with clarity – Just because you design a clear enterprise-level strategy, it doesn't mean that people will understand it. It has to be communicated clearly to maximize buy-in. This is something that many companies struggle with. This will also be discussed further in the final chapter.

- Have a process for aligning team-level strategies with higher-level strategy – It's important to design team-level strategies to be on the same page with the enterprise-level strategy. We accomplish this by incorporating a step within the strategic process that involves taking a step back and understanding the holistic viewpoint, and confirming alignment with the enterprise-level strategy. Many companies either overlook this element of strategy or underestimate its relevance. It can greatly reduce the misalignment and internal bureaucracy that commonly paralyzes many organizations.

- **Have a structured approval and resource allocation process** – A structured approval process can help maintain alignment when there are multiple strategies. This can help create a filter mechanism to ensure that only relevant strategies are being approved and resourced appropriately. If we don't have a system in place when there are multiple strategies being managed simultaneously, it may be time to consider introducing it.

- **Enable and guide bottom-up management** – It's obvious that strategies can come from a top-down direction, but how about a bottom-up direction? Are we encouraging this? Leaders should use idea proposals as an opportunity to connect with individuals and develop their ideas. They should coach to refine their proposals and approve the well-developed ones.

    Leaders should avoid outright rejecting ideas. Sometimes they sit on them and never return to them. Other times, they don't really connect with the individual during the ideation discussion. Interestingly, leaders who do this are often unaware that they're doing it, or they have a high distrust of others.

Tip #3: Provide Cross-Functional Support and Sponsorship of This Ecosystem

To promote an ecosystem of team-level strategies, it's important to establish a partnership mentality with the appropriate cross-functions to maximize support and sponsorship. Many of these strategies can get deterred or killed if they have insufficient support, and insufficient support can result in an unsustainable environment for team-level strategies. Let's take a look at a few ways that cross-functional support and sponsorship can enable this ecosystem.

- **Create margin** – If teams and people do not have the bandwidth, they cannot engage in strategy. Senior leaders need to partner with the teams to create appropriate margin. They can use that bandwidth to develop more skills, create space for research, or have time for "white space" for strategic thinking.

- **Transparency on data** – Be open to sharing knowledge and information. The more transparent we are, the more likely teams can be strategic with it. Of course, this shouldn't include confidential information. Data can include existing research, surveys, analytics, and trends. Transparency on this information can help more teams understand the overall landscape. In addition, teams can gather their own data as well. They have access to ground-level knowledge and could have their own data to process and internalize.

- **Access to knowledge capital** – An organization has a wealth of knowledge capital to have gotten to where it is today. This can include knowledge of processes that may be valuable to push strategies forward. However, access to this knowledge is often limited or unavailable to teams. This can make it difficult for teams to conceptualize and execute strategies. By granting greater access to the wealth of knowledge available within the organization, it equips teams to be in a better position to be strategic.

- **Readily deployable resources** – When there is significant delay, red tape, or distrust around deployment of resources, it can squander strategic efforts of teams. Rather, an environment of readily deployable resources can enable teams to expertly maneuver and adapt around obstacles. Obviously, this requires a mutual trust and partnership mentality to establish this. As teams demonstrate greater ownership and competence in strategic capabilities, it may become prudent to enable this.

- And more.

There are many large traditional companies that are trying to develop organization-wide innovation, but struggle to do so. When looking at the situation through this model, it becomes clearer where the issues are. If we are not adequately supporting team-level strategies, this will result in an unsustainable ecosystem, a higher failure rate of strategic efforts, misalignment, and underdeveloped/disengaged people.

Under such circumstances, it becomes extremely difficult or nearly impossible to enable engagement and innovation. It also forces them to frequently deal with misalignment issues in the back end of strategic initiatives throughout implementation. Therefore, it makes sense to reevaluate the ecosystem as a whole and consider a different approach.

Philosophical Differences in Traditional and Modern Companies

Senior leaders play a significant role in developing the strategy ecosystem by deciding what the priorities are and allocating resources accordingly. Overall, there is a large philosophical difference between how traditional and modern companies approach strategies. To illustrate this point, we will refer back to the strategy life cycle model and evaluate common differences in their top priorities.

First, we'll describe the common scenario for traditional companies that have a top-down focus. Typically, these companies allocate their attention and emphasis on:

- **Data** – Traditional senior leaders put a large emphasis on data to introduce objectivity and visibility in a scalable manner. It's not uncommon to see a strong preference toward objective data, numbers, sufficient sample size, statistics, analysis, and so on.

- **Enterprise-level strategy** – Traditional senior leaders interpret the current reality and conceptualize the enterprise-level strategy that addresses advanced strategic considerations, but may lack resonance with the majority of the people in the organization.

- **Strategic planning** – Traditional senior leaders often centralize planning, resulting in prescriptive strategic plans. This often entails extremely sophisticated plans, but lacks alignment and buy-in.

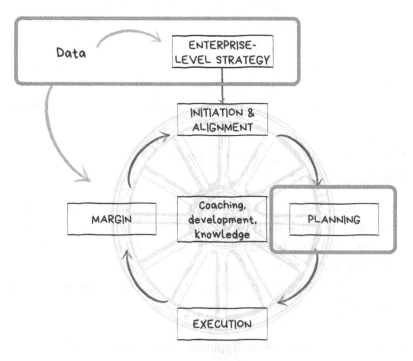

Visualization of top priorities in traditional approaches to strategy

Though these are valuable components, they don't harness the innovation of teams optimally. This doesn't get the team-level strategy "wheel" turning well. It forces a situation where they have to deal with misalignment and ownership challenges throughout their teams. This subsequently creates more issues in the back end of execution that involve cleaning up and putting out "fires."

Modern companies that focus on optimizing the strategy ecosystem have a different philosophical approach. The top priorities for this approach are different because the focus is on optimizing self-directed team-level strategies. Let's take a closer look at how this looks.

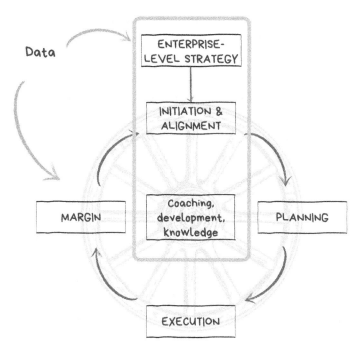

Visualization of top priorities in modern approaches to strategy

- **Enterprise-level strategy** – There is still a large focus on conceptualizing an enterprise-level strategic vision but with a greater emphasis on clarity and alignment.

- **Strategy initiation and alignment** – There is a much greater focus on strategic initiation and alignment to ensure that team-level strategies are going in the same direction. That's why there's a greater emphasis on clarity, communication, collaboration, and keeping people on the same page. Even if teams haven't fully developed strategic capabilities to own this step, it is still valuable to have people looking toward the same long-term direction.

- **Coaching, development, knowledge capital** – This is the centerpiece for the team-level strategies, like the "hub" of a wheel. This is about people development and leveraging existing knowledge capital within the organization. There needs to be a large emphasis on collaboration, management, leadership, and strategy development to "grease the wheels" for teams to handle strategy effectively. This is to ensure that the people infrastructure and strategic capabilities have been properly developed within the organization because without it, this approach will not be successful.

There'll still be moments where leaders need to help out by getting involved and coaching people throughout the planning and execution process. However, it's important to recognize that the endgame is to enable team-led strategies, which paves the road for greater leverage. That's why there's such a large focus on people development. When this is successful, it decentralizes most of the strategic processes to the teams. It gets the "wheel" of team-level strategies turning. This can be an extremely scalable way of harnessing organization-wide proactive thinking, and can ultimately pave the path for organic, scalable, sustainable, and exponential growth.

This Impacts How Senior Leaders Approach Strategy

This approach of building a strategy ecosystem can help us understand the need to rebalance the allocation of our resources and priorities to effectively enable team-level strategies. If we treat our alignment and people development efforts lightly, we will fail to create the innovation and forward-thinking atmosphere that many companies seek. If you're struggling to achieve this, ask yourself the following:

- Are we over-focusing on data and prescriptive planning?
- Does our existing strategic process account for alignment?
- If not, how can we adapt our process to incorporate it?
- Are we allocating enough of our resources for people development?
- What would a successful people development and strategy ecosystem program look like for your organization?

This mindset shift can make a world of difference, and it can change the way you approach strategy.

In this chapter, we brought together much of the content of this book in order to describe an ecosystem of strategy that is accomplished by leveraging culture. We discussed the paradigm shift required for this new approach to strategy, common areas of misalignment, and transitioning from linear to life cycle management. It requires deliberate effort to develop the strategic capabilities of teams and engage them as a leader. With this in mind, the final chapter will talk about the guiding light of your organization.

CHAPTER 18

ENTERPRISE-LEVEL STRATEGY

There are going to be moments of confusion and challenges throughout the course of our work. There are going to be difficult conversations with customers. There's going to be disagreement among staff members. There will be balls that are dropped and fires that need to be put out. In times like these, people may feel confused and would appreciate a beacon of light that acts as a guiding force to help them make decisions. Without this, they can easily get lost or feel like they're in the dark.

Even during moments when we are not lost, it provides clarity for how to take a proactive stance toward a future vision. In fact, it even helps define what our moments of success and triumph look like. It provides a baseline toward which we can calibrate. When faced with a decision, we can ask ourselves, "Will this move us closer to the vision?" In fact, people want to have this guiding force to know whether they are on the right track.

That's what the enterprise-level strategy is, the "guiding light" of the organization. However, fabricating an enterprise-level strategy is more involved than meets the eye. I know we already talked about strategy in previous chapters, but that was with an alignment and team-level strategy focus. In this chapter, we're going to focus on what everyone else is aligning to. It's what sets the tone of the organization, while keeping us going toward the right direction for maximizing value creation.

It's also important to recognize that the enterprise-level strategy works hand in hand with culture strategy. They have a mutualistic relationship and feed off of each other via two mechanisms.

- The enterprise-level strategy positions the organization to develop the internal culture.
- Culture strategy enables maximum leverage of the enterprise-level strategy.

In addition, enterprise-level strategies have additional and complicated nuances, so it's important to discuss them as their own topic. We'll be approaching this chapter by discussing:

- Strategic positioning of the enterprise-level strategy to maximize value
- Gaining alignment and engagement for the enterprise-level strategy
- Setting the priorities of the organization through the enterprise-level strategy

Some people ask, *How often do we evaluate the enterprise-level strategy?* We usually reevaluate the enterprise-level strategy every two to five years or when the current one is not adequately guiding the organization. This is such an overarching strategy that it usually takes years to materialize and doesn't need to be adapted as often as team-level strategies.

18.1. Strategic Positioning for Growth and Purpose

An enterprise-level strategy should be designed with a balanced approach. It should have elements that capitalize on market opportunities as well as having a purpose. One of the most common problems with enterprise-level strategies is that they have one or the other. This can lead to an imbalanced strategy that either fails to capture business value or doesn't resonate with people for engagement. Let's explore these elements further:

- **Opportunity-driven strategy** – Capitalizes on market trends to capture business value.
- **Purpose-driven strategy** – Maximizes engagement and emphasizes creating solutions to solve existing pain points.

Opportunity-Driven: Capturing Value through Strategic Positioning

First, we're going to talk about utilizing the enterprise-level strategy to position the organization for maximum value and growth. We have to recognize that there needs to be much more care and attention when designing this because it is extremely impactful.

You can be leading people to the "promised land" or be leading them off a cliff.

The enterprise-level strategy can be so impactful because it capitalizes on value that is created from its positioning. Some find this difficult to conceptualize because this is intangible value. They may find it challenging to recognize that there are ways to create substantial value in this manner. In fact, with a well-positioned enterprise-level strategy, we can generate significantly more value with the same set of resources, team(s), people, competencies, work dynamics, knowledge capital, and processes. This must be designed to capture the most opportunities, value, and synergy that we can anticipate. Let's explore a few different ways we can do this.

Being in the Right Industry and Market

When we're evaluating the enterprise-level strategy, we can adopt a bird's-eye view and evaluate whether we are in the right industry or market. This decision can make a large impact on whether we're dealing with a cutthroat or a bountiful market.

- **Blue Ocean Market** – This is a bountiful environment where margins are more generous, and there are less established competitors. This is a more forgiving market environment.

- **Red Ocean Market** – This is an extremely cutthroat and commoditized market environment that is oversaturated with competitors. Margins are extremely slim, and there is very little room for error.

If you want to dig deeper into evaluating the state of industries, consider looking into Porter's Five Forces. It is a great tool for assessing the market condition of industries. This looks at competitive rivals, potential new market entrants, suppliers, customers, and substitute products. Blue Ocean Strategy is another tool that is geared toward strategic positioning in markets that have more opportunity.

Synergy

By leveraging existing capabilities/assets in a strategic manner, we can create synergistic value. With such strategies, we can make 1 + 1 = 3, rather than 1 + 1 = 2. That difference between 3 and 2 is the extra synergistic value. This can be accomplished through:

- **Horizontal integration** – If you have a great product, process, or capability, then increasing your customer base through expanding to additional locations, increasing sales channels, or mergers and acquisitions (M&A) can create synergistic value. Those newly acquired consumers would get the same benefits as your current ones after they are integrated into your organization.

- **Vertical integration** – If you have a substantially large consumer base or buying power, then synergistic value can be created through taking over additional steps in the value chain. These can be steps in production, services, processes, or distribution along the same vertical value chain. Then, you can provide products to your own businesses, rather than utilizing vendors. Also, your customers can get more value as you offer more comprehensive solutions.

Reconciling culture is essential in extrapolating value from synergy. It's undeniable that strategic synergy can create an enormous amount of value. However, it's important to understand some of the potential challenges when implementing this. Creating synergy involves the integration of different business units to work in harmony. This can become an obstacle when each business unit has their own culture, especially if it was externally acquired. If there are stark differences in culture, then it can impede the proper capturing of this synergistic value. In fact, many synergistic efforts and M&A fail due to the challenges associated with business unit and culture integration. Therefore, it's prudent to mitigate this with:

- **Culture evaluation before integration** – It is wise to take culture into consideration before pulling the trigger on integration efforts. For example, if we are considering a M&A deal, it would be prudent to evaluate for culture compatibility during the due diligence process.

- **Leading culture integration** – Utilize principles that were discussed in this book to manage necessary culture integration efforts. Depending on how wide this gap is, it may be a simple or complex culture change process.

Anticipating the Market

Obviously, it's impossible to know the future for certain. However, we can use our understanding of the world to deduce patterns and trends. This goes beyond understanding external trends at a superficial level or simply listening to expert opinions. It requires cross-referencing information and trends with an extremely strong grasp of reality to forecast the future. Here are some sample patterns that we can use to do this:

- **Understanding the cyclical nature of economies** – There's a cyclical pattern to economies, which can make a large impact on businesses. Paying attention to this pattern helps us look past the hype and excitement of the news, as that could lead to poor decisions. Instead, it allows us to refocus on the fundamentals.

- **Understanding the sustainability of situations** – Ask yourself, is the current market situation sustainable? Is the current dynamic creating real value? If that is not the case, we may have an unsustainable market situation, and a correction may be overdue. This can impact how we play our chips and cards.

- **Having a clear mind and seeing opportunities in threats** – There will always be hardships. We also live in an era of information overload that highlights the threats more than the opportunities. This is often the result of hype and misinformation from the rest of the world. If we follow the same mentality, we will only perceive the threats around us, and be blind to the opportunities. Stick to the fundamentals to see these opportunities. Oftentimes, new trends arise out of troubling times, and can be harnessed. Like Warren Buffet said, "Be fearful when others are greedy. Be greedy when others are fearful."

- **Understanding the causes of industry category changers** – If we want to play a bigger hand, it's important to understand the causes of industry category changers (also known as disruptions). They have the potential to make such a large impact that it shifts the market dynamic of the entire industry. If we look at the pattern of what caused these disruptions, they were usually trigged by innovative solutions that had scalable impacts on technology, media, or labor force. You can reference disruptive business models to see how leaders applied these forces to reshape their industry, and figure out how to do it yourself.

Internal Culture Strategy

This is pretty much what this whole book was about. Internal culture strategy can have a massive impact on the organization by creating a trajectory for organic, sustainable, innovative, exponential growth. By positioning the organization to have a strong culture, it unlocks the potential to be a game changer in the industry.

Why Is This Important?

It's important to recognize the importance of positioning the organization for growth. Some may wonder, *Why is this important? Why can't we just do business without this?* It's true that you can do business without this, but bear in mind that it will create limitations. Strategic positioning for growth makes it easier to capture value, and as a result makes it:

- **Easier to penetrate the market** – It is easier to penetrate the market and capture value.

- **Easier to create growth opportunities** – It is easier to capture growth opportunities for the organization, which also creates opportunities for its people.

- **Easier to engage people** – If there are opportunities for people, it improves their engagement.

It's actually challenging to engage with people in a stagnant organization. It may still be possible to engage them, but it becomes an extremely difficult uphill battle to accomplish this. People who are interested in personal and professional growth will not find those opportunities in such situations. If the organization is positioned to capture more value, then it is easier to design *win-win* situations with employees. This creates a sustainable dynamic for the organization and its culture.

Purpose-Driven: Have Something People Can Engage With

Now, we're going to shift our discussion to designing enterprise-level strategies with a purpose-driven mindset. If we focus only on strategic positioning for capitalizing on market opportunities, it will not be enough to create a thriving business. You'll find that there's more involved when trying to maximize the value out of the enterprise-level strategy. It also needs to connect with people at a deeper level. A strategy that is solely based on market opportunities has the following challenges:

- **Doesn't engage people enough** – Without a purpose, the enterprise-level strategy will have challenges engaging people within the organization. It needs more. It needs a purpose that they believe in.

- **Lacks connecting with real pain points** – A business doesn't exist without its customers. Without a true connection to solving the pain points of its customers, it fails to deliver real value. A purpose-driven mindset helps the organization connect with those pain points to truly deliver solutions that are meaningful to them.

The enterprise-level strategy must be purpose-driven and create value for customers and employees to be truly sustainable. Without this, it becomes very difficult to apply culture strategy to the organization as people will simply not believe in it. It needs to answer:

Why **are we here?** – Answering this helps us define our purpose and gives us something to believe in and gather around. People don't want to congregate around a strategy designed to squeeze value out of our employees and customers. Focusing on the purpose allows us to remain vigilant as a value-creating business.

Ultimately, there needs to be a balance between encompassing opportunity-driven and purpose-driven strategic positioning. It's not simply one or the other. When you accomplish this, you get an organization that is capable of:

- **Organically identifying gaps in the market** – Having a combined purpose-driven and opportunity-driven mentality naturally identifies pain points. We can channel those pain points to identify gaps in the market. Then, we can focus on addressing those gaps with our products and services. This mindset can be a tremendous asset within the organization that allows for continuous innovation and adaptation.

- **Better engagement** – Purpose-driven strategies are easier for people to resonate with. That makes it easier to get their buy-in and engagement with the strategy. This allows for better alignment, ownership, problem solving, self-direction, and innovation.

I hope I made the point that it's more challenging to sustain a business without a purpose. However, some may ask, *Aren't there businesses that don't have a purpose that they believe in?* Yes, that may be the case. But you'll realize that many of them focus more on the transactions of business rather than delivering value. Some of them take it a step further and adapt the mentality: *There's a sucker born every minute.*

Eventually, even if their team(s) and customers are currently blind to these considerations, it will eventually catch up to them because it's not sustainable. This can manifest in different ways and can occur differently for every organization. This can happen through damage to the brand and reputation, regulatory backlash, entrants of new competitors who are willing to focus on creating value to capture market share and the best talent, and so on.

Leaders could try their best to prop up the situation. But how long can that last? Also, how can you build a self-directed organization when there's no purpose to engage people with?

18.2. Getting Alignment and Engagement with the Enterprise-Level Strategy

Now that we've discussed the importance of strategically positioning your enterprise-level strategy to be both purpose-driven and opportunity-driven, it's time to shift our focus to communicating those ideas with the rest of the organization and getting them on the same page. Here are the common challenges and obstacles associated with that:

- **People get confused about it** – It's not clear enough. People misinterpret it, and disagree with each other due to differing opinions on the priorities.

- **It doesn't penetrate multiple layers** – People don't connect with it and forget about it. It loses relevance after several rounds of interpretation from different layers of the organization.

An enterprise-level strategy has a unique challenge because it needs to stay relevant after several rounds of interpretation. This is because divisions, departments, and teams will use it to base their own strategies. Therefore, if it's not packaged properly, it won't resonate after multiple rounds of being interpreted.

Enterprise-Level MVV

We have to take the ideas from the previous section and package them so that the rest of the organization can understand and align with them. Utilizing the *mission, vision, and values* framework is a great initial vehicle for packaging those ideas into a cleaner format. Many people have heard of this framework, but they often get confused on how to use it, so here's a description of them.

- **Enterprise-level mission** – What's wrong with the world and how you intend to fix it.

- **Enterprise-level vision** – What the world will look like after you've finished changing it. Be bold with this! If it doesn't make you nervous, it's not bold enough!

- **Enterprise-level values** – These are values that make you who you are, make you competent, and make you stand out among your competitors. They need to be designed to keep the team together and move forward toward a strategic direction.

It's important to recognize that this isn't supposed to be a long-winded description, nor is it supposed to be a slogan. These are common mistakes that are made when people design their enterprise-level mission, vision, and values:

- **Long-winded mission or vision** – A long-winded description leads to a loss of clarity and resonance. It may be highly descriptive and accurate, but it's meaningless if you can't get people on board with it. Historically, mission and vision statements were written this way when only executives and board members looked at them. Nowadays, when we are trying to get more people bought into them, they need to be simpler.

- **Using the mission or vision as a slogan** – This isn't a slogan either. It's not about having a catchy phrase for getting people excited over something that doesn't have any real substance. Then, it would end up as a "poster on the wall" that collects dust and doesn't serve any function. Rather, it needs to paint a clear picture of who we are and where we're going.

- **Redundant values** – Try not to be redundant with obvious values. Personally, I find that the best values are the ones that focus on propagating culture strategy, at least the ones that resonate with your company. Other values tend to be extremely obvious, redundant, and self-explanatory, which makes them lose their meaning. Whenever possible, I recommend sticking with five values, as any more than that tends to lose resonance.

Once we have a well-written MVV, it's important to note that it is only as good as it gets used. This takes intentional alignment and reinforcement efforts. Many leaders have challenges with getting everyone on the same page with the strategy. This is because the scope of this task is more involved than meets the eye. Remember, there need to be sufficient team-level strategic capabilities built throughout the organization to smoothly achieve this alignment. We discussed this in the previous strategy chapters of the book. To recap, it involves:

- Increasing baseline strategic thinking skills
- Increasing essential strategy skills
- Focusing on the strategy ecosystem and alignment

On top of that, we need to utilize leadership tools to maximize resonance, optimize penetration of the enterprise-level strategy to multiple layers of the organization, and maintain strategic alignment. Let's discuss some of the tools that senior leaders can use to accomplish this.

Breaking the Enterprise-Level Strategy into Major Milestones

An enterprise-level strategy is very complex, no doubt about it. It's difficult to communicate it without overwhelming people. That's why one of the leader's responsibilities is to define reality and conceptualize a vision and enterprise-level strategy in a manner that is digestible for others. Then, they must communicate it in a clear manner for people to understand it. Otherwise, the strategy will fail to materialize.

To succeed at this, we need to share the vision in a manner that resonates with people and connects with their minds and hearts. However, the challenge in this is that enterprise-level strategies are overwhelming and complex. If we understand and recognize this, we can be cognizant of the fact that strategy can be challenging for most people. Therefore, a skilled leader can take the complex ideas and simplify them for people by breaking them down to bite-sized pieces. This can help create clarity. The clearer the vision is, the easier it is for people to understand it. That's why it's recommended to break the path down by smaller "line-of-sight" visions with phases and milestones.

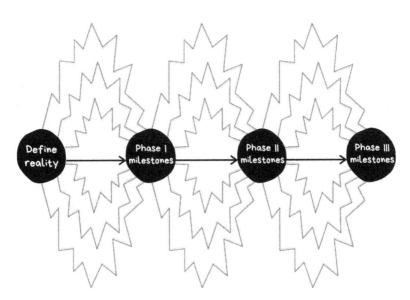

Visualization of a line-of-sight vision broken down into phases and milestones

Utilizing "Line-of-Sight" Visions

Oftentimes, vision statements have a two- to five-year run time to materialize. With such a long duration, it becomes obvious why so few people can resonate with it. Breaking the enterprise-level vision into smaller "line-of-sight" visions that have shorter durations (for example, one year) can greatly improve the visibility of the overarching strategy.

Creating Clarity by Using Phases and Milestones

Break down the "line-of-sight" vision into major phases with associated milestones. Paint a picture of how it would look. Connect with people by sharing stories to let them know what it would feel like to live in a world where we accomplished this. Use simplified imagery to minimize confusion. Encourage input on how we would get there. This can greatly help with resonance.

Consider using "three" phases or milestones. There's something magical about the number three when it comes to knowledge absorption and retention. Studies show that people retain three ideas better than they retain two or four ideas. If it's reasonable to do so, consider simplifying the line-of-sight vision to three landmark phases and create clarity around them by defining milestones and strategic goals. Remember, attention is a limited resource, and strategists need to know how to capitalize on it. As we move forward with the strategy, consider revisiting your progress in quarterly increments or other frequencies that make sense for your organization. In the spirit of remaining adaptable and agile, reassess the relevance of your overarching strategies and make any necessary updates and pivots before the next set of strategic goals is ironed out.

Tips When Communicating Strategy

It's also important to take the right tone when communicating the vision to people. It is best to communicate in a simple and deliberate manner to maximize resonance and absorption.

You Can't Micromanage and Tiptoe Strategy

The truth is you can't micromanage strategy. It's messy and goes in multiple directions at once. Even if you try to micromanage it, you'll quickly end up in a situation where you're dealing with an overwhelming amount of issues because you may end up having to micromanage the tactics and execution considerations as well. You'll quickly realize that the act of micromanaging strategies is unsustainable. It'll drive you and everyone around you crazy.

Instead, it is about setting the enterprise-level strategy, creating clarity, and developing people's strategic abilities. When you approach it this way, there will be increased ownership and a natural tendency for efforts to diverge in their own directions, hence the need for converging points within strategic phases and milestones. These are important because it gives you a tool to mobilize people toward a convergence point without having to micromanage them.

When we effectively communicate clear milestones, our team(s) can strategize on how to get there from their angle. This is valuable because you aren't involved in the day-to-day activities of the team and likely don't have firsthand information on what their obstacles are. They might even go in a different direction than you had imagined, but will converge back to the milestones as the strategy moves forward.

Even dictating process selection and procuring capabilities is borderline micromanagement. At the end of the day, if you are in a position to develop the enterprise-level strategy, and you are dictating which processes and capabilities to introduce, you may be micromanaging or may have the wrong people.

Minimize Using Cautious Language

Incremental language is not very effective when sharing the strategic vision with the rest of the organization. Minimize saying phrases such as "Let's do XYZ and we'll see what happens," because it won't get buy-in and move the strategy forward. It'll create confusion regarding where to converge at the relevant milestones.

Some strategic leaders naturally use a very cautious, noncommittal and incremental language when communicating. They take this tone because they understand that there is a great degree of uncertainty in strategic planning, and they want to encourage differing perspectives. There are definitely moments when it's appropriate to take such tones during strategic planning. However, this is extremely counterintuitive when strategists inadvertently carry that tone when communicating the vision to get buy-in. It overcomplicates issues and creates vague milestones, and people have challenges understanding where to converge.

Strategy Facilitation:
Connecting Strategic Plans across Multiple Layers

Facilitating strategy sessions is a great way to maintain alignment between higher-level strategies and the organization as a whole, thereby ensuring that we're on the same page. It accomplishes this by increasing involvement from managers and teams, which increases the reach and penetration of the enterprise-level strategy, bridges strategy skill gaps, and maximizes ownership, adaptability, and innovation. This helps to:

- **Maintain alignment with key cross-functions** – Essential cross-functions play a critical role in supporting the overarching strategy. The strategies, phases, and goals can be shared with these functions during facilitation sessions, so they can conceptualize their role and develop their own strategic goals that optimize support of the enterprise-level strategy, and even cover angles that only they can see.

- **Maintain alignment with vertical layers** – It should be pretty clear by now that strategy is not exclusive to the highest level. In fact, there can be a strategy for each relevant level. This can connect them across multiple vertical levels, including those from enterprise level, division level, department level, and team levels.

Furthermore, we can also use subsequent facilitation sessions to convert strategies into tangible plans through a co-creation process. This involves following up with tactical planning and execution. Through this approach, a team could take a strategy from the level above, fabricate their own, and subsequently create their own tactical plan for implementation.

This creates a chain of synchronized strategies and relevant tactical plans across different layers that have been co-created. This provides the following benefits: optimizes alignment with the higher-level strategic direction, and maximizes engagement, ownership, and situational adaptation in execution throughout multiple layers.

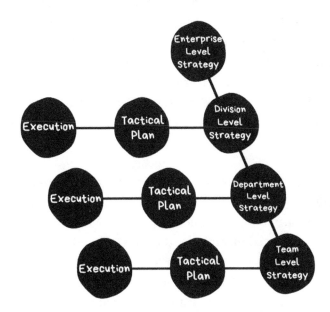

Visualization of interconnected strategies and subsequent tactical plans and execution

Overall, the feasibility of this facilitation approach is dependent on multiple factors, including: the collaboration skills of the team, strategy proficiencies of the team or representative, coaching/facilitative skills of the managers/leaders, size of the team, complexity, scope of the strategy, and so on. Furthermore, the follow-up facilitation for the tactical planning can be done in the following ways:

- **Team facilitates the plan and proposes** – If the manager and team have a good understanding of the vision and they have sufficient proficiencies, they can facilitate the tactical planning process and propose it to the senior leadership. This can involve components including but not limited to: diagnostics, strategies, goals, priorities, objectives, task breakdown, communication plan, budget, risk, and so on.

- **Senior leader facilitates** – This may be more of an interim solution to bridge skill gaps as it involves an overreaching situation until the team has developed adequate proficiencies. It can also be used as an opportunity for senior leaders to evaluate and develop the skills of their teams. Ultimately, the manager of the team should be able to handle the facilitation. Sometimes, the presence of a senior leader can disrupt the planning process due to the "boss versus facilitator paradox," because the leader is a stakeholder and may compromise the purity of the facilitation.

- **No facilitation (centralizing decisions)** – If the teams are not ready for facilitated planning sessions due to a lack of trust or chronic underdevelopment, then the planning will need to be centralized to minimize the risks of derailing situations. Ideally, this should also be an interim solution until sufficient people development efforts have taken root and mutual trust has been established, unless the scope of such effort is deemed unrealistic.

Of course, there are nuances to this facilitated approach. If it's haphazardly done, it can lead to disorganization, wasted resources, failing to get the right perspectives, and failing to meet the objectives. To prevent this, one of the biggest things to get right is: *get the right people involved for the planning sessions.* However, this can depend on the nuances of the organization, because each is built differently with its own set of established processes and structure. That being said, key perspectives can include those from:

- **Sponsorship** – This usually involves senior leaders who can provide the necessary authority, sponsorship, and influence that is required of the strategy.

- **Cross-functional support** – Sometimes, organizations have cross-functional requirements that necessitate their involvement to secure their support.

- **Expertise** – Some strategies require specialized expertise to build and push the strategy forward.

- **Execution** – Representation from the execution team is essential for implementation, as they have an understanding of ground-level considerations. However, they are often underrepresented or have underdeveloped strategy skills. Even if you get a representative from the execution team, they should demonstrate sufficient strategic capabilities. If their competencies are not adequately developed, then they may become the weak link and be the blocker to the alignment of strategy. That's why we should aim to develop them.

That being said, there can still be more nuanced or complicated situations in strategy facilitation. Let's explore some scenarios:

- **What if that involves too many people?** – Sometimes we find ourselves in a situation where there are too many people to have meaningful strategic planning sessions. One reason for this is that some larger organizations have a lot of hierarchal and cross-functional red tape, and it requires involving certain people in the planning stage due to approval or functional considerations. This leaves fewer openings for the execution team to get involved in the strategic planning table before it becomes too crowded.

Another reason for this may be due to having a large execution team under a centralized manager. That may already involve too many people in the discussion. Actually, that may indicate an unsustainable structure and it could be worthwhile to consider reorganizing. Having key representative(s) from the execution team, and "swinging by" with the rest of the team at appropriate moments when their input is required, mitigates this.

- **Bringing in an external facilitator** – Sometimes, there are circumstances that require specialized approaches or involve a larger scope where it makes more sense to have an external facilitator who is experienced in those matters perform the strategic planning facilitations. That person could get involved with specialized agendas, skills, or breakout sessions. Other times, the organization wants to use a facilitative approach, but doesn't have the know-how to do this and brings in an external facilitator.

- **And more.**

Overall, the most common mistakes in strategy facilitation are insufficient representation and perspectives, being unclear on how to do it, or not doing it at all! It's important to remember that it can be a valuable tool to promote strategic alignment in a manner that maximizes ownership, engagement, situational problem solving, and innovation.

If You Are Overseeing Multiple Strategies Simultaneously, Consider Using a Structured Process

When an organization has challenges in simultaneously managing multiple strategic directions, it may be time to introduce structured processes. If there are already existing processes within the organization, but they are suboptimized, it may be worth reevaluating those processes.

Structured strategy processes can create organization and standardization throughout the various steps, from strategy initiation to planning to execution. This can include organized steps for developing strategies, schedules, documentation, gaining approvals, deployment of resources, reporting, integration, closing procedures, and so on. This may be more applicable with larger organizations that need oversight for a larger number of strategies.

In regard to the topic of structuring strategies, many people are curious regarding the necessity of strategy documents. They wonder, *Do I need to convert my strategy into a document?* The answer, like many things, is it depends. Traditionally, strategic planning was centralized and written in a strategy document to highlight the key points to applicable readers. The challenge with utilizing this approach in a standalone manner is that it creates a large amount of misalignment, as there are fewer people who can read and understand the document. If this is created in an isolated situation, it's very easy for this to become prescriptive.

That's why a facilitative approach to co-create a strategic plan is helpful, as it gets more involvement and buy-in. In essence, it covers topics similar to those that are required to generate a strategy document. Many companies use a template during these facilitated strategic planning sessions. However, it is also important to recognize that there are many instances where these sessions may not be realistic in every scenario due to existing constraints. In those cases, strategy documents may be a good option to increase the reach of the plan.

Situational Reinforcement: As Sponsor, Facilitator, and Coach

As a leader, there will be many instances where you can reinforce the strategy situationally. In fact, to unlock the potential of the enterprise-level strategy, we need to be prudent with our situational reinforcement as a coach and facilitator. None of these approaches are possible without developing the strategic skills of the people within the organization. Therefore, use your everyday moments to coach and develop people's ideas. Encourage them to problem solve and help them refine their thinking skills.

We can use situational moments to reinforce the enterprise-level strategy by guiding the direction of the team-level strategies. Especially when leaders have sponsorship responsibilities, they wield significant influence on whether strategies get approved and continued. They can ensure that the strategies have a healthy focus and work toward the "guiding light." We'll explore how we can guide different levels of strategy to align with the relevant priorities of the enterprise-level strategy in the following section.

18.3. Specializations and Prioritization in Culture Strategy

One of the most common reasons why an enterprise-level strategy fails is because people have a poor understanding of it. It's important to understand the implications of it because it translates into business priorities. This allows us to be strategic in how we allocate our resources and efforts. Thus, it's essential to get clear on the following:

- What are our strategic priorities?
- As an organization, what do we specialize in?

This is important because there are a finite amount of resources. It's impossible to specialize in everything at once. If we don't get on the same page with this, we will surely fail to meet our goals. We will end up with:

- **Wasted resources** – Inadvertently allocating resources to efforts that do not help the strategic direction and thus are wasted.

- **Unnecessary politics and unhealthy interfaces** – When this is not clear, there will be needless debates and politics regarding the priorities of the organization. Therefore, it's important to clear the confusion and set the priorities straight.

- **Failed strategy** – Ultimately, a haphazard selection of priorities and specializations will result in failure to meet strategic goals.

This can cause significant damage to the organization. To get around this, we need to truly understand the implications of the enterprise-level strategy, make it explicitly clear, and get on the same page. That means that we need to understand:

- **Internal priorities** – Who we really are
- **External priorities** – What we are really selling

If you try to do everything by being the jack of all trades, you'll be great at nothing. It's very easy to fall into this trap. If we are not absolutely clear on what our strategic priorities and specializations are, then in the heat of the moment, we can make hasty decisions that are not truly in our best interests. To understand our priorities, we need to go beyond understanding who we are, and also understand who we are not.

Know both who we are and who we are not.

This gives us a guideline to decide which strategies to approve, but also to disapprove the ones that do not meet the criteria. This provides us with greater clarity and distinguishing factors as we move toward a strategic direction.

Internal Priorities: Who We Really Are

When we have clarity on who we really are, it guides us as we create our underlying internal strategies. Whether we are aware of this or not, all organizations need to demonstrate specialization, in one form or another, to stay relevant in the market. By setting clear organizational priorities, we can determine how we will choose to specialize and differentiate ourselves from our competitors. Here are three ways that we can select our specialization and double down on it by customizing our internal processes.

- **Customer Intimacy** – With a Customer Intimacy specialization, we are focusing on the broader customer problem and offering a total solution package. The priorities of this specialization are developing customer acquisition capabilities, developing customer solutions, becoming a problem expert, and customizing services.

- **Operational Excellence** – With an Operational Excellence specialization, we focus on having the best total costs, and we focus on efficiency. It's actually important to note that variety kills efficiency in this situation, which is a common mistake. The priorities of this specialization are end-to-end product delivery, streamlined customer service cycles, process redesign, and continuous improvement.

- **Product Leadership** – With a Product Leadership specialization, we are focusing on having the best product. In this situation, it's important to recognize that every product has a life cycle, and you must intentionally cannibalize your own success with innovation before your competitors do. The priorities of this specialization are innovation, commercialization, market exploitation, product technology, and research and development (R&D) cycle time.

You'll notice that it would be very difficult to do multiple specializations at the same time. Each of the underlying components involves extremely intentional strategies and investments. In fact, if we diversify our efforts too much, we will fail to double down on what really matters. However, if we play our chips right, we can extrapolate larger returns. This is the power of knowing who we are.

Some organizations actually think that they're in a different category than they really are. For example, many organizations think that they specialize in Customer Intimacy because they care about their customers. Obviously, they care about their customers, otherwise they wouldn't exist.

However, are they truly customizing their solutions to each individual need? Or have they continuously improved their operational processes to predictably address the needs of the majority?

Knowing the difference in such scenarios will impact how we make strategic decisions. That's why it's so critical that we have a strong understanding of the enterprise-level strategy, and what it really means. For a more granular exploration on this topic, refer to the Value Disciplines by Treacy and Wiersema.

External Priorities: What Are We Really Selling?

Customers are different, and they perceive value in different ways. How are we trying to differentiate ourselves from our competitors? What are we really selling?

When we are designing the enterprise-level strategy, it should be clear how we are trying to differentiate ourselves from others. This helps us gain clarity in our market segment, define our internal strategies, design our processes, interface with customers, and achieve alignment so that we move in the same direction. Below are several ways we can differentiate ourselves.

- **Cost** – Are we trying to win on price? If we are, we should be coupling this with the most efficient processes to reduce costs, otherwise it'll be unsustainable. There will always be a competitor who is willing to undercut you.

- **Efficiency** – Are we trying to win on fast service, being on time, and being reliable? If that's the case, we need to design our processes to streamline speed, response times, and reliability.

- **Communication** – Are we trying to win by having the best customer service? This will require personalized customer service training, engagement, team development, and adaptability.

- **Usability** – Are we trying to offer the best solution? If that's the case, we need to invest in our innovation and be willing to challenge the status quo.

Whichever our specialization and priorities are, culture strategy can help us achieve them. When we achieve a team that is self-directed and innovative, we can channel them toward those priorities. For example, even if our position is *cost*, we can develop innovative solutions to bring costs down.

Don't try to be everything. If you are the best solution, with the best service, with the highest reliability *and* the cheapest price, then you will bankrupt yourself. In reality, that solution will have expenses that are too costly to be able to offer it at the lowest prices.

Alternative Sub-Specializations

When we truly create an organization with a strong culture infrastructure, there are endless pathways we can take. There are many other alternative sub-specializations that can be integrated to further leverage the power of culture strategy. Here are a few examples:

- **Ecosystem-based product architecture** – Product architecture has many overlapping principles with strategy. In essence, it's being strategic with technology and engineering principles. Therefore, similar concepts can be applied when developing an overarching product architecture based on organizational communication structures. This maximizes partnerships with teams to maintain alignment with the overarching plan while developing their own team-level architecture to maximize their engagement, innovation, ownership, and self-direction.

- **Growth with a focus on culture integration** – Many of the challenges associated with growth and expansion are due to poor leadership and culture integration. Through a synchronized effort in people development, succession planning, change management, and integration, we can greatly improve the success rate of our growth efforts without diluting our quality and purpose.

- **Pave your own path!**

Dream big! Imagine what's possible with an enterprise that has the right culture infrastructure. What else can you do with an engaged and innovative company? Think about what's possible with an army of strategic and self-driven teams under one banner.

You could go on and create new business models: ones that we've never seen before. Solve some world problems, even the issues that have yet to be uncovered. Build a legacy and make an impact on this world. Go make us proud! When you do, share your stories with us. I look forward to hearing about them.

BRINGING IT ALL TOGETHER

Culture strategy is dear to me because it changed my life. It allowed me to gain control over my life, achieve freedom, and live with purpose. My objectives for this book were to share this knowledge by opening more minds on the moving pieces of culture strategy. I tried to do this by showing you the real path of culture strategy.

There's so much fluff and hype out there regarding this topic. I wanted to take the fluff out of it to help others gain a solid understanding of culture strategy, so it makes sense to implement it. This should, in turn, help you and more companies make this transformation. It's time that a no-nonsense, logical approach is available so we can properly size up the scope of this initiative and achieve the transformation in a more predictable manner with a higher success rate.

This is a genuine path that leads to results, and it doesn't involve shortcuts. It focuses on the strategies, tactics, and implementation for building a real infrastructure through people and culture. I can show you the path that leads to this value creation through culture strategy, but it's still up to you to decide to walk it. I'll be upfront: it may not be an easy and straightforward journey. But you'll be moving forward in a more impactful and sustainable direction.

Why You Should Lead through Culture

Culture strategy is a powerful tool. As a leader, manager, or entrepreneur, you can greatly benefit through applying these concepts. Imagine the potential impact of self-directed teams that organically create innovative, sustainable, and exponential growth. You should choose to lead through culture strategy because it can do the following:

- **Benefit you directly** – You'll find that leading with culture strategy benefits you as a leader in many ways. It will pave the path for making a larger impact, accomplish more with less effort, recapture balance in life, give you a sense of purpose, and build a legacy. This can lead to financial freedom as a business owner or promotional opportunities as an employed leader. Whatever your goals are, culture strategy can help you build the life that you always wanted.

- **Benefit others** – Not only can culture strategy help you live a better life, it can benefit others as well. It positively impacts the lives of the employees within your organization, as they find a home and oasis in a society of dysfunction. This strengthens their psychological well-being, helps stabilize their personal lives and families, and provides professional growth opportunities, if so desired. Additionally, consumers receive improved customer service or products/services that better resonate to their needs.

- **The time is now** – There has never been a more relevant time to implement culture strategy. The market is ripe for organizations that can better adapt to consumer needs, provide purpose for talent, and provide innovative solutions. In the past, the banana may have been green to implement this, but the banana is yellow now. Even if you don't choose to implement culture strategy, enough of your competitors will do it and overtake the market. If you react when it's hitting your bottom line, it may be too late, as culture strategy doesn't materialize overnight.

Tips on Getting Started

You may be wondering, *I'm interested, but where do I begin?* This may have been an overwhelming amount of content for many readers. First of all, don't worry, that's normal. Here are some tips on how to get started.

One Step at a Time

This can be a daunting and overwhelming effort. Rather than absorbing everything at once, take one step at a time. This is not going to be an overnight process. Depending on your situation, it may be useful to adopt a "crawl, walk, run" mentality.

Even if you were equipped with all of the realizations and skills, the rest of the world did not have the same breakthroughs with you. Sometimes introducing too much change at once can destabilize situations because managing the change is a process—there is no button that's pushed to magically alter everything according to your vision. There may be a need to reconcile the psychological aspects of change and the organization's political considerations. Rather, take it one step at a time and try to enjoy the process. The important thing is that you're heading toward the right direction. If you do this and stick with it, next thing you notice, you'll be there.

Put It into Practice, Connect the Dots

You have to live it. It's not the knowledge of the concepts that translates into results. It's more about the depth of understanding and transferring those ideas into your daily habits and instincts. This transformation only occurs when you put it into practice. It's going to require a series of trying, failing, and recalibrating to succeed at it.

This also requires a flexible mind and a solution mentality. This is because it may go against the way you currently do things. Sometimes experienced managers are the ones who struggle grasping the concepts the most, especially if they were doing things differently their whole lives. However, with the right mindset, they can do it too.

Use This Book as a Reference Guide along Your Journey

This book was designed to be an overview of culture strategy and introduce relevant topics and how they relate with each other. It touched on a broad range of skillsets that can actually be explored further with deeper dives. I encourage having a lifelong endeavor of continuous learning to develop and master these skills.

This book was written in a way to be a continuous resource throughout your journey of becoming a transformative leader and walking this path. There are many realizations that won't seem apparent until you are personally faced with such an obstacle. Keep the book close and refer to relevant sections when you encounter those experiences.

Use This Book as a Tool to Get People in Your Organization on the Same Page

Culture strategy depends on being able to get people on various levels of the organization on the same page because we all play a role in this. This book can be used as a reference tool to get alignment among different people.

These people can include business owners who want to grow their business, stabilize it for sustainability, recapture life, or have a sense of purpose. It can help investors and board members who are interested in maximizing the ROI of their investment portfolio or sustainability of their companies. It can help senior leaders accomplish their objectives by demonstrating an approach using culture strategy that will help them develop transformative leadership skills and design or sponsor the right initiatives that will take the company to the next level. Cross-functional department heads can gain clarity on how to play their part in supporting culture strategy. This book can be an effective tool for aligning with middle managers by helping them understand their role in becoming a culture-focused manager, which can create enormous value for both the organization and people within their teams. Finally, it can help create clarity for individual contributors to understand how self-directed teams function differently, and how they can play their part.

Consider an Advisor, Coach, or Consultant

Depending on your experience level, this may or may not have been an overwhelming amount of information. If it was a lot to take in at once, it may be worthwhile to consider leveraging an expert's help. There can be tremendous value in being pointed in the right direction for your unique situation.

Sometimes, people have a tendency to regress and go back inside the rabbit hole of their ways. Left to their own elements, after years or even decades, they may end up in a situation where it's too late to turn the organization around due to a downward spiral. Or otherwise, they continue to walk in the wrong direction for the remainder of their lives. They'll look backward at the tail end of their careers and realize they haven't lived the life they wanted, which can lead to regret. Unfortunately, many people make this realization when it's too late. Remember, we only live once.

Even if you can do it on your own, it takes most people an exorbitant amount of time to get all the necessary breakthroughs to lead this effort. By the time they truly understand it, the opportunity cost has added up to a tremendous amount. Or at worst, you're already at the tail end of your life or your organization is already failing. Unfortunately, we can't go back in time to fix the past, but we can change the trajectory moving forward.

A simple calibration of efforts can tremendously change the trajectory of your results. An advisor, coach, or consultant who you resonate with and is familiar with the path that you wish to walk can help you stay on the path and pull you out of the rabbit hole. It's important to understand that this is a journey, and we should begin walking the right direction as soon as possible.

Closing Words

Beyond giving you the tools to transform your business and take it to the next level, I believe this topic can have a profound impact on society. Collectively, organizations have an enormous amount of influence because of their extensive reach and impact on a large number of employees and customers. By aiding more companies in making this transformation, we can pave a path for a sustainable society with organizations that raise the bar by demonstrating competitiveness through adaptively solving existing and future problems. This will also help companies provide a home for employees to give it their all, grow, and deliver value by innovatively solving real issues in society. One day, I hope companies like this become the majority rather than the minority.

From another angle, this topic has the potential to open the eyes of our current leaders to groom the leaders of tomorrow to make an impact. They can help them understand this approach, live it, and pay it forward by committing to groom others as well. This would ensure that our society is in good hands, even in the future.

Getting culture strategy implemented may be initially challenging, as it may involve restructuring the foundations of your organization. However, once you overcome the hurdles and it succeeds, you may establish an organic growth trajectory that can occur while maintaining your personal enjoyment in life. Imagine how your life, your career, your satisfaction can improve if you actually succeed in implementing this. It may even unlock the potential to make an impact that you didn't know was possible—through transformative leadership and culture strategy.

Thank you for reading and best wishes. Go and make a difference!

REFERENCES

A Guide to the Project Management Body of Knowledge PMBOK Guide. 6th ed. Newtowne Square: Project Management Institute, 2017. Print.

Bergman, Stanley. "Why Companies That Only Care About Investors Won't Thrive." LinkedIn Pulse. April 15, 2015. https://www.linkedin.com/pulse/ why-companies-only-care-investors-wont-thrive-stanley-bergman/.

Brassard, Michael, and Diane Ritter. *The Memory Jogger 2: Tools for Continuous Improvement and Effective Planning.* 2nd ed. Methuen: GoalQPC, 2018. Print.

Clifton, Jim, and Jim Hart. *It's the Manager.* New York: Gallup Press, 2019. Print.

Covey, Stephen R. *The 7 Habits of Highly Effective People.* New York: Simon and Schuster, 2004. Print.

Coyle, Daniel. *The Culture Code: The Secrets of Highly Successful Groups.* New York: Bantam Books, 2018. Print.

Drucker, P. F. *Managing Oneself.* Boston: Harvard Business School Press, 2008. Print.

Galbraith, Jay R. *Designing Organizations: An Executive Guide to Strategy, Structure, and Process.* 1st ed. San Francisco: Jossey-Bass, 2002. Print.

Goffee, Rob, and Gareth Jones. "What Holds the Modern Company Together?" *Harvard Business Review* (November–December 1996).

HBR Guide to Emotional Intelligence. Boston: Harvard Business Review Press, 2017. Print.

Hersey, Paul, and Ken H. Blanchard. "Life Cycle Theory of Leadership." *Training and Development Journal* 23, no. 5 (May 1969): 26–34.

Katzenbach, Jon R., and Douglas K. Smith. *The Wisdom of Teams.* Boston: Harvard Business Review Press, 1993.

Kayser, Thomas A. *Building Team Power: How to Unleash the Collaborative Genius of Teams for Increased Engagement, Productivity, and Results.* 2nd ed. New York: McGraw-Hill Books, 2011. Print.

Kayser, Thomas A. *Mining Group Gold: How to Cash in on the Collaborative Brain Power of a Team for Innovation and Results*. 3rd ed. New York: McGraw-Hill Books, 2011. Print.

Kotter, John P., and James L. Heskett. *Corporate Culture and Performance*. New York: The Free Press, 1992. Print.

Lencioni, Patrick. *The Five Dysfunctions of a Team*. San Francisco: Jossey-Bass, 2002. Print.

Lombardo, Michael M., and Robert W. Eichinger. *The Career Architect Development Planner*. 1st ed. Minneapolis: Lominger, 1996.

Marston, William M. *Emotions of Normal People*. London: K. Paul, Trench, Trubner and Co., 1928. Print.

Schein, Edgar H. *Organizational Culture and Leadership*. 5th ed. Hoboken: John Wiley and Sons, 2017. Print.

Scholtes, Peter R., Brian L. Joiner, and Barbara J. Streibel. *The Team Handbook*. 3rd ed. Madison: Oriel Incorporated, 2003. Print.

Thomas, Kenneth W., and Ralph H. Kilmann. *The Thomas-Kilmann Conflict Mode Instrument*. Mountain View: CPP, Inc., 1974.

Treacy, Michael, and Fred Wiersema. *The Discipline of Market Leaders: Choose Your Customers, Narrow Your Focus, Dominate Your Market*. Reading: Addison-Wesley Books, 1995. Print.

Tuckman, Bruce W. "Developmental Sequence in Small Groups." *Psychological Bulletin* 63, no. 6 (June 1965): 384–99.

White, Colin. *Strategic Management*. New York: Palgrave Macmillan, 2004. Print.

Yount, Jennifer L., and Johannah Jones. *Strategic Planning*. American Management Association, 2019.

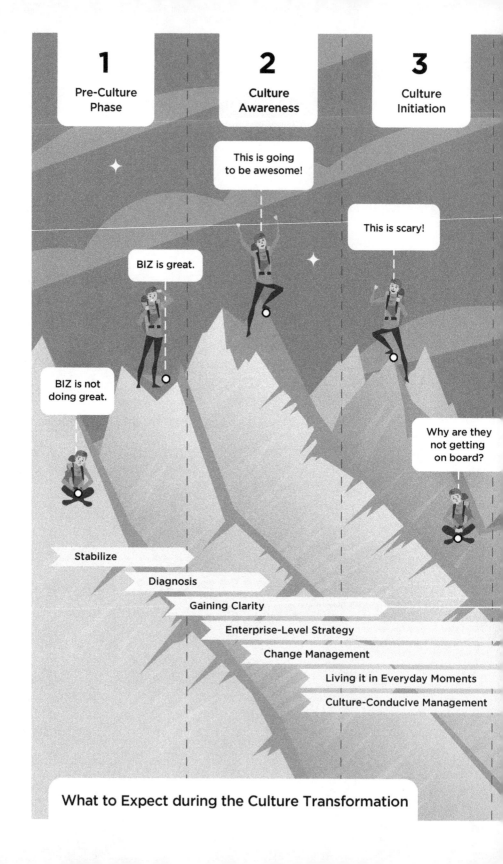

What to Expect during the Culture Transformation

CPSIA information can be obtained
at www.ICGtesting.com
Printed in the USA
BVHW031720210721
612424BV00004B/302/J

9 781544 519753